D1356788

Contours of Ableism

Contours of Ableism

The Production of Disability and Abledness

Fiona Kumari Campbell

Griffith University, Australia

First published 2009 by
PALGRAVE MACMILLAN

Palgrave Macmillan in the UK is an imprint of Macmillan Publishers Limited,
registered in England, company number 785998, of Houndmills, Basingstoke,
Hampshire RG21 6XS.

Palgrave Macmillan in the US is a division of St Martin's Press LLC,
175 Fifth Avenue, New York, NY 10010.

Palgrave Macmillan is the global academic imprint of the above companies
and has companies and representatives throughout the world.

Palgrave® and Macmillan® are registered trademarks in the United States,
the United Kingdom, Europe and other countries.

ISBN-13: 978–0–230–57928–6 hardback

This book is printed on paper suitable for recycling and made from fully
managed and sustained forest sources. Logging, pulping and manufacturing
processes are expected to conform to the environmental regulations of the
country of origin.

A catalogue record for this book is available from the British Library.

A catalog record for this book is available from the Library of Congress.

Printed and bound in Great Britain by
CPI Antony Rowe, Chippenham and Eastbourne

This work is dedicated to my daughter Revati Arden Campbell

Contents

List of Figures

Foreword

Dan Goodley
Professor of Psychology and Disability Studies, Manchester
Metropolitan University, UK

This is an important book. All forewords say that, though, don't they? But this book *is* important because it comes at a crucial time in the development of disability studies across the globe, where disabled theory and activism have matured to such a stage that they are entering a key period. Through increased alliances with feminist, queer and postcolonial comrades, disability studies is continuing with its emancipation of disabled people at the same time as destabilising the dominant social order. This period of activism and theory has been defined by Lennard Davis (2002) as *dismodernism*: where the values of modernism and the ambitions of postmodernism are directly conveyed by the theory and activism of disabled people. Key to this dismodernist turn is a critique of the dominant order, the other or alterity. For Campbell this alterity is *ableism*. That Campbell's book is written from her location in the Global South is not coincidental. As I have noticed more and more in my own reading for a book on disability (Goodley, 2010), of which Campbells' work has been very influential, scholars from outside of the Anglo-American traditions of disability studies have consistently demonstrated a willingness to be trans-disciplinary in approach. Campbell's book not only builds on this tradition but take it further by introducing *ableism* as a novel and ground-breaking analysis to disability studies.

There is also something of the Global South about the way in which Campbell directs her analysis. This text gazes and writes back at the Global North: at the ableism it insists on rolling out as part of what Hardt and Negri (2000) defined as *Empire*: the globalised bio-political machine of supranational organisations and rich nations, which aim to instil (and install) forms of subjectivity, ways of living and forms of governance in all corners of the world. Campbell not only takes to task ableism, she grabs it kicking and screaming from its perch aboard the good ship Empire and tears it apart. This is a book that is beautifully conceived and clearly argued. On page 6, Campbell outlines one of her (soon to be) victims of deconstruction, the able/ideal citizen of contemporary society:

> Whether it be the 'species typical body' (in science), the 'normative citizen' (in political theory), the 'reasonable man' (in law), all these signifiers point to a fabrication that reaches into the very soul that sweeps us into life and as such is the outcome and instrument of a political constitution: a hostage of the body.

Her point is that alterity for all of us is empty: we never match up to the ableist ideal. For disabled people, though, the alterity is further emptied, captured in common terms and couplets that indicate their exclusion from the symbolic, such as suffering from, afflicted with, persistent vegetative state, the mentality of an eight-year-old, useless limb, good and bad leg, mentally unstable, deranged and abnormal. As Campbell (2009, p. 17) argues, instead of embracing disability at the level of beingness (i.e. as an intrinsic part of the person's Self), the processes of ableism, like those of racism, induce an internalisation or self-loathing which devalues disabled people. In short, normality and normalcy is achieved through an unsaying: an absence of descriptions of what it is to be normal. And ableism has potentially massive impacts upon disabled people:

> regimes of ableism have produced a depth of disability negation that reaches into the caverns of collective subjectivity to the extent that the notion of disability as inherently negative is seen as a 'naturalized' reaction to an aberration.
>
> (Campbell, 2009, p. 166)

But, this is a book not simply about queering the various pitches of ableism such as norms, laws and antecedents; cultural forms of disability production; the medicalisation of Deafness through the selling of Cochlear Implants, the biosocial and medical dramas of transplanting body parts; the performance of disability in teaching; the co-constitution of disabled and female bodies; sexuality and disabled people. This text also looks for possibility, resistance and disruption. As Campbell notes on page 45:

> More than ever, I argue we are witnessing a new kind of human subjectivity – intersubjectivity if you like – technological humans – hybrids, cyborgs, or monsters. What better place to extend our ideas about ableism and the production of disability than the subject

of transhumanism with all its incumbent issues around ontology, humanness and of course the place of technology.

In true transdiscplinary style, and drawing on a wonderful Smörgåsbord of theories including Latour, Butler and Heidegger and Fukuyama, Campbell firmly plants disability studies concerns in the arenas of transhumanism, postmodernism and, I would suggest, what Rose has termed thanatopolitics: the increasingly ableist obsessed nature of everyday life (Rose, 2001). For example, Campbell draws on the work of Haraway, which some of us in disability studies are finding more and more useful. But what emerges in Campbell's analysis is a carefully resolute anti-romanticist view of the hybrid or post-human destination that undergirds a lot of feminist and critical technoscience ideas. In particular, Campbell raises some important ethical and political questions about the kinds of transhuman – or hybrids – that are valued in an ableist system:

> the transhuman project because it is founded on an unbridled form of ableism combined with an 'obsessive technological compulsion' – will involve a meager shuffling of the deckchairs – a rearranging of 'bums in seats'.
>
> (p. 73)

This is important stuff. It warns us, as disability scholars, to be mindful of the assumptions that underpin contemporary understandings of 'good', 'better' or 'future' lives. Some of the key questions raised in this book, which will be of interest to readers from the social sciences and humanities, include:

- What kind of society is technology advancing us into?
- What forms of alterity are disabled identities being forged against and with?
- What values underpin the schools, societies, institutions or cultural narrative that disabled people are, arguably, becoming more included within?
- To what extent can alternative non-ableist notions of personhood be developed and valued?
- How can a revisioning of ableist society influence the pedagogy, teaching and learning of disability studies?
- How can the disabled body be desired and desiring in ways that subvert the ableist gaze?

On page 197 of the book, Campbell reminds us of the place of her analysis:

> A move towards studies in ableism *must not* spell a separation with disability studies, rather the focus on ableism is meant to reconfigure a disability studies perspective and extend it. There is a real danger of those who come to studies in ableism without being exposed to the rich canon of critical disability studies will not feel inclined, accountable or committed to broader disability studies scholarship.
>
> (Campbell, 2009, p. 197)

This health warning reminds us of the conviction to the politics of disability that underpins all the arguments of this book. It also reminds us that disability is not a minority nor a peripheral issue: dis/abled people all face the threats of an increasingly punitive and governing ableist society.

References

Campbell, F. K. (2009). *Contours of Ableism: The Production of Disability and Abledness*. London: Palgrave Macmillan.

Davis, L. J. (2002). *Bending Over Backwards. Disability, Dismodernism and Other Difficult Positions*. New York: New York University Press.

Goodley, D. (2010). *Disability: Psyche, Culture and Society*. London: Sage.

Hardt, M. and Negri, A. (2000). *Empire*. Massachusetts: Harvard University Press.

Rose, N. (2001). The politics of life itself. *Theory, Culture & Society*, 18(6), 1–30.

Acknowledgements

Writing this book has been an intensely personal experience. My theoretical reflections and discussions with others have encouraged me to reflect upon my own journey and struggles as a disabled person in an ableist society. I write from a lonely place where there is limited opportunity to consider theoretically some of the topics of this book, where theory in its own right is valued and appreciated. The global critical disability studies community where time, networks and costs permit have been my partner along the way. Writing/thinking is not really an individual enterprise so I would like to pay homage to the people whose works have most influenced this book: Giorgio Agamben, Judith Butler, Wendy Brown, Martin Heidegger, Bill Hughes, James Overboe, Gregor Wolbring, Primo Levi and Owen Wrigley (please write another book!!). More personally this book is a tribute to the courage of the late Dr. Patricia Morrigan (Gowland), who inspired me as a 16 year old to think otherwise about social inequality and resistance through the power of imagination. Of course without Hashem who bestows all gifts there would be nothing.

This work would not have come to completion without the tremendous encouragement of Lesley Chenoweth and Elizabeth Kendall from my home institution, the School of Human Services & Social Work at Griffith University. Along the way, during times of doubt about the work's merit I received kind words and support from Bernadette Baker, Himali De Silva, Scot Danforth, Leslie Roman, Dan Goodley, William MacNeil, Andrea Rhodes-Little, Naomi Sunderland and especially Gerard Goggin. Conversations are the digestive system of thinking theoretically. I am indebted to the challenging discussions with my graduate students in particular Lyn O Hamilton, Therese Crisp, the late Margaret Corney and especially Kathryn Duncan.

Between juggling teaching schedules and writing grant applications I received immeasurable research assistance in formatting, updating sections of the book and receiving critical feedback from Josephine Seguna, book manager extraordinaire Gail Pritchard and Ann-Marie Tripp.

Thanks to Belinda Mason for permission to use her photographic image 'Embracing Life' from 'Intimate Encounters – an exhibition of photographs by Belinda Mason', Catalogue, p. 16, 2004.

I feel privileged to be able to use the front cover painting *On the Bars* by Quentin Blayney, a young man who transformed his giftedness when confronted with disability and illness. Thanks to Paula de Burgh for permission to use this image.

Part 1
Cogitating Ableism

1
The Project of Ableism

Feminist Rosemary Tong (1999) long ago alluded to the profound possibilities of using critical disability studies theory to re-comprehend and re-spatialise the landscape of thinking about race and gender as sites of signification. This Chapter presents a preliminary conversation in the emergent field of studies in ableism and desires to not only problematise but refuse the notion of able(ness). Our attention is on ableism's production and performance. Such an exploratory work is indebted to conversations already commenced by Campbell (2008), Hughes (2007) and Overboe (1999, 2007).

My approach is three pronged. First, I explore the problem of speaking/thinking/feeling about the Other (in this case persons referred to as 'disabled people') and the 'extraordinary' Other, the 'Abled'. This conversation is captured under the banner of 'The Ableist Project'. Here I argue it is necessary to shift the gaze of contemporary scholarship away from the spotlight on disability to a more nuanced exploration of epistemologies and ontologies of ableism. As part of this project of exposure my second task then will be to tease out the strands of what can be called 'Ableist Relations', including the effects of the compulsion to emulate ableist regulatory norms. Finally, as part of a commitment to make the necessary connections between theory and practice, I look at the tasks ahead in the refusal of ability and the commitment to a disability/not-abled imaginary.

Shifting the gaze – 'The Ableist Project'

Typically literature within disability and cultural studies has concentrated on the practices and production of disablism, specifically by examining those attitudes and barriers that contribute to the subordination of people with disabilities in liberal society. *Disablism* is a set of assumptions (conscious or unconscious) and practices that promote the differential or unequal treatment of people because of actual or presumed disabilities. On this basis the strategic positions adopted to facilitate emancipatory social change whilst diverse, essentially relate to reforming those negative attitudes, assimilating people with disabilities into normative civil society and providing compensatory initiatives and safety nets in cases of enduring vulnerability. In other words, the site of reformation has been at the intermediate level of function, structure and institution in civil society and shifting values in the cultural arena. Such an emphasis produces scholarship that contains serious distortions, gaps and omissions regarding the production of disability and re-inscribes an able-bodied voice/lens towards disability. Disability, often quite unconsciously, continues to be examined and taught from the perspective of the Other (Marks, 1996; Solis, 2006). The challenge then is to reverse, to invert this traditional approach, to shift our gaze and concentrate on what the study of disability tells us about the production, operation and maintenance of ableism.

The earlier work of Tom Shakespeare concludes, 'perhaps the maintenance of a non-disabled identity...is a more useful problem with which to be concerned; rather than interrogating the other, let us deconstruct the normality-which-is-to-be-assumed' (1999, p. 28). Hughes captures this project forcefully by calling for a study of 'the pathologies of non-disablement' (2007, p. 683). An Abled imaginary relies upon the existence of a hitherto unacknowledged imagined shared community of able-bodied/minded people held together by a common ableist homosocial world view that asserts the preferability and compulsoriness of the norms of ableism. Least we believe that people who fail to meet the ableist imaginary might think otherwise about human ontology and corporealities. Overboe (1999, 2007) and Campbell (2007, 2008) point to the compulsion to emulate the norm through the internalisation of ableism. Ableistnormativity results in compulsive passing, wherein there is a failure to ask about difference, to imagine human be-ingness differently.

Compulsory ableness and its conviction to and seduction of sameness as the basis to equality claims results in a resistance to consider ontologically peripheral lives as distinct ways of being human least they produce a heightened devaluation. Ontological reframing poses different preoccupations: what does the study of the politics of 'deafness' tell us about what it means to be 'hearing'? Indeed how is the very conceptualisation of 'hearing' framed in the light of discourses of 'deafness'? By decentring abledness, it is possible 'to look at the world from the inside out' (Linton, 1998b, p. 13) and unveil the 'non-disabled/ableist' stance. In a different context Haraway (1989, p. 152) exclaims, '...[this] cannot be said quite out loud, or it loses its crucial position as a pre-condition of vision and becomes the object of scrutiny'.

So what is meant by the concept of 'ableism'? A survey of the literature suggests that the term is often referred to in a fleeting way with limited definitional or conceptual specificity (Clear, 1999; Iwasaki & Mactavish, 2005; Watts & Erevelles, 2004). When there is commentary, ableism is described as denoting an attitude that devalues or differentiates disability through the valuation of able-bodiedness equated to normalcy (Ho, 2008). For some, the term *ableism* is used interchangeably with the term *disablism*. I argue however that these two words render quite radically different understandings of the status of disability to the norm. Furthermore, as a conceptual tool, ableism transcends the procedures, structures, for governing civil society, and locates itself clearly in the arena of genealogies of knowledge. There is little consensus as to what practices and behaviours constitute ableism. We can, nevertheless, say that a chief feature of an ableist viewpoint is a belief that impairment or disability (irrespective of 'type') is inherently negative and should the opportunity present itself, be ameliorated, cured or indeed eliminated. Ableism refers to:

> A network of beliefs, processes and practices that produces a particular kind of self and body (the corporeal standard) that is projected as the perfect, species-typical and therefore essential and fully human. Disability then is cast as a diminished state of being human.
>
> (Campbell, 2001, p. 44)

In a similar vein, Veronica Chouinard defines ableism as 'ideas, practices, institutions and social relations that presume ablebodiedness, and by so doing, construct persons with disabilities as marginalised...and largely invisible "others"' (1997, p. 380). In contrast, Amundson and Taira attribute a doctrinal posture to ableism in their suggestion that 'ableism is a doctrine that falsely treats impairments as inherently and naturally horrible and blames the impairments themselves for the problems experienced by the people who have them' (2005, p. 54). Whilst there is little argument with this presupposition, what is absent from the definition is any mention of ableism's function in inaugurating the norm. The Campbell (2001; Chouinard, 1997) approach is less about the coherency and intentionalities of ableism; rather their emphasis is on a conception of ableism as a hub network functioning around shifting interest convergences. Linton defines ableism as 'includ[ing] the idea that a person's abilities or characteristics are determined by disability or that people with disabilities as a group are inferior to non-disabled people' (1998b, p. 9). There are problems with simply endorsing a schema that posits a particular worldview that either favours or disfavours disabled/able-bodied people as if each category is discrete, self-evident and fixed. As I will argue later, ableism sets up a binary dynamic that is not simply comparative but rather co-relationally constitutive. Campbell's (2001) formulation of ableism not only problematises the signifier disability but points to the fact that the essential core of ableism is the formation of a naturalised understanding of being fully human and this, as Chouinard (1997) notes, is articulated on a basis of an enforced presumption that erases difference.

Whether it be the 'species typical body' (in science), the 'normative citizen' (in political theory), the 'reasonable man' (in law), all these signifiers point to a fabrication that reaches into the very soul that sweeps us into life and as such is the outcome and instrument of a political constitution: a hostage of the body. The creation of such regimes of ontological separation appears disassociated from power. Bodies in this way become elements that may be moved, used, transformed, demarcated, improved and articulated with others. Daily the identities of *disabled* and *abled* are performed repeatedly. An ethos of compulsory abled-bodiedness as McRuer (2002, p. 93) puts it 'showcase[d] for able-bodied performance' pursuant to the incessant consuming of objects of health, beauty, strength and capability. In the next section, the dividing practices of ableism are considered in more detail.

'Ableist Relations'

Central to regimes of ableism are two core elements that feature irrespective of its localised enactment, namely *the notion of the* normative (and normate individual) and the enforcement of a *constitutional divide* between perfected naturalised humanity and the aberrant, the unthinkable, quasi-human hybrid and therefore non-human. This constitution provides the layout, the blueprint for the scaling and marking of bodies and the ordering of their terms of relation. It is not possible to have a concept of *difference* without ableism. Let us take each of these two elements separately and explore them more closely.

The able/not-able divide

It is necessary to establish and enforce a constitutional divide. The divide is at the levels of ontology, materiality and sentiency. I wish to focus on the constitutionality of that divide between the normal and the pathological and mechanisms of ordering. This analysis is influenced by the proposals advanced by Bruno Latour in *We Have Never been Modern* (1993).

Latour's main proposition is that post-enlightenment modernity and atomistic man have never been modern, for the concept of Modern delineates two sets of independent practices that must remain distinct in order for them to work/function. In recent times, Latour suggests, these practices, *translation* and *purification,* have begun to be less clear and ambiguous:

'Translation', creates mixtures between entirely new types of being, hybrids of nature and culture. The second, by 'purification': creates two entirely distinct ontological zones: that of human beings on the one hand; that of nonhumans on the other.

(Latour, 1993, pp. 10–11)

The devices of translation and purification can assist us to grapple with that which seems 'unholdable' and elusive; the uncontainability of the disabled body. 'Translation' is based on the notion that structures or networks are not obvious or self-contained. Latour uses the example of a chain flowing from the upper atmosphere, industrial strategies and onto the concerns of government and greenies. 'Purification', in contrast, engages in the creation of divides of ontological distinctions, which espouse a foundational (almost first cause) self-evidence. Here, Latour (1993) cites that partition between nature (as self-contained), non-humans and culture (created and driven by humans). This 'modern critical stance', as Latour calls it, acts as the ethos or template of modernity.

In the context of ableism, Latour's schema proves helpful (see Figure 1). The processes and practices of translation cannot be separated from the creation of that ordering category termed 'disability'. For many people deemed disabled, in the world of technoscience their relationship with non-human actants has been profoundly cyborgical and hybridisable (e.g. the use of communication and adaptive devices, implants and transplants). As such the networks of association between human and non-human (sentient beings and machines) have always been and increasingly are pushing the boundaries of the practices of

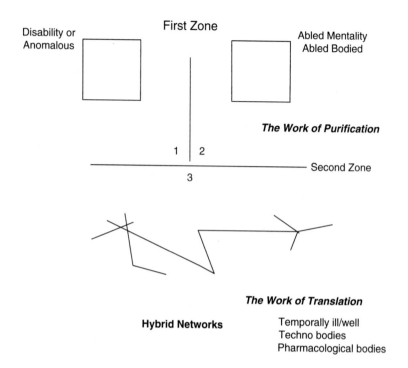

Source: the author

Figure 1   Purification and translation.

purification. The disabled body induces a fear as being a body out of control because of its appearance of uncontainability. The practices of purification insist on this being the case. Ableism's constitutional divide posits two distinct and entirely clear ontological zones: disabled and abled (normate). Latour (1993, p. 11) explains,

> Without the first set, the practices of purification would be fruitless or pointless. Without the second, the work of translation would be slowed down, limited, or even ruled out.... So long as we consider these two practices of translation and purification separately, we are truly modern – that is willingly subscribe to the critical project, even though that project is developed only through the proliferation of hybrids down below. As soon as we direct our attention simultaneously to the work of purification and the work of hybridization [translation], we immediately stop being wholly modern, and our future begins to change.

The challenge then is to look *beyond* social context, at the interactivity between the processes and techniques of purification and translation, in particular to investigate what this interactivity clarifies and obfuscates. Even though Latour claims that purification is not an ideology in disguise, I would assert that the existence of processes of purification creates a simulation, if you like, of the conditions of naturalism. Latour's discussion of whether relations are conscious and unconscious or are illusion and reality is an important one. He concludes that moderns are not unaware of what they do; rather it is the holding steadfast to dichotomies, the divides, which makes possible the processes of translation. We can, by analogy, argue that matters of intentionality or discourse and so forth are not critical to the emerging technologies of ableism, but rather it is the act of holding stoically to the distinction between abledness and disabledness.

In contemporary developments in high-tech and biotechnologies, it is occasionally possible to witness the glitches in the purview of purification, whether that is in the debates over transhumanism, xenotransplantation or the emergent of new 'life' in the form of artificial intelligences (A.I's). The confusion about where human life begins and ends harks back to the Enlightenment era where philosopher's like Locke inquired 'What is It?' in trying to make sense of the humanness of changelings (Campbell, 1999; Locke, 1979). The fortunes of technoscience continue to disrupt the fixity of defining disability and normalcy especially within the arenas of law and bioethics. Whilst anomalous bodies are *undecidable* in being open to endless and differing interpretations, an essentialised disabled body is subject to constant deferral – standing in reserve, awaiting and escaping able(edness) through morphing technologies and as such exists in an ontologically *tentative* or *provisional* state.

Latour points out the ultimate paradox of this modern constitutional divide is that whilst the proliferation of hybrids is allowed for, at the same time this constitution continues to deny the very existence of hybrid entities within its formulation (Latour, 1993). Contemporary conditions suggest that it is not the event of denial that is operational; rather it is the 'place' or significance given to such ambiguous entities that disrupt the rather neat demarcation zones. Practices of purification continue to rein in (successfully or otherwise) the chaos created by increasing 'grey zones' along the continuum of human/non-human difference. In the governing of prostitution, Razack (1998) points to the creation of an 'anomalous zone' to contain and tolerate the deviance. In dealing with political prisoners, the despised, those interned in concentration camps and institutions, Agamben (1998, 2005) indicates the

manufacturing of states of exception that exist beyond the law and spatiality to enable 'treatments' of those existing in the realm of a *bare
life*. The significance of the enforcement of a constitutional divide, for
the practices of ableism, is that such orderings are not just repressive
but they are ultimately productive; they tell us stories, they contain
narratives as to 'whom' we are and how we 'should be'.

In the closing pages of *We Have Never been Modern* (1993), Latour
argues that as science creates new definitions of being human, these
new formations do not displace the older versions rather humanism is
redistributed. I am not entirely convinced of this emergent multiplicity and expansion of ontologies of humanness. Contra Latour, Hayles
(1999) argues that should sentiency be conceptualised on the basis of
informationalcy, this new rendering would amount to a profound shift
in the theoretical markers used to categorise all life (or what is 'life').
In this moment there is a rallying of networks scurrying to squeeze
new ontological formations of dis/ability into 'old' systems of ordering
and thus attempt to avoid re-cognising an abundance of (post-marginal,
post-peripheral) morphisms. Anthropomorphism becomes the catch cry
of ableism. As Latour (1993) rejoices,

> Morphism is the place where technomorpisms, zoomorphisms,
> phusimorphisms, ideomorphisms, theomorphisms, sociomorphisms,
> psyomorphisms, all come together. These alliances and their
> exchanges, taken together, are what define the anthropos. A weaver
> of morphisms – isn't that enough of a definition? (p. 137)

What normate . . . ableist normativity?

Georges Canguilhem (1978, p. 69) states, 'every generality is the sign
of an essence, and every perfection the realisation of the essence . . . a
common characteristic, the value of an ideal type'. If this is the case,
what then is the essence of normative abled(ness)? Such a question
poses significant conceptual challenges including the dangers of bifur-
cation. It is reasonably easy to speculate about the knowingness of life
forms deemed disabled in spite of the neologism disability's catachre-
sis orientation. In contrast, able-bodied, corporeal perfectedness has an
elusive core (other than being posed as transparently average or normal). Charting a criterion of abled to gain definitional clarity can result
in a game of circular reductionism – saying what it *is* in relation to
what it *isn't*, that which falls away. Disability performances are invoked
to mean 'any body capable of being narrated as outside the norm'
(Mitchell, 2002, p. 17). Such an analysis belies the issue whether, at their

core, women's, black and queer bodies are ultimately ontologically and materially disabled. Parsons (1999) commented,

> Women talk about being proud of who they are – proud *because* they are women; aborigines talk about being proud *because* they are aborigines; gay men and lesbians about being proud because of their sexuality. But throughout the disability movement we are much more likely to hear people with disabilities talking about pride in themselves *despite* their disability (p. 14).

Inscribing certain bodies in terms of deficiency and essential inadequacy privileges a particular understanding of normalcy that is commensurate with the interests of dominant groups (and the assumed interests of subordinated groups). Indeed, the formation of ableist relations requires the normate individual to depend upon the self of 'disabled' bodies being rendered beyond the realm of civility, thus becoming an unthinkable object of apprehension. The unruly, uncivil, disabled body is necessary for the reiteration of the 'truth' of the 'real/essential' human self who is endowed with masculinist attributes of certainty, mastery and autonomy. The discursive practices that mark out bodies of preferability are vindicated by abject life forms that populate the constitutive outside of the thinkable (that which can be imagined and re-presented) and those forms of existence that are unimaginable and therefore unspeakable. The emptying (*kenosis*) of normalcy occurs through the purging of those beings that confuse, are misrecognisable or as Mitchell (2002, p. 17) describes as 'recalcitrant corporeal matter' into a *bare life* (see Agamben, 1998) residing in the/a zone of exceptionality. This foreclosure depends on necessary unspeakability to maintain the continued operation of hegemonic power. For every outside there is an inside that demands differentiation and consolidation as a unity. To borrow from Heidegger (1977) – in every *aletheia* (unveiling or revealedness) of representation there lies a concealedness. The visibility of the ableist project is therefore only possible through the interrogation of the revealedness of disability/not-health and abled(ness), Marcel Detienne (1979) summarises this system of thought aptly:

> [Such a] . . . system is founded on a series of acts of partition whose ambiguity, here as elsewhere, is to open up the terrain of their transgression at the very moment when they mark off a limit. To discover the complete horizon of a society's symbolic values, it is also necessary to map out its transgressions, its deviants (p. ix).

Viewing the disabled body as simply *matter out of place* that needs to be dispensed with or at least cleaned up is erroneous. The disabled body *has* a place, a place in liminality to secure the performative enactment of the normal. Detienne's summation points to what we may call the double bind of ableism when performed within Western neo-liberal polities. The double bind folds in on itself – for whilst claiming 'inclusion', ableism simultaneously always restates and enshrines itself. On the one hand, discourses of equality promote 'inclusion' by way of promoting positive attitudes (sometimes legislated in mission statements, marketing campaigns, equal opportunity protections) and yet on the other hand, ableist discourses proclaim quite emphatically that disability is inherently negative, ontologically intolerable and in the end, a dispensable remnant. This casting results in an ontological foreclosure wherein positive signification of disability becomes unspeakable.

> I've always believed that within tragedy, there is incredible life and emotion. So my condition is not something I think of as sad; I think it's something so beautifully human. It doesn't make me less of a human being. It makes me so rich...I see my life as an active experiment; to grasp at greatness I must risk failure. I put instinct before caution, ideals before reality and possibility before negativity. As a result, my life is not easy but it's not boring either.
>
> (Byrnes, 2000)

Disability cannot be thought of/spoken about on any other basis than the negative, to do so, to invoke oppositional discourses, is to run the risk of further pathologisation. An example of this is the attempt at desiring, or celebrating, disability that is reduced to a fetish or facticity disorder. So to explicate ourselves out of this double bind we need to persistently and continually return to the matter of disability as negative ontology, as a malignancy, that is, as the property of a body constituted by what Michael Oliver (1996, p. 32) refers to as, 'the personal tragedy theory of disability.'

Returning to the matter of definitional clarity around abled(ness), Robert McRuer (2002) is one of the few scholars to journey into ableism's non-axiomatic life. He argues that ableism (McRuer refers to compulsory abled-bodiedness) emanates from everywhere and nowhere, and can only be deduced by crafty reductionisms. Contra the assertions about the uncontainability of disabled bodies which are (re)contained by the hyper-prescription and enumeration, the abled body mediated through its assumption of compulsion is absent in its presence – it just is – but resists being fully deducible. Drawing on Butler's work, McRuer (2002) writes,

> Everyone is virtually disabled, both in the sense that able-bodied norms are 'intrinsically impossible to embody' fully and in the sense that able-bodied status is always temporary, disability being the one identity category that all people will embody if they live long enough. What we might call a critical disability position, however, would differ from such a virtually disabled positions [to engagements that have] resisted the demands of compulsory able-bodiedness (pp. 95–96).

My argument is that insofar as this conception of disability is assumed within discourses of ableism, the presence of disability upsets the modernist craving for ontological security.

The conundrum, disability, is not a mere fear of the unknown, or an apprehensiveness towards that which is foreign or strange. Rather, disability and disabled bodies are effectively positioned in the nether regions of 'unthought'. For the ongoing stability of ableism, a diffuse network of thought depends upon the capacity of that network to 'shut away', to exteriorise, and unthink disability and its resemblance to the essential (ableist) human self. This unthought has been given much consideration through the systematisation and classification of knowledges about pathology, aberration and deviance. That which is thought about (the Abled norm) rather ironically in its delimitation becomes vacuous and elusive. In order for the notion of ableness to exist and to transmogrify into the sovereign subject, the normate individual of liberalism, it must have a constitutive outside – that is, it must participate in a logic of supplementarity. When looking at relations of disability and ableism we can expand on this idea of symbiosis, an 'unavoidable duality' by putting forward another metaphor, that of the mirror. Here I argue that people deemed disabled take on the performative act of mirroring in the lives of normative subjects:

> ... To be a Mirror is different from being a Face that looks back ... with a range of expression and responsiveness that are responses of a Subject-in-Its-Own-Right. To be positioned as a Mirror is to be Put Out of Countenance, to Lose Face.
>
> (Narayan, 1997, p. 141)

In this respect, we can speak in ontological terms of the history of disability as a history of that which is unthought, to be put out of countenance; this figuring should not be confused with erasure that occurs due to mere absence or exclusion. On the contrary, disability is always present (despite its seeming absence) in the ableist talk of normalcy, normalisation and humanness (cf. Overboe, 2007, on the idea of *normative shadows*). Disability's truth-claims are dependent upon discourses of ableism for their very legitimisation.

Disability imaginaries – reconceptualising the human?

Phenomenological studies have long recognised the importance of focusing on the *experience* of the *animated living body (der Leib)*, in recognition that we dwell in our bodies and live so fundamentally *through* them. This intensity is captured by Kalekin-Fishman (2001):

> Before every action, there is a pause...and a beginning again. The pause is for description, for mulling over the requirements of balance, for comparing the proposed action with movements that are familiar, and for explaining to myself why I can or cannot do what is at hand... In the course of daily living, the thinking is not observable; the behaviour just happens, part of what this person does naturally. The physiology of 'a slight limp' is part of the unmediated expression of what my 'I' is (p. 36).

In short, we cannot 'know' existence without being rooted to our bodies. To this extent, it is problematic to speak of bodies in their materiality in a way that distinguishes between emotions and cognition. This generative body is shaped by relations of power, complex histories and interpreted through a bricolage of complex interwoven subjectivities. This approach to perceiving the body in terms of *geist* or animation can be applied to re-thinking peripheral bodies deemed disabled. It is this body that infuses the discourses and animates representations. Refusing able(ness) necessitates a letting go of the strategy of using the sameness for equality arguments as the basis of liberal freedom. Instead of wasting time on the violence of normalisation, theoretical and cultural producers could more meaningfully concentrate on developing a semiotics of exchange, an ontological decoder to recover and apprehend the lifeworlds of humans living peripherally. Ontological differences, be that on the basis of problematical signifiers of race, sex, sexuality and dis/ability, need to be unhinged from evaluative ranking and be re-cognised in their various nuances and complexities without being re-presented in fixed absolute terms. It is only then, in this release that we can find possibilities in ambiguity and resistance in marginality.

Instead of asking 'how do you manage not being like (the non-stated) *us?*' (the negation argument), disability imaginaries think/speak/gesture and feel different landscapes not just for being – in-the-world, but on the conduction of perception, mobilities and temporalities. Linton (1998a, p. 530) points out that the 'kinaesthetic, proprioceptive, sensory and cognitive experiences' of disabled people as they go about their daily life have received limited attention. Nancy Mairs (1996) notes that a disability gaze is imbricated in every aspect of action, perception, occurrence and knowing.

In order to return bodies back to difference – in-the-human – a re-conceptualisation of knowing (episteme) is paramount. Only this knowledge is of a carnal kind, where thinking, sensing and understanding mutually enfold. Whilst ever present in ableist normalising dialogue, disability's veracity is undeniably contingent upon conversations of ableism, its production and performance, to confer validity.

2
Internalised Ableism: The Tyranny Within

> Internalized oppression is not the cause of our mistreatment; it is the result of our mistreatment. It would not exist without the real external oppression that forms the social climate in which we exist. Once oppression has been internalized, little force is needed to keep us submissive. We harbour inside ourselves the pain and the memories, the fears and the confusions, the negative self-images and the low expectations, turning them into weapons with which to re-injure ourselves, every day of our lives.
>
> (Marks, 1999, p. 25)

Although there are many debates in disability studies and the disability services fields, most people would agree with the proposition that disabled people[1] experience various degrees of subordinated and diminished lives through economic, social, legal, religious and cultural discrimination. These problems were recently formally recognised by the United Nations in the form of the UN *Convention on the Rights of Persons with Disabilities*, which bind member nations who become signatories. In the light of this recognition, it is important to pause and think about the nature of harm that disabled people experience and the very concept of *harm*. For instance, is it the impairment itself that causes the harm? If so, we should focus on reducing or indeed eliminating the impairment, which is a common perspective. Such a view interprets disability as harmful in and of itself. In contrast, there is a view among some disabled people that whilst impairments at times cause inconvenience, tiredness and even pain, the primary source of harm is external to the person, situated in the realm of belief.

From the moment a child is born, he/she emerges into a world where he/she receives messages that to be disabled is to be *less than*, a world where disability may be *tolerated* but in the *final instance*, is *inherently negative*. We are all, regardless of our status, shaped and formed by the politics of ableism. This chapter is about theory – it is an attempt to theorise about the way disabled people live with ableism. One assumption underpinning my argument is that ableism is essentially harmful and, instead of providing solace to disabled people, it actually involves practices and attitudes that induce other forms of impairment and injury.

> The way you see me, it's not me, not the real me. You see the sham-bling, the stumbling, the lunge, and you don't see me. Except for the feet, I'm almost you. But most of all, I'd like a chance to show you the way I see myself, the way I know I am. It's not that bad once you get used to it. Please, just a day, no, not that – a minute, a second, a *second* – that's all I need, a *second* – you would all love me.
>
> (Bell, 2000, p. 285)

So this chapter will relate the experience of disability to 'race' by explor-ing the concept of internalised racism, its use in Critical Race Theory (CRT) and its possible application to critical disability studies. The dis-cussion and explanation of CRT through the framework of ableism, provided in the previous chapter, will allow for discussion of inter-nalised racism and consideration of its connection to the phenomena of internalised ableism.

Critical race theory

CRT has not only brought into question the notion of race as a perma-nent and abiding classification system, but has also made a contribution to the notion of race as a practice that is constantly negotiating, shaping and forming the individual[2] resulting in internalised racism (Frankenberg, 1993; McClintock, 1995). CRT considers racism not as aberrant, but rather as a natural part of Western life. Expanding on this perception, Delgado and Stefancic (2000) declared,

> Because racism is an ingrained feature of our landscape, it looks ordinary and natural to persons in the culture. Formal equal oppor-tunity – rules and laws that insists in treating blacks and whites (for example) alike – can thus remedy only the more extreme and

shocking forms of injustice.... It can do little about the business-as-usual forms of racism that people of color confront everyday and that account for much misery, alienation, and despair (p. xvi).

Applying similar reasoning to the state of disablement, the 'business-as-usual' forms of ableism are so absorbed into the function of Western societies that ableism as a site of social theorisation (even within critical disability studies) represents the last frontier of inquiry. Disability studies is still preoccupied with debating the distinctions between 'impairment' and 'disability'. Although there is recognition that the term *disability* can be both culturally and economically constructed, the state of impairment remains under theorised (see Corker, 2001; Tremain, 2005 for notable exceptions). Cultural practices of shaping bodies can affect the aetiology of 'typical' human functioning. The ranking of bodies occurs through dividing and partitioning according to clear-cut descriptors of 'race' 'gender', 'caste' and 'disability' (Mitchell & Snyder, 2003). Gordon and Rosenblum (2001) suggested that similar approaches to disability, as have been applied to race, might lead to new and productive sites of engagement. They argued that there are likenesses and distinctions in the ways disabled people and other stigmatised groups are named, enumerated, dis-enumerated, partitioned and denied attributes valued in the culture. One example of this process is the enshrinement in Indian law of the 'backward' class, which refers to a specific segment of the population grouped by social order and location. 'Backwardness' is rendered visible through intelligence quotient scales and categorisations such as 'sub-normalcy' and 'retardation' (Scheerenberger, 1983).

   Certain theories of development have described whole nations of the 'Third World' as 'backward' and 'undevelopable' (Baster, 1954). CRT draws on the notion of 'interest convergence' (Bell, 1995), a concept that describes situations where white people with power endure or foster black advancements to the extent that these advancements promote white interests (Delgado & Stefancic, 2000; Smith & Stovall, 2008). Interest convergence has sometimes resulted in unlikely bedfellows (i.e. groups in the community forming alliances where normally their interests might be different or even conflicting). Consider the alliance between the Roman Catholic Church and World Islamic Council at the 1994 UN International Conference on Population and Development (Moffett, 1994). A critical disability studies perspective invites us to explore the limits of liberal tolerance of disability, interest convergence and the points of departure away from the interests of ableism.

Hahn (1986) testified that there was a close link between the attitude of paternalism, the subordination of disabled people and the 'interests' of ableism:

> Paternalism enables the dominant elements of a society to express profound and sincere sympathy for the members of a minority group while, at the same time, keeping them in a position of social and economic subordination. It has allowed the non-disabled to act as the protectors, guides, leaders, role models, and intermediates for disabled individuals who, like children, are often assumed to be helpless, dependent, asexual, economically unproductive, physically limited, emotional immature, and acceptable only when they are unobtrusive.
>
> (p. 130)

Jones's (1972, p. 172) seminal work on racism argued that race-based power relations are galvanised 'with the intentional or unintentional support of the entire culture'. In this regard, Delgado (2000) claimed that the situation of members of racial minorities was akin to persons with physical impairment. Supporting this conclusion, Delgado cited the work of Oliver Cromwell Cox (1948) who claimed,

> A *rebuff* due to one's skin color puts [the victim] in very much the situation of the very ugly person or one suffering from a loathsome disease. The suffering... may be aggravated by a consciousness of incurability and even blameworthiness, a self-reproaching which tends to leave the individual still more aware of his [sic] loneliness and unwantedness.
>
> (cited Delgado, 2000, p. 132)

Therefore to recap the previous discussion, ableism as a conceptual tool, goes beyond procedures, structure, institutions and values of civil society, situates itself clearly within the histories *of knowledge* and is embedded deeply and subliminally within culture. Many people are familiar with the concepts of sexism and racism, to denote negative differentiation on the basis of sex or racial origin; but ableism is generally perceived as a strange and unfamiliar concept and it is important to refute a rigid understanding of ableism from the outset. The intention is not to propose ableism as another explanatory 'grand narrative', a universalised and systematised conception of disability oppression but rather highlight a convergence of networks of association that produce exclusionary categories and ontologies (i.e. ways of being human). It is my contention, therefore, that focussing on the study of ableism instead of focussing on the study of disability/disablement may produce different questions and sites of study, for the nuances of ableism close off certain aspects of the imagination. As Butler (1997a) put it:

> The operation of foreclosure is tacitly referenced in those instances in which we ask: what must remain unspeakable for the contemporary regimes of discourse to continue to exercise power?
>
> (p. 139)

Butler's (1997a) comments are complex, dense and needs unpacking. Imagination is integral to human growth. To imagine is to consider desire, to dream of possibilities, to see life differently. Sometimes it is not possible to imagine: maybe there is an overwhelming sense of gloom or maybe the consequences of imagining differently would result in being ridiculed, pathologised or at best, ignored. Butler (1997a) made the point that for systems of thinking to be maintained, certain ways of imagining need to remain unspeakable and unspoken. In some countries, this is achievable due to the actual absence of words in the vocabulary to describe a certain kind of difference. So is it possible to imagine disability outside of the context of tragedy or catastrophe?

Internalisation

Instead of embracing disability at the level of beingness (i.e. as an intrinsic part of the person's Self), the processes of ableism, like those of racism, induce an internalisation or self-loathing which devalues disablement. Unspeakable silences exist regarding the study of certain aspects of race. Pyke and Dang (2003) noted that there is an intellectual taboo/fear surrounding the study of internalised racism, presumably because attention to internalised racism may undermine the political potency of the African-American rights movement and eclipse liberalism's black 'success' stories. What then about the hidden stories of the 'can do' generation of successful, assimilated professionals with disability? Do disabled people experience a sense of inadequacy dissonant to their success? A lack of focus on the costs of ableism has led to a shortage of research around the themes of suicide, drug and alcohol use and additional mental health stressors amongst 'successful' disabled people. One might be led to believe that the pathologisation of the disability 'problem' has, in contrast to matters of race, meant an acceptance and awareness of internalised ableism. The pathologisation of disability has meant that therapy predominantly concentrates on normalisation and is not necessarily directed to attending to the harms of ableism (e.g. living with prejudice).

Kovel (1970) presented a bleak but pertinent testimony of the impact of internalised racism, noting that the 'accumulation of negative images...presents [racial minorities] with one massive and destructive choice: either to hate one's self, as culture so systematically demands, or to have no self at all, to be nothing' (p. 195). Rosenwasser (2000), writing in the context of anti-Semitism defined what she termed 'internalised oppression' as:

> An involuntary reaction to oppression which originates outside one's group and which results in group members loathing themselves, disliking others in their group, and blaming themselves for the oppression – rather than realizing that these beliefs are constructed in them by oppressive socio-economic political systems.
>
> (p. 1)

The key ingredients of CRT are negative representations of human be-ingness (perverted sexualities, ambiguous bodies and skins) which continually shape an individual's sense of self and regulate behaviours. CRT's notion of internalised racism indicates a process whereby people of colour absorb and internalise aspects of racism (Freire, 1970; Harvey, 1995). The nature of *differentially situated realities* means that there will be many different relationships with internalised racism. For instance, Watts-Jones (2002) argued that for people of European Christian decent, internalised racism can empower, if not privilege, feelings of superiority. 'It is an experience of self-aggrandizement on an individual, socio-cultural and institutional level' (p. 592), whereas for coloured people, internalised racism induces self-mortification and estrangement. Internalised racism compels people of colour to adopt strategies of colour disavowal in that 'enjoyment or privileges we accrue are by virtue of abandoning our identity to approximate that of the extolled group. There is no entitlement or sense of entitlement' (pp. 592–593). Similarly the lack of discussion about ableism and internalised ableism, in particular, means that the casting of disability into the background through a re-emphasis on personhood (e.g. person-first language) often erases or disavows disability. In effect this non-recognition of ableism suggests that *disability does not matter* and makes it difficult to enquire as to the ways that different knowledge standpoints place us in different relationships not just to disability, but also to power and marginality. It is all too easy to become silent about the costs of living with disability in an ableist world and the differences between disabled and non-disabled people.

Recent research correlates the experience of racism to low socioeconomic status and the acquisition of physical and psychological impairment (Williams & Collins, 1995) in that racism not only causes distress, but impacts on mental health status (Krieger, 1999). Racism can be experienced as a personal deficiency on the part of the discriminated, that is what have I done or not done to bring about this behaviour or response ('blaming the victim') rather than being aware that the experience of racism is due to racism and not the person's own interaction. Pyke and Dang (2003) argued that because internalised racism is an adaptive response to racism, where both compliance and resistance in interrelated ways reproduce or replicate racism.

In examining sites for the internalisation of racism, Burstow (2003) made it clear that we should not be looking at a single event or site of impact, rather internalisation occurs through the accumulative, residual and reoccurring experiences of racism. Burstow remarked that 'the point is oppressed people are routinely worn down by the insidious trauma involved in living day after day in a sexist, racist, classist, homophobic, and ableist society' (p. 1296). Within ableism, the existence of disability is tolerated rather than celebrated as a part of human diversification. I contend that internalised ableism utilises a two-pronged strategy, the distancing of disabled people from each other (dispersal) and the adoption by disabled people of ableist norms (emulation). These two strategies are described below.

Tactics of dispersal

The experience of disablement can arguably be spoken of not in terms of individualised personal tragedy, but in terms of communal trauma where the legacies of ableism pervade both conscious and unconscious realms. Although the prevailing theme has been the individualisation of disability through the domination of medicine, nonetheless histories of catastrophe, negative portrayals of disability and an absence of celebratory role models collectively saturate the lives of disabled people. Unlike other minority groups, disabled people have had fewer opportunities to develop a collective conscious, identity or culture. The connection between epistemologies (knowledge-forms) of ableism and the production of internalised ableism can be seen in Social Role Valorisation Theory (SRV) as articulated by Wolf Wolfensberger (1972). This theory is also known by the name of 'normalisation'. His strategy of 'conservatism corollary' *explicitly* discourages fellowship amongst persons with disabilities and other minorities. According to Wolfensberger (1972), the 'conservatism corollary' posits that:

> The greater the number, severity, and/or variety of deviances or stigmata of an individual person, or the greater number of deviant/ stigmatized persons there are in a group, the more impactful it is to: (a) reduce one or few of the individual stigmata within the group, (b) reduce the proportion or number of deviant people in the group, or (c) balance (compensate for) the stigmata or deviancies by the presence, or addition, of positively valued manifestations.
>
> (Wolfensberger & Thomas, 1983, p. 26)

Wolfensberger (1972) argued that 'When a significant proportion of people within a distinct or compact group have one or more such *oddities*, then the whole group including non-stigmatised members is apt to be negatively stereotyped (Wolfensberger & Thomas, 1983, p. 26, emphasis added)'. In other words, the consequence requires that disability service workers overcompensate to reduce or minimise any 'devaluing characteristics'. The reality of the outcome is that it does nothing to interrogate and challenge hegemonic ideas that exclude, separate and subordinate people with disabilities. Instead, the approach actively promotes separation between and within groups of the so-called 'stigmatised' peoples. Clearly, this is a precursor to a strategy of dispersal, predicated on the belief that disabled people should not draw attention to each other via associating (with other culturally devalued people) (Szivos, 1992). This 'dilution of deviancy' is familiar in the histories of other marginalised populations such as indigenous, coloured, gay and lesbian peoples. The consequences of dispersal generate internalised ableism in that mixing with other people with impairments is interpreted as a negative, inadvisable choice. Dispersal policies are only permissible because the *integration imperative* exists and receives support from the disability services sector. The integration imperative is based on the belief that mainstream institutions and methods are superior to other separate settings (O'Brien & Murray, 1996) that include sub-cultural environments. These sub-cultural spaces should not be confused with segregated or institutional environments. As Watts-Jones (2002) pointed out, 'within group' processes can act as a sanctuary for healing internalised oppression. However, dispersal strategies deny disabled people access to this sanctuary.

Emulating the norm

Schwalbe & Mason-Schrock (1996) argued that for Asian-Americans to deflect stigma, they often engage in 'defensive Othering'. Defensive Othering occurs when the marginalised person attempts to emulate the hegemonic norm, whiteness or ableism, and assumes the 'legitimacy of a devalued identity imposed by the dominant group, but then saying, in effect, "there are indeed Others to whom this applies, but it does not apply to me" ' (1996, p. 425). This attitude is evident in a State-supported system of diagnostic apartheid based on the evaluative ranking of bodies according to type and severity of impairment:

> The 'naturalness' of the notion of the abled-bodied liberal individual coupled with the negation of a disabled sensibility makes many disabled people queue for the chance to be anointed as 'people first', whilst simultaneously disavowing their previous embodied positions as 'gimps;' and 'cripples'. Ironically, disabled people who achieve 'people first' status are not achieving full normative status but are only legitimizing an able-bodied resemblance through their desire for normality.
>
> (Overboe, 1999, p. 24)

The desire to emulate the Other (the norm) establishes and maintains a wide gap between those who are loathed and that which is desired. The linkage between internalised racism as a 'rational' response to oppression makes it possible to examine the operation of 'dishonour'. Watt-Jones (2002) noted two levels of shame; the first is linked with being a person of colour, the second relates to a shame induced by being consciously aware of one's shamefulness. Kuusisto's (1998) autobiographical extract, *Planet of the Blind,* captures this sense of shame for disabled people:

> Raised to know I was blind but taught to disavow it, I grew bent over like the dry tinder grass. I couldn't stand up proudly, nor could I retreat. I reflected my mother's complex bravery and denial and marched everywhere at dizzying speeds without a cane. Still, I remained ashamed of my blind self, that blackened [sic] dolmen.
>
> (p. 7)

Shamefulness is magnified in culture where the rhetoric of being a survivor, a non-victim, is powerful and being a victim is to be 'passive or deficient' (Watt-Jones, 2002, p. 594). For 'enlightened' disabled people, such shame taps into a wellspring of discourses of residual disability deficiency. The emerging counter-story of the disability survivor prevents us from exploring the personal costs of disability subordination and normalisation. For instance, in my own scholarly community, the few staff members with disability report privately struggling with demands to perform, live up to leadership challenges and mentoring expectations. As an isolated minority, there are few opportunities to find a sanctuary for healing/sheltering from the forces of ableism. In Australia, there is an awareness that many of our disability rights movement leaders are suffering 'burnout', have had emotional collapses or just moved on in order to cope with the realities of living in a hostile world.

Internalised ableism can mean that the disabled person is caught 'between a rock and a hard place'. In order to attain the benefit of a 'disabled identity' one must constantly participate in the processes of disability disavowal, aspire towards the norm, reach a state of near-ablebodiedness, or at the very least to effect a state of 'passing'. As Kimberlyn Leary (1999) described,

> Passing occurs when there is perceived danger in disclosure.... It represents a form of self-protection that nevertheless usually disables, and sometimes destroys, the self it means to safeguard.
>
> (p. 85)

The workings of internalised ableism by way of 'passing' are only possible by moving the focus from the impaired individual to the arena of relationships. Ableist passing is not just an individual hiding their impairment or morphing their disability; ableism involves the *failure* to ask about difference, that is disability/impairment. For internalised ableism to occur there needs to be an existing *a priori* presumption of *compulsory ableness*. Such passing is about not disturbing the peace, containing the matter that is potentially out of place.[3] An example of 'passing' under these circumstances would be experiencing trepidation about revealing one's impairment status fearing stigma and workplace discrimination, despite the fact that work colleagues would benefit from disability focused mentoring and exposure (see Bishop, 1999; Monaghan, 1998).

A *benchmark* of successful inclusion is the acquisition of new skills for performing the part(s) of a disembodied abled self. Although there can be no denial of an injured body, one 'solution' is to emphasise those aspects of self that are able to mimic the qualities of ableist personhood. The disabled body is constantly in a state of deferral, in a holding pattern, waiting for the day it will be not just repaired but made anew (cured). Until then the conditions of fabrication, of mimicking the abled-body, are usually of a disembodied kind because it is assumed that flight from the body will act as a distraction towards those assimilating qualities of social conduct and deportment. In time, we will be able to re-create normalcy by rebuilding or morphing the injured body to a form that for all practical purposes replicates the old (whole) form (see Campbell, 2004). New technologies, therefore, have the effect of re-conceptualising impairment in terms of provisional or tentative disability (Campbell, 2005a, 2007), thus promoting ableism.

Internalisation involves apprehending that which 'belongs to the "other" [and incorporating it as] one's own' (Wertsch, 1998, p. 53). Clearly the processes of internalisation are not straightforward and predictable. As Fanon (1963) remarked, 'In the colonial context the settler only ends his work of breaking in the native when the latter admits loudly and intelligibly the supremacy of the white man's values' (Fanon, 1963, cited McClintock (1995), p. 329). The internalisation process requires something that '...only their superior dominators have or can give them' (Oliver, 2004, p. 78). Internalised ableism means that to emulate the norm, the disabled individual is required to embrace, indeed to assume, an 'identity' other than one's own. I am not implying that people have only one true or real essence. Indeed, identity formation is in a constant state of fluidity, multiplicity and (re)formation. However, disabled people often feel compelled to manufacture 'who' they are – to adopt aspects that are additional to self. It is useful to concentrate on what Butler (1997b) aptly referred to as the 'psychic life' of power. She describes this psycho-social dimension as:

> An account of subjection, it seems, must be traced in the turns of psychic life. More specifically, it must be traced in the peculiar turning of a subject against itself that takes place in acts of self-reproach, conscience, and melancholia that work in tandem with processes of social regulation.
>
> (p. 19)

Sometimes disabled people adopt the labels of disablement 'strategically' to gain access to social benefits. This adoption of a disability category or classification does not mean that an individual with disability holds to a belief that 'they are disabled', an example being Deaf people registering for disability programmes even if sections of this group do not identify as 'disabled'. Rather without a classification or diagnosis it is very difficult to have certain needs arising out of bodily or mental differences recognised. This approach might initially seem commendable and even viewed as an act of subversion against government regulation; however, it also may produce a conflicted self. In other words, the processes of identity formation *cannot be* separated from the individual who is brought into being through those very subjectifying processes. Butler (1997b) describes this process of the 'carrying of a mnemic trace':

> One need only consider the way in which the history of having been called an injurious name is embodied, how the words enter the limbs, craft the gesture, bend the spine ... how these slurs accumulate over time, dissimulating their history, taking on the semblance of the natural, configuring and restricting the doxa that counts as 'reality'.
>
> (p. 159)

It is beyond the scope of this chapter to discuss these complex processes in detail suffice to say that disabled people do not passively and uncritically absorb negative representations of disability, rather life involves a constant negotiation with competing responses to disability (both positive, negative and contradictory) often resulting in an ongoing state of ambivalence.

Philosopher Linda Purdy (1996) contended that it is important to resist conflating disability with the disabled person. She writes,

> My disability is not me, no matter how much it may affect my choices. With this point firmly in mind, it should be possible mentally to separate my existences from the existence of my disability.
>
> (p. 68)

The problem with Purdy's conclusion is that it is psychically untenable, not only because it is posited around a type of dualism, that simply separates being-ness (the mind and emotions) from embodiment (matter, in this case the body), but also because this kind of reasoning disregards the dynamics of identity formation. The experience of impairment within an ableist context *can* and *does* effect the formation of self – in other words 'disability *is* me', but that 'me' does not need to be imbued with a negative sense of self-ness. Purdy's (1996) bodily detachment appears locked into a loop that is filled with internalised ableism, a state with negative views of impairment, from which the only escape is disembodiment and the penalty of denial is a flight from her body. By unwittingly performing ableism, disabled people become complicit in their own demise, reinforcing impairment as an undesirable state.

What begins as an attempt to gain benefits and potentially usurp the forces of classification and calculation in the governing of disability often ends up becoming complicit, reproducing the constitutional ontologies essential to the continued power of ableism. The deployment of the denotation of disability strategically cannot be undertaken without some incorporation of internalised ableism, either at a conscious or at an unconscious level. Within ableism disability cannot be detached from its negative association. People, living with an impairment, face these two co-existing dynamics, sometimes jostling in tension, even when adopting outlaw and resistant subjectivities and lifestyles:

> I HATE [it] when people tell me how well I've overcome my disability. To me, it's suggesting that I am separate from my body. But my body is me and I am my body. This includes my disability. It is part of who I am and a part of what makes my body beautiful and a part of what makes me a beautiful person. My disability CANNOT be separated from who I am. I cannot overcome my own body.
>
> (Shain, 2002)

By applying CRT (c.f. Delgado & Stefancic, 2000) to an analysis of ableism, I have pointed to its embeddedness in our society. The very existence of ableism and its effects, like racism, are covert, but more often profoundly hidden. Ableism is an epistemology (a knowledge framework) and an ontological modality (a way of being) that frames an individual's identity formation and, thus, becomes the power 'that animates ones emergence', through complicity and resistance (Butler, 1997b, p. 198). At the end of this chapter, two strong images of living with impairment emerge. The first is of disabled people as *survivors*. Disabled people labour under the pain and burden of violence. This labouring has resulted in lives of *ontological vulnerability*. There is an ethical imperative for us to interrogate the impact of ableism and speak of the injuries it causes for disabled people. By exposing the practices of ableism and the hidden process of internalised ableism, I am mindful of the necessity to not cause further injury. An example here could be the continual use of photographic images of people exhibited as freaks when alive, and re-exhibited to illustrate ableist practices. To do so reinforces the notion of an overwhelming vision of catastrophe, where disabled people are forever sucked into the vortex of being perpetual victims. This chapter invites the reader to enter the field of critical ableism studies. It argues the critical need to investigate internalised ableism and its effects on the psychic life of our community. One of the approaches of CRT is storytelling, or counter-storytelling, in combination with the 'historical triangulation of facts that have an impact on present-day discrimination' (Parker & Stovall, 2004). The historical silence of disabled people has been overcome through the emergence of the disability rights movement and the development of critical disability studies. However, the study of ableism, especially internalised ableism, moves outside the narrow confines of individualised life-stories and squarely locates itself within a collectivist history of ideas and the field of discursive practices. For example, further research could explore the process of counter-story telling about the so-called 'disability success stories'. Normally these stories are often based on the notion of 'success *in spite of* impairment' which is profoundly different to stories that embrace impairment and are based on the notion of 'success *because of* disability' or stories about living with ableism.

The second image is of disabled people engaged in guerrilla activity – rejecting the promises of liberalism and looking elsewhere, daring to think in *alternative ways* about impairment. For too long, marginality and liminality have been viewed as places of exile from which the emarginated are to be 'brought in from the cold' and integrated so they too can sit beside the 'warm fires' of liberalism (and all will be well). However, as bell hooks (1990) reminded us, the margin can be '... more than a site of deprivation ... it is also the site of radical possibility, a space of resistance' (hooks, 1990, p. 149).

3
Tentative Disability – Mitigation and Its Discontents

Increasingly law mediates medico-technological formulations of impairment. Many years ago it was hard to imagine a scenario where disabled people could be pressured into obtaining surgical, prosthetic or pharmacological interventions in order to avail themselves of the identity of the 'disabled person', thus enabling them to access social services and legislative protections. This chapter first explores how law operates as a narrative and provides an outline of legal baggage and backdrops. The legal story-teller makes certain unconscious and implicit *choices* regarding the spaces and places within which the narrative or story of disability unfolds. Rather than being neutral, these choices reinforce a performative compulsion for sameness and a notion that disability is *inherently* negative. I then explore disabled peoples' encounter with the law and the matter of mitigation of disability in law. Finally, I demonstrate how these legal formulations have the capacity to redefine disability as being *provisional* or *tentative*.

Legal baggage and backdrops

Law has traditionally had an ambivalent attitude towards disabled people, restricting itself to being an arbiter of rules and policies about care and protection. The rule of law and its enactment in common law, constitutions focus on the rights of individuals, as enforced by courts. A frequent motif in the literature on the rule of law is that the rule protects against the use of arbitrary power by governments against individuals. Joseph Raz (1977) notes elasticity of the notion of arbitrary power, concluding that 'many forms of arbitrary rule are complementary with the rule of law', (p. 2). One aspect of this chapter's focal concerns asks the question – does the trend towards representing disablement in terms of mitigation represent a slide towards the arbitrary use of power by government through the apparatus of law? The insights of legal geography have pointed to the intersection of law, space and power, whereby the spatial order of things (political, economic, ontological and cultural) are lived before they are recited and theorised. Legal texts invoke narratives that involve choices about which spaces and places to include and exclude. These spatial partitions can mask and obscure power relations and power dynamics. Doreen Massey (1997) explains,

> Social space can helpfully be understood as a social product, as constituted out of social relations, social interactions. Moreover, precisely because it is constituted out of social relations, *spatiality is always and everywhere an expression and a medium of power.*
>
> (p. 104)

Thus, critical legal geographers, the 'space invaders', contest the notion of neutral or empty space and point to the centrality of law as enacting spatial hierarchies (c.f. Aoki, 2000). Such cartographical dividing and partitioning, John Comaroff asserts, exposes law as 'the cutting edge of colonialism, an instrument of the power of an alien state and part of the process of coercion... [which became a] tool for pacifying and governing colonized peoples' (2001, pp. 305, 306). What role has law played in the colonisation of disabled people in asserting the rule of ableism? Law is more comfortable in focusing on a *singular place* in the form of an individual person – case by case diachronically, rather than in interrogating communally inherited beliefs synchronically. This has resulted in a process of decontextualisation, whereby action is reduced to individual volition rather than being connected to context, history and legacies. This topographical denial does not present any real difficulties and is quite in keeping with the common law tradition, which as Wesley Pue (1990) readily points out is already *anti-geographical* – deriving its meaning in an abstracted, acontextual way, removed from the spatially materialities in which it is contested. When courts construct legal doctrine and write judicial opinions, they do so by organising and interpreting events and ontologies of personhood according to a narrative in which the events and characters 'relate to one another and to some overarching structure, in the context of an opposition or struggle' (Ewick & Sibley, 1995, p. 200). However, the elusive nature of impairment (particular when lived out in a social context) and the problematical difficulties, in some instances, of forecasting prognosis do not neatly fit with the law's focus on rules, formulae and predictability.

Legal responses to the challenges of disablement persistently demonstrate a *performative passion for sameness* (Stiker, 1999). Not just *any* sameness, but paradoxically and deliberately, a sameness underpinned by an ontological separation between 'abled' and 'disabled', where 'mixtures' are absorbed through processes of fabricating or simulating ableness. In many ways, law is an attempt to create order out of disorder (i.e. diversity and difference) through the process of purification – the establishment and demarcation of distinct zones (disabled/abled, human/non-human) and translation that acknowledges the reality of mixtures between these extremes (refer to Chapter 1). States of disability and health are far more ambiguous and ambivalent than the establishment zones suggest. The health/disability continuum is continually meditated through context (e.g. certain mobility differences *matter* more in distinct environments than others), always fluid and fluctuating according to both internal (organic) and external (environmental) stressors and cultural modalities. Law is uneasy with bodies that ooze or are leaky, especially those that are fat, distressed, sick, dying, addicted and appear impermanent.

I argue that law reflects a broader desire to *drive down disability* – thus ensuring that this class of enumerated persons remains problematically in a *state of exceptionality*, defined by law, rather than being a significant part of a country's population. The state of exceptionality refuses to conceive of disability as a form of difference within the population. The role of biomedicalism coupled with regulative aspects of the law can be found in many legal definitions of disability. For instance, in the Indian *The Person with Disabilities (Equal Opportunities, Protection of Rights and Full Participation) Act*, 1995, disability is reduced to diagnostic types: s. 2 (i) and a 'person with a disability' to 'a person suffering from not less than 40% of any disability as certified by a medical authority' (s. 2 (t)). In this example, the legal enactment of purification zones attempts to settle the matter of disability by way of enumerative exactness and reduction of disability to a medical model. The motif of disability is *much more* than a state of being. Nationalism demands that the archetypal normative citizen be free from flaws and matters of possible degeneracy. In these times of economic rationalism and panics over risk and terror, the sentiments of famous US eugenist case *Buck v Bell*[1] find new credence:

> We have seen more than once that the public welfare may call upon the best citizens for their lives. It would be strange if it could not call upon those who already sap the strength of the State for these lesser sacrifices, often not felt to be such by those concerned, in order to

prevent our being swamped with incompetence. It is better for all the world, if instead of waiting to execute degenerate offspring for crime, or to let them starve for their imbecility, society can prevent those who are manifestly unfit from continuing their kind.... Three generations of imbeciles are enough.

[274 U.S. 200, 208]

The utilisation of legal remedies by disabled people, especially after acquisition of impairment, occurs within a broader sociological context of an increasing 'culture of blame'. The disabled litigant is required to show that they have suffered (Brown, 1993, 1995). For example, when a court declares that a disabled litigant does or does not conform to a legal rendering of disability, the court has to first construct a narrative in which a character (the disabled plaintiff) is faced with an obstacle or conundrum (disability discrimination) posed by an antagonist (a disability discriminatory employer, for instance). In framing a disability discrimination case in this way, a court is assembling a set of circumstances into an intelligible whole, into a coherent narrative in which the actions and events are endowed with intentionality, meaning and purpose. Indeed the whole goal of legal pleadings is *context reduction* and reconstruction through the transmogrification of complex and often contrary realities in the lives of disabled people into coherent, factual 'stock stories'. There are some aspects of non-conforming disability realities which are, so to speak, 'zoned out' because they dispute the seemingly coherent ontology of what a disabled person should be like. On occasion these outlaw realities of disability are subject to being governed and therefore regulated by absorption into *anomalous zones*. According to Razack (1998), these anomalous zones are spaces that tolerate departures from norms and therefore are places where there is the possibility of norm subversion. Legal consciousness, combined with a matrix of scientific ableism (biomedicalism), has produced a fabricated sense of a 'natural' (albeit colonised space) where the juridical tentacles of the law are difficult to trace, let alone to assess what those fabricated 'spaces' enable.

It is the claim of this chapter that spatial realities within disability law, due to the ontological basis of spatiality, have produced the contours of disabled subjectivity. This subjectivity in turn shapes debates about the purview of citizenship, and about which impairments (and the degree thereof) are to be seen as 'acceptable' in advanced capitalist liberal nation-states. In contrast, in the so-called 'developing nations', there are disputes regarding the best way to discern the field of not-disability (i.e. the healthy comparator). Without the specifically marked space of the *disabled person* where human corporeal differences are partitioned from each other, it would not have been possible to *see* the person who is 'disabled' (and who is not), to make visible the disabled gaze. In analysing the law as it pertains to disabled people, I have returned to the concept of 'interest convergence', or situations where white people with power endure or foster black advancement only to the extent that such advancement promotes white interests (Delgado & Stefancic, 2000). Within the arena of the subordination of people of colour, *Richmond* v. *Croson*[2] revealed the limits of race-based interest convergence. In that decision, the Court proclaimed that African-Americans had accomplished racial equity with white people, and as a consequence of their 'success', African-Americans could no longer rely on a history of racial discrimination to argue for the maintenance and introduction of affirmative action programmes.

Studies in ableism invite us to explore the limits of liberal tolerance of disability and the points of departure away from the interests of ableism. Thus, the trend in courts of narrowing the definition of disability by reframing disablement in terms of mitigation has already occurred in the United States and is likely to have international implications (Zugelder & Champagne, 2003). Theresia Degener and Gerard Quinn (2000) note that although US Federal law is jurisdictionally autonomous from the domestic law of other nation states, its flagship disability statute, the *Americans with Disabilities Act 1990* [hereinafter ADA], has become a template globally, to the extent '...that the international impact of this law [the ADA] is larger than its domestic effect'. Regardless of where we live, the notion of mitigation will transform civic understandings of disablement as something that is provisional and tentative. This trend is of concern when the tendency towards a universalised codification of disability (norms) is on the increase.

When law meets disability – possibilities and dangers

The production and designation of the neologism 'disability' (especially in law) cannot occur outside of the purview of the processes and practices of ableism. Legal reasoning is fundamentally ableist, just as it has been argued elsewhere that hegemonic tropes of legal reasoning are inherently masculinist (c.f. MacKinnon, 1989; Minow, 1990). Biomedicalism assumes that impairment encroaches on the psychic life of the disabled person because it asserts that disability is internal, inaugurating a crisis within the person's bodily or cerebral self. Disability is a state that warrants medical interventions, curative treatment and mitigation of the impairment or compensatory legal remedies wherever possible. Whilst the alleviation of discomfort and suffering is critical it cannot be assumed that having a disability automatically results in suffering or disease. Many of the affects of impairment are able to be adequately managed by affordable access to a range of supports, strategies and technologies. It is too easy to assume that impairment is the source of a 'disability problem' rather than the way society responses to impairment as a form of difference.

Medicine in cooperation with law is brought in to assess the 'damaged' body by utilising scaled enumerative scripts such as those typified by the *Table of Maims* whose fiction is legislated into existence. Law's investment in biomedicalism invokes a moral landscape wherein the unruly body is culpable and blameworthy (and thus held responsible) whereas the 'real' disabled body is innocent (thus deserving legal protection). Discourses around medical research, new technologies and practices contain implicit narratives of disability as a *personal medical tragedy*; the existence of impairment and the experience of disability to be inherently negative. As Michael Oliver (1996, p. 32) puts it: 'disability is [viewed as] some terrible chance event which occurs at random to unfortunate individuals'. Biomedical fabrications of ontologies of disability as tragic are policed by law, that has the authorising power to say what disability *is* and *is not*. By showing that a story achieves its meaning and persuasiveness by burying and discounting relevant facts and often by restricting and fixing the spatial scope of a narrative, dominant legal narratives fail to correspond with material reality.

Increasingly, legal regimes are utilised by disabled people to access greater resources and services to mitigate the effects of impairment, and as a vehicle for the monetary compensation of loss. However, recent studies have suggested the emergence of a paradox, wherein the application for disability benefits and compensation can generate feelings of despondency as the disabled person engages in a process of altered perceptions and puts on the 'clothes of a disabled identity' (Holloway, 1994; Sayer et al., 2004). Throughout these processes, the disabled litigant is required to 'identify' with the disabled person before even commencing the process of articulating a breach of rights or securing protective remedies. The litigant needs to draw on a wellspring of suffering and future damage. Under the *Americans with Disabilities Act* 1990 (ADA) disabled people are viewed as a 'discrete, insular minority' (Barhorst, 1999–2000, p. 139; Hasday, 2004), reinforcing the belief that disability is exceptional rather than normative. This *insular version* of disablement

Figure 2 Shifts in legal performances of disability.

carries with it a negative connotation that Rovner (2001, p. 250) argued is 'hard wired into law'.

A 'good citizen' is one who does the 'right thing' by mitigating an assumed burden associated with their impairment (see Figure 2). Legal discourses play a critical role in maintaining the distinction between those designated as 'sick', 'well', 'deserving' and 'undeserving'. Disabled peoples' interactions with law necessitate that disabled people act in ways that are in accordance with discourses norm of abled-ness. Maybe the spectacle of a disabled litigant acting out a part (the 'disabled role') in court would be amusing; a performance necessary to achieve a remedy, were it not for the enduring psychic consequences of playing to such a drama. It is important to not just look at what is confessed or how disability is spoken of in trial judgments, but also there is a need to interrogate the silences and uncontested assumptions about disablement. *Injury* then, and its companion response: mitigation of impairment has become the interpretative lens from which to speak of the experiences of impairment and its performative and economic impacts. In short, the entry point of disability into law is through the doors of 'deficiency' – an assumed deficiency in the body, merging into a deficiency in character.

The art of lawyering is a process that involves fictional creations of truth, where as Cain (1994, p. 33) described 'lawyers are imaginative traders in words. But these symbols traders are also creative. They invent categories and these categories constitute the practices and institutions within which their clients can achieve their objectives.' In so far as deficiency and the tragedy of impairment are assumed, liminality created by an ableist culture, and the ways law culturally mediates difference and marginality become curtailed and hidden. The necessity to embrace the narrative of suffering signifies disability as a negative state. The burden of negative formulations of disablement means that the disabled litigant would have difficulty if she wished to present an affirmative approach to living with an impairment coloured, by a mixture of joy and despair. Such a representation is diametrically opposed to dominant cultural narratives of disablement as catastrophe and therefore as Rovner (2001, p. 277) observed 'law's constraints make it impossible for [those] stories...to be heard and recognized'.

In summary, the inscription of certain figurations of legal disability requires that disabled people's 'experiences' be regulated within the confines of juridical formations, ultimately foreclosing any alternative perspectives. Interestingly, the delimitation and marking of certain bodies as 'disabled' or 'injured' bears little resemblance to the views of impaired people and is ostensibly 'imposed through policies of repression and coercion' (Emecke, 2000, p. 494). Legal rendering of disability through statutory definitions and case law can produce a dissonance between those 'official' and private realities. The self-understanding of impairment is very complex. It is not clear about the extent to which individual with impairments internalise the tragic scripts (known as internalised ableism) not refashion them as acts of resistance. See Campbell (2008) and Emecke (2000).

Mitigation Compulsions or 'The most envenomed serpents admit of some mitigation, and will not bite their benefactors' (Josephus, 1974, p. xvii. v. §5).

Philosophical conversations about *mitigation* raise a number of questions related to the quandary of impairment, such as: What does it mean to mitigate impairment? What is the justification for mitigation? Do disabled people have a *duty* to mitigate their impairment? In exploring these questions, I argue that it is important to also think about how answers to these questions would differ (or not) if we were responding to mitigation in the context of people of colour, gay men, lesbians and women. In which case, what difference does having a disability make and why does disability make a difference? The borderlands of disability and the security of impassable crossings between the realities of able-bodiedness and disablement mean that such orderings are not just repressive but ultimately productive; they tell us stories, they contain narratives as to 'who' we are and how we 'should be'. In other words, as John Law rightly concludes, 'ethics will derive from ontology. And ontology, what there is, is being made at least in part in narratives' (Law, 1999). The fact is that hegemonic narratives of disablement undoubtedly assume that disability *qua* disability is inherently negative.

I want to start, rather unusually on my part, with a dictionary definition of 'mitigation':

> **Mitigation: 1.** Compassion, mercy, favour. Obs.
> **2a.** The action of mitigating or moderating; the fact or condition of being mitigated; an instance of this; spec. abatement or relaxation of the severity or rigour of a law, penalty, etc.; extenuation or palliation of an offence, fault, etc.; abatement or minimization of the loss or damage resulting from a wrongful act. **in mitigation** (Law): by way of extenuation or palliation (esp. of an offence) in order to obtain a favourable modification (of judgment, a penalty, damages).
>   **b.** Something that serves to mitigate; a mitigating circumstance or provision; a palliative. Later also in Criminal Law: mitigating circumstances collectively esp. presented or accepted in extenuation of an offence.
> **3.** Prob.: a soothing remedy. Obs.
> **4.** Softening or qualification of wording, etc. Obs.
> **5.** Taming (of an animal). Obs.(Oxford English Dictionary Online, 1989)

At the outset, 'mitigation' signals a desire to soothe, to make mild or gentle[3] that which is being mitigated. When applying such sentiments to disablement, the vision of soothing the suffering body under the guise of care and compassion comes to mind. Moving through the definition, phrases like 'minimisation of the loss or damage' appear as 'a palliative' response (Definition 2b), but interestingly, also as a 'taming' of an animal (Definition 5). Does mitigation then, transcend a therapeutic response and become a strategy for taming the unruly disabled body? One development that has attracted the attention of some legal scholars is the use of terminology such as 'elective' or 'voluntary' disability. Proponents of the legal concept of *elective disability* have argued that legislatures should distinguish between two categories of 'disability' when they make assessments for coverage (protection) under anti-discrimination legislation, namely, the categories of *immutable* and *elective* (or *voluntary*) disability. As these legal theorists explain, the category of 'immutable disability' should apply to situations in which it is not possible (at least, not at present) to eliminate the disability (where this term usually means 'impairment'). Under these circumstances, a plaintiff should be deemed innocent and, therefore, deserving of support and care. The category of 'voluntary' ('elective')[4] disability should, on the other hand, be used in situations where disabilities were caused, continue to exist, or have been worsened by individual 'voluntary' conduct (Hasday, 2004; Key, 1996; Tucker, 1998).

The philosophical discussion of these proposed concepts is heavily laden with the language of moral judgement. In an argument about the need to ensure the integrity of the ADA and to maintain public support for that statute, Lisa Key remarked that extending protections to those people who she identifies as 'voluntarily disabled' may result in 'the loss of protection for those who are truly deserving' (Key, 1996, p. 80). In another hypothetical case of a janitor with a back injury who did not attend therapy, she stated, '[he] refused to help himself, while at the same time expecting others, ... to bear the costs of accommodation' (Key, 1996, p. 82). No reason is proffered as to why the janitor may not have attended therapy. She used another hypothetical example of a man who sustained a spinal injury through the 'reckless' behaviour of diving in shallow water. Key (1996) painted a picture of an individual who failed to lift more than 30 pounds in a rehabilitation programme. She concludes,

> He is making an informed, conscious decision to continue living with the impairment. This is his prerogative. However, society should not be obligated to bear the cost of his choice.
>
> (p. 84)

The perspective of Key (1996) reveals a kind of reasoning which denies the reality of competing demands and values in the lives of disabled people. These legal arguments occur within the politico-juridical context that disability is ontologically intolerable, a corporeal state that slips closely towards the precipice of the human underbelly. Further, I contend that this argument is underscored by the presupposition that disability *is* harm and impairment is harmful to disabled people psychologically, spiritually and bodily and that the existence of impairment is harmful to the social order, in particular economic life. The law's role in scaling suffering and injury according to biomedical perspectives can be contrasted with an alternative way of rendering suffering or more specifically 'injury'. Emecke (2000) argued that 'injury' captures those asymmetrical power relations between self-referentiality and external retort or perception, in this instance in the reasoning and pronouncements of courts. This conclusion finds support in the writing of Laura Rovner, a legal practitioner and academic who argues that under the ADA the disabled person carries the burden of proving that they have been harmed. In order to do so, the person is required to adopt a victim identity, which may not only be in conflict with her own sense of self but reinforces the very negative figuring of disablement (as weak, passive, suffering victims) that the ADA purports to challenge (Rovner, 2001, pp. 252–253). This negative clothing of disablement remains even after the litigation has ended and is difficult to shake off.

Casing disability

Contestations over the meaning of disability under the ADA are exemplified in a series of cases brought in the U.S. Supreme Court in 1999 known as the *mitigation trilogy*,[5] More recently, the High Court in Australia, in *Purvis*[6] was asked to decide the definition (delimitation) of 'disability' under the *Disability Discrimination Act* 1992 (Cth). Disputes over the definition of 'disability' in disability discrimination cases under domestic laws are more often than not about broader philosophical issues about where to 'draw a line in the sand' about disability and non-disability. These disputes go to the heart of 'dilemmas of difference', and how archaeologies of difference are mapped. One thing that becomes clear in a number of ADA judgments is the struggles by judges to deal with the arbitrariness of impairment. In the District court case of *Lawson v. CSX Transportation*[7] (2000), this conundrum is brought to the foreground. The Court argued that if it failed to account for mitigating measures taken by disabled individuals, then 'all diabetics would be considered disabled... A diabetic whose illness does not impair his or her daily activities would therefore be considered disabled simply because he or she is diabetic.'[8] Later, the judges claimed that a proposal to broaden the definition of major life activities 'would open the ADA to countless potential plaintiffs who have innumerable conditions that cause their bodies to function in ways outside normal parameters, notwithstanding the condition's impacts on the plaintiffs' daily activities'.[9] Justice Antonio Scalia in *Murphy v United Parcel Service* (1999) is reported to have removed his glasses to reveal his 'sightlessness' and his potential inclusion as 'disabled' when acting without the mitigation of his glasses (Wasserman, 2000).

The juridical power of law and its capacity to name or erase different ways of framing disability were put to the test in a series of decisions that the U.S. Supreme Court handed down in 1999. There were three cases that altered the definition of disability under *Title 1 (Employment)* of the *ADA*. The central question in the trio of cases was whether disability should be measured in its 'untreated' state, or in light of any corrective measures that would give the appearance of normal function-ing. In its examination of the meaning of the term 'disability' in the context of the ADA, the U.S. Supreme Court held that determination of whether a person is 'disabled' or not should be made by evaluating impairment in its unmitigated state (*Sutton* 2146–2147, per O'Connor). However, the Majority judgment of Justice Sandra Day O'Connor held that:

> ... if a person is taking measures to correct for, or mitigate, a physical or mental impairment, the effects of those measures – both positive and negative – must be taken into account when judging whether that person is 'substantially limited' in a major life activity and thus 'disabled' under the Act (2146, per O'Connor).

The courts complicity in the semantic recuperation of what constitutes a mitigating measure may open a Pandora's Box as various Court's attempt to discern the difference between compensatory measures and correc-tions. Barhorst (1999–2000, p. 164) concluded, '... disabled persons who must mitigate their impairment to survive will have no recourse against an employer's decision'. What is interesting about these cases is that they illustrate some of the ways that technological applications mediate various discourses about the ontology of disability in law, and dis-putes over disability discrimination enact discourses that traumatise and penalise the resistant impaired body. Such structures require the Courts to anticipate 'a person's decision whether or not to pursue medical inter-ventions [as well as evaluate the status of] an operation [that] would have ameliorated the effects of an impairment but was rejected as too risky?' (Mayerson & Mayer, 2000). Instead of clarifying the meaning of disability, the trilogy of ADA cases (*Sutton*, *Murphy* and *Albertson*) has provoked a series of new questions with respect to the techno-logical morphing of normalcy. The Court in all three cases concluded that individuals who 'mitigate' their impairments must have this fac-tor considered when evaluation is made with respect to their coverage under the lawful 'disability' definitions of the ADA. However, none of those cases addressed the question of whether individuals have a *duty* to mitigate impairment; that is, if individuals 'choose' not to engage technologies (aids, prescriptions drugs and so on) that seem to mitigate their impairments, should they still be considered disabled? For exam-ple, should a woman without arms be required to wear a prosthesis or have a hand transplant in order to be considered 'disabled' under the ADA? Whilst this line of argument was raised in the District Court case of *Finical* v. *Collection Unlimited* (1999),[10] it was soundly rejected by the Supreme Court. We might extend these questions further in order to ask this question: will current (and future) morphing technologies contribute to the framing of a benchmark mitigated disabled body which is used to assess definitional conformity irrespective of the matter of usage or 'choice'? Will today's 'normal' body be superseded, that is, become tomorrow's 'abnormal' body?

Aftermaths: disability as provisional or tentative

> For constitutions … are like principles that claim to be general, to govern, to regulate. Despite the fact that they never did, this is no doubt a sometimes useful fiction. One we will hold onto sometimes, perhaps even much of the time – but also one which we give up here and there in order to interfere and try to make specific differences to the arrangements of specific institutions (Law, 1999).
>
> … The ADA, as constructed by the current Court, can hardly be said to do much of anything to protect disabled people. Instead the Court's activist interventionism has done a great deal to shield both private employers and public officials, in addition to denying the importance of past discrimination while preserving as much of the pre-ADA status quo as possible. The Court's central message to disabled people seems to be 'Get over it.'
>
> (Soifer, 2003)

In Australia, one method of discouraging full entry into the Australian community, complete with full rights and responsibilities, is to give certain classes of immigrants temporary visas. Likewise, other classes of immigrants who are deemed to be acceptable as 'new' Australians have the opportunity to avail themselves of permanent resident status or indeed to become a full Australian citizen. Keeping this motif in mind, disabled people, to a greater or lesser extent, are still busy articulating entitlements to full citizenship status – that is, having access to economic, political and cultural resources available to other classes of citizens. Australia's particular brand of welfare liberalism is characterised by a *residual orientation* primarily reliant on paid employment with a sharply targeted (restrictive) safety net of benefits for individuals who for 'no fault of their own' are not in the paid workforce. The residualist approach means that even those groups provided with assistance are positioned out-of-bounds of citizenry – they are, so to speak, 'remainders', euphemistically labelled welfare recipients. Harris (2001) provided a definition of the 'moral-behavioural dimension' of welfare rationalities as one that:

> Revolves around constructs such as responsibility, independence, motive and effort. It embodies governmental evaluations of proper/improper and responsible/irresponsible behaviours, suggests how people ought to behave, and sets out governmental strategies to achieve the desired ends.
>
> (p. 6)

This chapter has pointed to the emergence of conceptual and judicial realities that err towards the notion of mitigated impairment in one country and is already having various ramifications in countries such as Australia and Canada. This is what *has* already happened. Yet, what *could* happen, should the notion of mitigated impairment, and its associated state of tentative or provisional disability, become mainstreamed within law and service provision? As part of this paper's focal concerns there are two spatial faultlines that are easy to miss that no doubt frequently, but silently coincide and occasionally collide. The *first faultline's* purview is jurisprudence and involves the cause of action and scope of discrimination. In this scenario judicial reasoning oscillates between seeing discrimination in 'a cut and dry manner... anticipat[ing] all possible scenarios and deciding which should be regulated and how' and the converse response, where discrimination is conceptualised as 'a problem of human interaction that is fluid and constantly manifesting itself in new forms such that we have no clear sense of all the circumstances in which it might arise in future or what to do about them' (Réaume, 2002, p. 122).

The *second faultline* is specific to the theorisation of disability within critical disability studies and the activist movement as a whole. Disability is viewed catachrestically, as an unstable, spatially and historically contingent concept. Yet rather paradoxically, the notion of disabled people as a protected class is often engaged strategically as '...a valid and unifying identity that reflects the real experiences and culture of a large group of people' (Eichhorn, 1998–1999, p. 1414). The American Courts, when confronted with knowledge about the fluidity of impairment and its potential unboundedness, have sought to make disability more *workable* by attempting to delimit and contain impairment. This lack of acceptance of impairment in it's 'untreatable state' and the consequential concept of disability as provisional or tentative re-asserts the belief that disability is inherently negative – a bodily order that is waiting to be expunged. In the meantime, the mitigation compulsion leaves disabled people with the sense that the only kind of impairment acceptable is one that is veiled or hidden. Passing becomes an esteemed attribute.

Passing is not just about the impaired person hiding their impairment or morphing their disability. This strategy occurs in a culture of 'ableism', which involves a failure to ask about difference, in this instance, disability/impairment. For, as seen in the previous chapter, internalised ableism needs to have an existing *a priori* presumption of *compulsory ableness* (or at least the aspiration of ableness). Such passing is about keeping the coloniser happy by not disturbing the peace, containing the matter that is potentially out of place. The proposal to conceptualise disability as tentative or provisional, to assign it spatially to a 'temporary zone', should not be confused with the Jacques Derrida's notion of deferability, where in our case the signifier disability has its meaning deferred for the present, still impending and awaiting (Campbell, 1999). Instead, positioning disability as tentative conjures up the notion of disability *in waiting*, disability *standing in reserve* for technologies that can restore wholeness. This view of disablement has the potential to realign social planning away from a focus on 'care' to that of 'cure'. A shift away from the notion of permanence may mean that governments will become hesitant to invest in long-term service provision infrastructure and cordon off citizenship rights only to those with immutable disability. The political and civil rights implications of these speculations are unimaginable – disabled people who wish to seek good fortunes are likely to feel compelled to resort to mitigation measures, least they be prepared to feel the full weight of being assigned the label of having a voluntary disability. Hard to imagine – let us feel compelled to imagine so that we can be prepared to act.

4
Love Objects and Transhuman Beasts? Riding the Technologies

Introduction

Technologies in the form of sentiency, objects, spatialisation not only enact the demarcations between nature and culture, human and alterate; technologies mediate the conditions of ableism remediating the ways the abled body and mentality can be known. This chapter implores the reader to think more deeply about technologies and disability. Although disabled people more so than other kinds of humans have had an erotic consubstantial liaison with technologies, it can be argued that more recent developments in the world of techno-science materially and ontologically usher in a kind of somatic fusion between the corporeally anomalous body and the artefact.[1] More than ever, I argue we are witnessing a new kind of human subjectivity – intersubjectivity if you like – technological humans – hybrids, cyborgs or monsters. What better place to extend our ideas about ableism and the production of disability than the subject of transhumanism with all its incumbent issues around ontology, humanness and of course the place of technology. We visit the relational ontology formed and invested through technologies as well as the Brave New World of the enhanced human, the extropian ideal of the *überman* who proclaims disability as a designation for the non-(re)constructed bodies of the Old World. An underlying question of the chapter asks whether there is a new relation between nature and culture, between human relations with objects, or are we just witnessing a new configuration of ableist relations based on an intrinsic human–technological relation?

Rather than holding to a simplistic view that technologies are inherently dangerous or implicitly beneficial, this chapter attends to ways technology is engaged, its disjunctures and constructed boundaries. I begin with a discussion of the work of a number of philosophers of technology (Martin Heidegger, Robert McGinn, to name a few) arguing that certain aspects of their thought can be appropriated as useful tools from which to assess technological formations. This exploration continues by looking at what I have called 'dis/technologies' – particular kinds of artefacts that fuse with the disabled body and incorporate subjectivity. The latter part of the chapter outlines developments in enhancement technologies and the shift towards transhumanism and what this means for concepts of normalcy.

Technological enframing

Martin Heidegger's thinking about technology is a good point at which to start to consider the ontological effects of technological intercourse. The strength of Heidegger's work concerning technology lies in his refusal to essentialise the existence of technology and thus lapse into mitigation projects that seek to arrest technological determinism. In fact he adamantly rejects both instrumentalist and anthological definitions of technology (Heidegger, 1977). Both approaches seem quite futile, being locked into a permanent vortex/tussle over domination and subordination concerns. Heidegger does recognise the 'dangers' counter posed by the 'promise' of technologies. Instead, Heidegger attempts to refigure, reframe our orientation to technological concerns by moving discourse out of the realm of the mechanistic to the philosophical, linking technological investigation to the meaning of being (*der Sim von Sein*). 'Being' provides the framework for working out which entities are entities, Life (*Leben*) as Life, how we come to an entity and sort them through. Very early in the lecture *The Question Concerning Technology* (1977), Heidegger makes it quite clear that it is not possible to 'opt out' of the technological matrix – just like power, technology cannot be escaped, there is not inside and outside to technology and human subjectification:

> Thus we shall never experience our relationship to the essence of technology so long as we merely conceive and usher forward the technological, put up with it, or evade it. Everywhere we remain unfree and chained to technology, whether we passionately affirm or deny it.
>
> (p. 287)

Hence technology is intrinsic to metaphysics and is a mode of revealing being. Now it would be easy to assume from this statement a kind of technological nihilism. On the contrary, our consubstantiality with technology presents new openings to rethinking technological relationality and materiality, thus breaking away from the rigid circular thinking that dominates much of the debate about disabilities and technology. Heidegger's new episteme can open up the conversation about the connectedness of ontology, corporeality and artefact. Heidegger proposes a new discipline, metaphysics, a new way of figuring the essence of technology that precedes the development of the nineteenth-century mechanised forms – indeed he returns us to Greek philosophy. After revisiting the philosophical question of causality, Heidegger exacts the Aristotelian understanding of 'cause' as 'effecting'. Using the example of the creation of a Communion Chalice, Heidegger introduces the notion of an artefact coming into being – not just as a mere object, but its 'chaliceness' (or essence). Such a bringing forth *poeisis* results in a kind of enlightened *aletheia*, an 'unveiling' or 'revealing' of a concealed essence of technology:

> Technology is therefore no mere means. Technology is a way of revealing. If we give heed to this, then another whole realm for the essence of technology will open itself up to us (Heidegger, 1977, p. 294) (emphasis added).

At this point it is possible to talk of *dis/technologies*[2] as having a normative essence – crafted around the conditions of ableism wherein certain technologies are assigned to rein in anomaly in particularised fashions. The history of dis/technology is to purge, restrain, realign and normalise ableist comportment. Modern trends are to de-crip technology and assign to new and more marketable meaning, to induce technological attractions – the super limits of the prosthetic leg or the sexed up colours of the cochlear implant. In conjunction with this understanding, Heidegger (1977) returns to the etymological source of 'technology' – stemming from *technikon*, meaning that which belongs to *techné* (p. 294). Imbued within this definition is not only the skilled craft, but also a poetic bringing forth – a kind of desirous knowing that discloses 'technologies essence constitut[ing] the meaning of being in our age' (Dahlstrom, 1988, p. 150). In contrast, modern technology's mode of revealing itself to the world is one of 'challenging forth' (*herausforden*), where there is an obsession with techniques of extraction, exploitation and exhaustion enframed[3] within a 'resource' paradigm

(Heidegger, 1977, p. 296). This is more than a Luddite anti-technological stance. As Dreyfus (1995, p. 54) draws together the perspective:

> The threat is not a *problem* for which there can be a *solution* but an ontological *condition* from which we can be *saved*. Heidegger's concern is the human distress caused by the *technological understanding of being*, rather than the destruction caused by specific technologies.
>
> (p. 99)

The hegemony of challenging forth revealing most often results in ontological transformation of living beings and artefacts. Heidegger uses the example of the Rhine River to support his argument (Heidegger, 1977, p. 297). The Rhine is transmogrified from a source of philosophical, aesthetic and cultural inspiration to mere energy source/resources when coupled with a hydroelectric dam. In terms of the perfectible human body we can see a similar patterning and re-ontologising. For instance, the demands of labour and operationalisation of mechanics may reinvent the productive, resourceful human body (under the sign of ableism), one that is permanently 'standing in reserve',[4] one not of value for itself, but only of use for something – a 'human resource'. It is a body that can be surveyed and cartographically inscribed in terms of species-typical functioning. We can argue then that this dominant process of technological enframing and revealing that ontologically converts the productive body also creates its constitutive outside – the useless body. For Heidegger threat is when 'calculative thinking...come(s) to be accepted and practiced as the only way of thinking' thus flat lining the constitution of being (Heidegger, 1966, p. 56).

It is important however not to become stuck here, for Heidegger suggests it is possible to have a renewed orientation, revealing of technology as enframing occurs as the point of its interaction with the world. So there is always a possibility of play, of resistance, of 'saving power' by employing a poiesistic orientation – a taking part in the processes of coming to being. Heidegger's conclusions provide a firm basis for developing an analytics of disability and technological intersections. By employing a strategy of techne, a mindfulness towards 'things', it is possible to move with technologies. As Daniel Dahlstrom (1988) summarises,

> Such composure demands that thinking and not mere reckoning, be brought into play as, a measure of things. In other words, maintaining this equanimity towards things requires seeing them for what

they are, a kind of thinking that does not pre-emptively subordinate things to special interests or to a particular scheme of organization. Heidegger was in dead earnest about the necessity of searching for a way out of the danger presented by modern technology, but the search can only begin with this composure toward things and the kind of thinking that sees the technological world for what it is, a world of danger and promise.

(p. 153)

Heidegger's insight provides an opportunity to develop a counter-ableist disposition towards technologies. How does one see dis/technologies for 'what they are'? What are the particular ways that disabled people interpolate those technologies to integrate/to fuse it with their own beingness. Does having composure towards things mean that there is a demand to sense corporeality and spatiality differently. We can summarise Heidegger's ideas about technology by arguing that the very essence of technology not only constitutes the meaning of contemporary being – but that human life, *geist* and action (*poiesis*) are technologies in a constant state of disclosing and unfolding. It is this denial or mis-recognition of such 'truth' that prompts a separation between being and doing – and incites a suspicion of not only technologies but a mis-negotiation of necessary equipmentality and the prosthetic imagination. What do we see in the wheelchair user – their confinement, the contraption, the not-possible rather than the smooth gliding carrying device that sometimes speeds? Is the composure in terms of design and aesthetics towards the invalid aid, or a counter-revealing of a transmogrified person who has an expanded corporeality – the norm does not possess? Alternatively dis/technology can foster the birthing of the abled-disabled or nearly-abled who in morphing normalcy through a dis/technological embrace can turn towards participation in society by dis-attending to disability. Moving along this reflective path can unveil the hidden if not unsayable life world of dis/technology engagers that refuses ableist rendering of difference. The *poesis* of dis/technology is distributed in the *wheelchairness* of the wheelchair. The composure towards wheelchairness or artificial speech transmission sees these devices not as mere mechanism but as an extension of body type, a somatic expansion. Disabled people may feel some ambivalence towards the human/machine interface as the device is meant to be an external object of functionality rather than a form of assistive embodiness that not only can be personalised but invoked characterlogically – but negatively marks the person as visibly disabled and therefore a hybrid. In his 1982 lecture *Technologies of Self* (1997b), Michel Foucault made reference to four kinds of technologies that govern how human beings come to knowledge about themselves, namely technologies of production, of sign systems, of power and of self. *Technologies of self* refer to instances/ practices that:

> Permit individuals to effect by their own Means, or with the help of others, a certain number of operations on their own bodies and souls, thoughts, conduct, and way of being, so as to transform themselves in order to attain a certain state of happiness, purity, wisdom, perfection, or immortality.
>
> (p. 225)

Such assemblages of technologies both interact and overlap and extend to the material, productive and attitudinal. There is no doubt that Foucault's work takes up and has been significantly influenced by the challenges of the Heideggerian ethos (Kendall & Michael, 2000). Like Heidegger, Foucault turns his attention to the ancient Greek understanding of *techné* and the way in which *technai* are played out in the daily routine of *souci de soi* (care of self). In this sense, Foucault extends the notion of technology, using it in the wider sense to explore problems of self to work on the question of 'how have certain interdictions required the price of certain kinds of knowledge about oneself? What must one know about oneself in order to be willing to renounce anything?' (Foucault, 1997b, p. 224). Despite the importance of this issue there has been considerable research silence around the onto-technological dimensions of dis/technology. This should come as no surprise. Ableism's research agendas keep the focus on functionality and issues of dependence. Although dis/technologies are pitched as assistive they are nonetheless marked as technologies of *inconvenience*, because disability *qua* disability is inconvenient. The negative ontologisation of disability aids is captured in the denotation '*(in)valid* aids'. The social order of dis/technologies patterns the social, although the interface between machine and humans is not necessarily determinate but co-relational. In response to the high levels of technology abandonment, Hocking asserts that the role of assistive devices on identity formation requires 'therapists to be alert to social and cultural meanings' (Hocking, 1999, p. 8).

Whilst Foucault's insertion of the self within the technological is significant, he does not go as far as Heidegger (and later Latour) to extend technological being to flora, fauna, inert nature and artificial artefacts. Nonetheless, a Foucauldian analytics of technologies or a technique of self offers us a device from which to investigate the formation of subjectivities of disability through the lens of technological mechanisms, apparatus and corporeal prosthesis. This linking of episteme and praxis provides a framework to examine local understanding of the productive and docile body's relationship to 'normalization', 'enhancement' and the so-called 'restorative' technologies. As Foucault rightly points out, the fashioning of self is not a private-orientated venture, rather the subject in formation draws upon, inserts tropes of self 'he finds in his culture and are proposed, suggested, imposed upon him by his culture, his society, and his social group' (1988, p. 291).

Technology as characterological and fabricative

> What there is to be mastered, handled, or owned derives from Smokie and me – alone together. At times, we conceive of our togetherness in terms of mastering and handling the social world. We get through it, one as blind, the other as a dog. We own blindness insofar as we treat it as *belonging* to us. This is one of the possibilities of the two-in-one.
> (Michalko, 1999, p. 184)

Technology always has a context – its use, characterological nature, the kinds of relationships we form with such 'objects'. From a critical disability studies perspective it is crucial that we search for the ethos or drivers of technological innovation and critically appraise the ontological relations produced by the intermingling of corporealities and devices. I would suggest that technophilic and technophobic stance frame technological practices/representations (Drengson, 1990). The rein of technocracy induces a pursuit of technology as love object – 'humans are technologized by their own love of the technical and of techniques. Life has become mere mechanism' (Drengson, 1990, p. 30). The assessment of technology has developed into two approaches: one that is *instrumental* relying heavily on the speculations of 'experts' and the other of a *discursive* nature where the public engages in educative and consultation processes. In either approach, Technological Assessment (TA) practices have become wedged in advisory governmental apparatuses. The technological laboratory itself is a site or acts as a hub of power, a centre of calculation constantly self-assessing and respond-ing to a range of levels/sources of mobilisation of support. Ableist technological regimes hold the locus of control in the hands of the device and not in the personalised integration of this technology by disabled people.

We may wish to ask that within this vacuum of activity–assessment, various networks of association, what position and degree of lever-age do consumers have of disability-orientated technologies. Johnson and Moxon (1998) suggest very little. Technologies when conceptu-alised as a form of 'care' become susceptible to administering to the biomedical/functional/normalising needs of disabled bodies as com-monly defined by service providers, designers, retailers and rehabil-itative experts – bearing minimal resemblance and thus potentially subverting the coupling requirements of disabled persons. As Hasler (1993) puts it:

> The [disability] movement does not reject the idea of gadgets. One of the basic requirements for independent living is appropriate tech-nological equipment. But even here, appropriate can be defined differently by a non-disabled person and a disabled one.
>
> (p. 15)

Schumacher suggested that the development, pursuit and implemen-tation of technologies be conceived of in terms of a metaphysical practice (Schumacher, 1973). Whilst being created out of the human hand, Schumacher proposes technological devices take on a 'life' or agency of their own engaging in forms of enrolment that are not self-limiting. Rather paradoxically, instead of relieving the burden of the so-called 'human limitation', the non-human artefact simultane-ously fabricates a reduction in 'burden', whilst inducing new, pervasive and unpredictable other kinds of 'burden', for example, technological maintenance. Consider the growth of the ergonomics industry as a con-sequence of computerised changes in the workplace. The solution to this conundrum is to ask of technologies – 'what does it do?', and 'what should it do?' Indeed, is it possible for technologies to reveal a 'human face'? (Schumacher, 1973, p. 123). I am not really sure what qualities are imbued in the 'human face' – rather than being essentialised we return again the question of subjectivity and the rejection of a uni-versalised human condition. Schumacher's early ruminations in *Small is Beautiful* have influenced *inter alia* the eco-philosophical approach to technology appraisal. Here appropriate technology starts from the assumption that the artefact is 'neutral' and formulations of 'appropriateness' are governed largely by situational indictors. Restraint as such should not be deemed to imply hostility to technologies. Ableist conditioning means that the dominant marking of dis/technology is in terms of anti-dependency devices that chauffeur assimilation.

Robert McGinn's (1990, 1991) approach to philosophising about technology provides a refreshing alternative to dominant romanticism and determinist tendencies of much of the literature. McGinn's (1990) 'spin' on technologies not only dismantles this deadlock, but also offers a re-visioning of explanatory frameworks around disability and technologies. Whilst there is little agreement as to the definition of technology, McGinn does offer a framework in an attempt to systematise technology. He suggests that technology be viewed as material, fabricative, purposive, resource-base expending, knowledge, method, enabling/informing activity, including the practitioners own [mind] mental set. I am interested here in McGinn's departure from the usual understanding of technology in definitional terms, towards a description of *technologies as characterological* (e.g. having a character, behaviour and personality) and as a form of human activity that can lead one to the conclusion that there is no 'inside or outside' of technology. Technology is this sense is *evoking ontologies*.

It is the fabricative dimension that is also worthy of further investigation. According to McGinn (1990) the processes by which technics (material outputs of technological production) are produced are ontologically fabricative:

> Some of the significant features of the technic are due primarily to the technologist working of his or her will on the constituent ingredients or parts, rather than their all being primarily the result of the operation of chemical...laws....In sum, the fabricative character of technology pertains to the nature of the processes in which its issue is brought into being.
>
> (p. 12)

McGinn's formulation unifies and merges the relationship between the object and the creator. Leaving aside the birthing imagery, the practices of technology incarnate and embody aspects of the comported 'will'. In other words, drawing upon McGinn's notion of the fabricative, we can say that such practice draw in, interface and are prefaced by an ontological process of subjectification, that is, techniques of self coitally unifying with the art of techné. As McGinn (1990) suggests,

Technologies maybe individuated or related by characterising the substantial differences or similarities in technics, specific purposes, methods, bodies of knowledge, resource bases, contexts and practitioners mental sets associated with the different incarnations or embodiments of the activity – form. Technology is the practice of the technologies under consideration.

(p. 23)

On this basis, an analytics of technologies can act as a rich font for the extrapolation of techniques of boundary policing between artefact, human and mis-confirmed beings. This is a kind of conglomerate of categories which includes all sorts of corporeal misfits assigned to the edges of human subjectivity – changelings, abominations, sub-humans, freaks, post-human, cyborgs. Indeed McGinn's approach helps us to keep in mind that technology is not just mere mechanism, but always has as its subject ontological concerns.

Technologies are situated and constrained/produced by power relations engaged to varying degrees in *commodity fetishism*. I am calling upon the notion of *commodity fetishism* embraced by Donna Haraway (1997) to denote that kind of exhilarating erotic-economic zeal for reshaping/recreating/translating the boundaries between nature/culture, what Latour (1993, pp. 99–100) calls the 'first great internal divide'. The sexual illusion to fetishism I do not believe is incidental – for many disabled people technology cuts to the core of be-ingness, a point understood by Heidegger long ago who used thinking about technology to consider ontology. Filmmaker and erotic artist Lori Erickson is adamant that she 'moves through the world in a wheelchair', which she considers part of her (quoted in Vogels, 2008).

Dis/technology characteristics

Technology is characterological not just in the sense of having a purposive essence (as Heidegger suggests) but also in its unification and transmogrification of the corporeal and psychic life of the person with disability:

> People don't get that when they kick our chair, move our chair while we're in it, or touch our chair without necessarily touching our body, there's no difference...The chair is part of me! People don't understand that this is not a place to sit, it is not a piece of furniture, it is who we are, it's an extension of ourselves.
>
> (Ruthee, cited Smith, 2005, p. 26)

Gibson reports some examples of wheelchair users being horrified at a non-wheelchair user playing with their chair. In this case the technology of the chair, cane, voice machine is not mere prosthetic but signifies an ontological emergence that is not able to be cut off from the visceral. In discussing of one her interviewees, 'Jack', Gibson remarks, 'it [the wheelchair] *is* Jack, that is becoming – Jack … [where a sense of self] has leaked into a machine' (Gibson, 2006, p. 194). We can see from this perspective that space is opened up for an in-depth analysis of the nature of being humaned, the hybridity and mixtures produced by technological liaisons and coupling in an enduring performance. The Cyberkinetics *BrainGate* system (http://cyberkineticsinc.com) enables impaired individuals, such as those with locked in syndrome, to control computer signals through thought. The user imagines speaking and therefore incites the possibility of engaging in understandable outerworld communication. The technology decodes the neural firing patterns of cells and hence acts as cerebral supplement to the organism. These interventions into and through the body can change notions of the self whereby processes 'outside' of the body become constitutive elements of cognition. Hence it is possible to speak in terms of human subjectivity as an assemblage; wherein technologies are networks folding into our-selves morphed into punctualised and fixed actants. This corporeal arising and intermingling is captured by Rod Michalko's (1999) meditation on his relationship with his guide dog Smokie. As a sentient dis/technology, Smokie confuses and confounds atomistic individualism and animal spaces. Rod elicits an incompleteness without the dog – and the dog without the human:

> We are alone together in our identities and this togetherness binds them into our identity'. Together and separate we are alone and alone we are one.
>
> (p. 170)

Ontologically Michalko distils this relationship as *alone- together*:

> Alone – together suggests that we possess unity with each other as well as separateness from each other. Our separateness or difference from each other, originates and is steeped in the distinction between nature and humanity.
>
> (p. 172)

There is a sense in 'alone-together', a form of *kenosis* or self-emptying . . . a molecular transfer? Mialet picks up in an intuitive sensing communication by Stephen Hawking's secretary 'she does not wait for him to speak; by merely looking at his eyes she knows his answers, as one does' (Mialet, 1999, p. 566). In exploring the production of disability we can say that what is inscribed as a 'disabled body' is an effect generated by performance of bodies and bodies in a heterogeneous network of association. *Alone-together* is not restricted to sentiency – but 'inanimate' objects. As Kendall and Michael (2000) remind us there is no such thing as a pure human – *we are always* combined with non-humans wherein the environment is mediated through a layer of technologies (wrappers). McGinn's (1990, 1991) assertion that technology is characterological is given weight by extended mind theory, which argues that the self is always embodied and therefore any interventions into the body are likely to transform the self. Dis/technologies, it should come as no surprise produce different forms of embodiment. The extended mind takes in certain processes and events as constitutive elements that form cognitive processes (see Fenton & Alpert, 2008). Not all dis/technologies lead to ontological animation but conversely can produce a reconfiguration that almost leads to ontological banishment due to the extreme separation of materiality and ontology. Consider the example of physicist Stephen Hawking. Whilst the corporeal expansion/elasticity of his beingness is exemplified in the surprise of Roseanne Allucquère Stone (1996) when she attended a lecture by Hawking:

> And there is Hawking. Sitting, as he always does, in his wheelchair, utterly motionless, except for his fingers on the 'joystick of the laptop; and on the floor to one side of him is the PA system microphone, nuzzling into the Votrax's tiny loudspeaker. And a thing happens in my head. Exactly where, I say to myself, is Hawking? Am I any closer to him now than I was outside? Who is it doing the talking up there on stage? In an important sense, Hawking doesn't stop being Hawking at the edge of his visible body. There is the obvious physical Hawking, vividly outlined by the way our social conditioning teaches us to see a person as a person. But a serious part of Hawking extends into the box in his lap. In mirror image, a serious part of that silicon and plastic assemblage in his lap extends into him as well . . . not to mention the 'invisible ways, displaced in time and space, in which discourses of medical technology and their physical accretions already permeate him and us. No box, no discourse; in the absence of the prosthetic, Hawking's intellect becomes a tree falling

in the forest with nobody around to hear it. On the other hand, with the box his voice is auditory and simultaneously electric, in a radically different way from that of a person speaking into a microphone. Where does he stop? Where are his edges?

(pp. 4–5)

Nonetheless, there is a sense that there is something more at work here in how academics at least engage in readings of Stephen Hawking's persona. Whilst C. B. MacPherson's notion of possessive individualism is retained in the sense that Hawking is able to engage technologies to enable his brain to function as a command centre for sensing and communicating in the world, the 'just a head' metaphor or the machine-like brain dominates (Mialet, 2003). The enabling technology is incorporated to work his mind; hence his self is more thoroughly displaced as aspects of Hawking's modality are intertwined in a series of objects: computers, nurses, secretaries, batteries, voice machine, wheelchair and so forth. This reconfigured space extends the body zone and consequently the ontological topography. One outstanding issue is how displacement is figured – following a command centre model with network hubs moving outwards or in a loose dialectical shifting way – where technological revelations are subjects to constant recitations and renegotiations. Theories of extended minds and bodies raise the thorny issues of how 'essence' is retained. Essence, not in a static sense but in the sense of an enfolding subjectivity. Again in the instance of Hawking, Mailet (2003) proposes,

> With Hawking we have seen that it is not his flesh and blood that becomes 'the basic instrument of [his] intellectual and practical control over [his] surroundings' but the computer itself. The computer is the center of the network through which (almost) all interactions are negotiated because they are rendered visible and public (the computer distributes competencies between what is appropriate to/for Hawking's flesh-and-blood body, his identity, his assistants, his computer, and me.
>
> (p. 591)

Mialet's movement towards translation in acknowledging reconfigured body is halted and recuperated by the need to demarcate the inside and outsides of ontological agency (to purify, in Latour's terms) – by placing the computer in a distinct bounded zone. Far from being a distributed-centred subject that is not distracted by the daily disciplining of impairment, the dis/technologies are able to be figured as singularised and independent – disability appears as displaced. The distributed-centred subject neologism still tries to reproduce a singularised body so typical of liberalism. Hawking's essence and that of many disabled people involves constant negotiation that induce mindfulness not only of the dis/technology's workability but also of negotiations that deal with the relational aspects of copresence. I am inclined to err towards Law (1999) notion of networked living along the lines of the 'punctualised subject', wherein 'punctionalisation is always precarious, it faces resistances, and may degenerate into a failing network' (Law, 1999, p. 5). This rendering would seem to square better with the French view of disability (*situation de handicap*) as a relational and intersubjective confrontation:

> Disability as a *confrontation* between the ability of a person and situations she encounters in life 'macro-situations', such as work or schooling, or 'micro-situations' such as cutting meat or using the keyboard of a computer. The disabling situations are not only structural and material, they are also (especially) cultural [my emphasis & translation].[5]
>
> (Hamonet, 2006, p. 1)

The model moves beyond abilities and limitations and embraces subjectivity (*Ce dernier apaect représente, pour personne, sa façon de percevior différences de son corps*[6]) acknowledging the person's perception of difference in his /her body. If we seriously take onboard the conceptual notion of disability as a relational concept then the production of disability must not be a by-product of our faulty interaction with differences in mentalities and corporealities. This understanding is similar to the framework contained in the *Convention on the Rights of Persons with Disabilities*. The Preamble of the Convention describes,

> Disability [a]s an *evolving concept* and that disability *results from the interaction* between persons with impairments and attitudinal and environmental barriers that hinders their full and effective participation in society on an equal basis with others (emphasis added).[7]

Whilst many of the barriers to inclusion are *external* to the disabled person (laws, resources, environmental and educational barriers), barriers also exist that are *internal* to the person (self-image, internalisation

of negative views of disability, learned helplessness, and the legacies of incarceration). Although the conditions of ableism may allow
dis/technology to mediate an ontology, it is questionable that the
dis/technologised person actually morphs the abled ontology. Indeed
what is produced is something different, a not-quite-abled, or as examined later in the chapter, a transhuman 'person'.

Different mind/soma styles . . .

> Sweet Florence refuses to speak to me unless I first breathe noisily
> into the [telephone] receiver which Sandrine holds glued to my ear.
> 'Are you there, Jean-Do?' she asks anxiously over the air. And I have
> to admit that at times I do not know any more.
>
> (Bauby, 1997, pp. 49–510)

The Actor Network Theory (ANT) method lends itself to the unpacking
of such disabled-hybrid-assemblages through its explication of the generative processes (in Latourian language) of translation and purification.
Mention has already been made of Latour's formulation of two distinct
dichotomies of the 'modern condition' that need to be demarcated in
order to be 'effective' (see Chapter 1). Translation involves those time-
honoured practices of creating blends/fusions 'between entirely new
types of beings, hybrids of nature and culture' (Latour, 1993, p. 10).
It is Latour's ascription of practices of purification, the creation and
boundary policing of two distinct, apartheid zone of the 'human' and
'non-human' that lends itself to review the boundaries of normalcy (the
real human) and disability (the non-human, cyborg, changeling). So
how does copresence operate when dis/technologies are engaged and
how is the disabled body/mentality to be read to speak otherwise about
ableism? Copresence defined here consists of two dimensions: copresence as *mode* of being with others, and copresence as *sense* of being
with others. Mode of copresence refers to the physical conditions that
structure human interaction, whereas a sense of copresence refers to the
subjective experience of being with others that an individual acquires in
interaction. With dis/technologies the mode of copresence affects sense
of copresence, and knowledge of how the former affects the latter will
benefit copresence design. The presence-absence conundrum explodes
with disability – first through the different proprioceptive ways of being
human impairment–mediated sensing/(re)memorying ontologies and
through the usage of specific dis/technologies.

Feminist technoscience has the capacity to negotiate and bring the
concept of marginality into the debate. The technological enterprise

operates with a domain, a network of power relations, what Donna Haraway refers to as an 'informatics of domination'. This is not the place to rehash and rehearse Haraway's early writings on cyborgs; we can however hone in on those aspects of her work that are relevant to our focal concerns. Haraway deploys a feminist critical analytic of technological practices the figuring of scientific expertise. In *Simians, Cyborgs and Women*, Haraway (1991a) provides several elaborations of her understanding of 'cyborg':

> A cyborg is a cybernetic organism, a hybrid machine and organism, a creature of social reality as well as a creature of fiction. Social reality is lived social relations, our most important political construction, a world changing fiction.

> (p. 149)

Later Haraway states coupling and coded devices are 'text, machine, body, and metaphor – all theorized and engaged in practice in terms of communications' (p. 212). Indeed it is this symbiotic coupling that most disturbs, for the cyborg refers to more than mere additions or extensions to the body, but rather to humans and machines in interaction, refiguring, blurring (and weakening) border relations between humans, other living beings and machines – that ultimately challenge the coherence of the human form as self-contained, delimited and organic unity.

In later work Haraway (1997) argues that heterogeneous technoscience practices act as 'wormholes' wherein 'the laboratory continues to suck us into uncharted regions of technical, cultural, and political space' (p. 211) and as such are a form of life that move in and out of the domains of collective life. All objects whether animate or otherwise can be absorbed into the 'wormholes' reappearing as transmogrified, refigured entities. For instance, Haraway uses the example of field mice being transformed into 'finely tailored laboratory rodents' or 'model systems' (1997, p. 211). Based on Haraway's proposition, in context of impairment, it follows that the individual who is short statured (or a 'dwarf', to use the old fashion term) when propelled through the laboratory 'worm hole' has an existence that is reduced (transmogrified) into a 'gene defect'. More specifically in the example of pseudoachondroplasia to an 'abnormal gene' located on chromosome 19 called the cartilage oligomeric matrix protein (COMP) for short.

Despite Haraway's interest in forms of 'hybrid' and the pleasure of such boundary confusion and fruitful coupling, she has little to say about the relationship between the discursive production of 'disabled' and cyborg bodies. It is difficult to reckon with this silence and the lack of connection Haraway makes between technoscience's redefinition of the 'disabled body' as an object for technological reconstruction (the morphing of ableism) and the creation of cyborgs. Some possibilities for exploration are raised, but have not been fully developed. Haraway (1991a) argues that with the increased interconnectedness between machines and humans

> It is not always clear who makes and who is made. Biological organisms have become biotic systems, communications devices like others. There is no fundamental, ontological separation in our formal knowledge of machine and organism, of technical and organic.... One consequence is that our sense of connection to our tools is heightened...Perhaps paraplegics and severely handicapped [sic] people can (and sometimes do) have the most intense experiences of complex hybridization with other communication devices.
>
> (p. 178)

And later:

> Why should our bodies end at the skin, or include at best other beings encapsulated by skin?...For us, in imagination and in other practice, machines can be prosthetic devices, intimate components, friendly selves. We don't need organic holism to give impermeable wholeness, the total woman and her feminist variants (mutants).
>
> (p. 178)

The problem here is that Haraway presents an uncritical and overly optimistic perspective on prosthetic relationality, almost ignoring cultural practices that generate and fuel the prosthetic imagination. Where is Heidegger's sense of technological 'dangerousness' now? Can we read into Haraway's work an understanding of cyborg prosthesis that assumes supplementation, supplying/cancelling 'deficiency'? As Mark Seltzer (1992, p. 157) remarks, prosthetic/cyborg imbues a 'double logic' as self-extension, self-mutilation or even self-cancelling making visible the fragility and fragmentation of such concepts as atomistic agency and an essentialised human ontology. Just as the knowing self is always partial, in a process of unfolding '...never finished, whole, simply there and original,...always constructed and stitched together imperfectly' (Seltzer, 1992, p. 193), so is knowledge situated and technological perspectives partial. In Haraway's early work (1991b) she develops the concept of situated knowledges to alert us to the embodied and positioned nature of scientific objectivity that grounds the imagination of scientific vision.

In more recent work concerning reproductive technologies and genetic engineering, *Modest_Witness@Second_Millennium. FemaleMan_ Meets_OncoMouse*, Haraway (1997) examines those practices that count as knowledge. She calls upon the 'Modest Witness', one who has epistemic authority to testify, to act and reveal their presence in the sociotechnical order. In describing the practice of witnessing, Haraway recalls,

> Witnessing is seeing, attesting; standing publicly accountable for, and psychically vulnerable to, one's visions and representations. Witnessing is a collective, limited practice that depends on the constructed and never finished credibility of those who do it, of whom are mortal, fallible, and fraught with the consequences of unconscious and disowned desires and fears.
>
> (p. 267)

For the prospects of witnessing to be transgressive, technological practice needs to be cognizant of knowledges from subjugated standpoints. Feminist technoscience yearns for knowledge practices to be coupled with freedom projects.

Whither impairment? Disabled bodies metamorphosed into the transhuman

> You can increasingly tell the background of a young person by his or her looks and intelligence; if someone doesn't live up to social expectations, he tends to blame bad genetic choices by his parents rather then himself.... Scientists have not dared to produce a full-scale chimera, half human and half ape, though they could; but young people begin to suspect that classmates who do much less well than they do are in fact genetically not fully human. Because, in fact, they aren't...
>
> (Fukuyama, 2002, p. 9)

In 'developed' nations at least, disabled people are living on the cusp of a wide reaching transmogrification, entering a new plane of embodiment where new technological practices may 'cure' their impairment, or at best enable us to morph or simulate ableism (normalcy) and in the not so distant future, leave our bodies via teleportation or cyborghood. The field of post-humanism and transhumanism has been alive with activity since the late 1990s. These fields raise a number of concerns in relation to the status and parameters of human impairment and by extension that which is to be defined as residual and in turn be marked as 'disability'. Concisely, two lines of inquiry will be explored further in this section. Namely, is the evolution of the post-human figure/entity a 'way out' of impairment? Indeed, does the adoption of particular kinds of post-humanism by disabled people elevate their status to being suprahuman – a shift from 'deficiency' to being 'hyperendowed'? In other words, what kinds of beingness or to use Heidegger's (1977) term of phrase 'enframing' are being produced and how are these figurations accorded value? What transformed notions of productivity and uselessness are being formed? In contrast to these first set of questions exists the second inquiry that relates to those matters concerning the 'hiddenness' or unintended consequences of post-human technological practices.

Transhumanists argue that their agenda is to 'move on and out of bodies' into another spectrum of beingness, a Promethean animal who is contingently embodied and thus on a negentropic journey. This eschatological vision of enhancement may present dangers to impaired individuals and really be a 'wolf in sheep's clothing', not just in terms of a fabrication of ableness but rather as a *re-encryption* of the binary opposition of the normal and pathological (the deficient, mediocre and mundane). In these strands nothing has really changed, the conceptual schemas and mind maps of ableism remain intact – and the pool of the remnant, the 'have not's' and 'not quite's' grows larger and more diverse.

With all these jumbled questions laid out, this section will explore post-humanism and the production of (dis)ableism. I start with an outline of a selection of technological developments related to 'enhancement' and move into a discussion about the rationality and conceptualisation of post-humanism. I close with a consideration of contemporary impacts related to the treatment of impairment and future scenarios.

Übermensche city! Worlds of transhumanism and post-humanism

The phenomena referred to today as 'posthumanism' has been developing since the early 1940s but one can identify its antecedents in the world of fiction (Mary Shelley's (1818) *Frankenstein*), and film

(Fritz Lang's (1927) *Metropolis*). Indeed if one conceives of transhumanism as the quest to transcend species-typical boundaries then this desire can be traced back to the Sumerian *Epic of Gilgamesh* (1700 BCE) (see Bostrom, 2005). Despite the uncertainty confusion about the term 'enhancement', it can be said that transhuman enhancement is concerned to 'increase in value' (Savulescu, 2006). Today transhuman technologies have converged, known by the acronym NBIC (nanoscience, biotechnologies, information technologies and cognitive sciences). Naomedicine's taxonomies include biopharmaceutics, implantable materials, implantable devices, surgical aids, diagnostics tools (Gordon & Sagman, 2003). Katherine Hayles (1999) provides a three-point trajectory of cybernetic development in the post-human. The first period in the 1940s until the 1960s centred on the operational concept of *homeostasis and control* where artefacts performed as servants or protectors of human beings (i.e. robot in the sitcom *Lost in Space*). The second stage throughout the 1960s until the 1980s represent a period of *reflexivity* wherein freedom beyond human control was contemplated and the quest for 'life-like' temptations emerged. The third stage, in the contemporary moment, concentrates on *virtuality* and the breaking of the divide between human and machine.

Hayles (1999) notes that the significant point of departure from the other two phases lies in the emergent character of *artificial life* (A.L) into a realm and beingness that supersedes the control and anticipations of the designer/creator, taking on an identity (or consciousness) of its own. The new kid on the block to eclipse the light of cosmetic surgery is cosmetic neurology, 'the practice of intervening to improve cognition and affect in healthy individuals' (Chatterjee, 2007, p. 129). This ontological eruption is brought into sharp relief by Hayles (1999, p. 11), who indicates that some researchers believe that A.Ls. are not 'merely models of life but are themselves life'. Hayles goes on to argue that this conclusion is philosophically sustainable if one views sentiency in terms of *informationalcy*. On this basis, A.Ls 'are life forms because they have the form of life, that is, an informational code. As a result the theoretical bases used to categorise all life undergoes a significant shift' (1999, p. 11). This assertion is supported by Kurzweil (1999b, p. 60), who uses the hypothetical situation of scanning a person's brain and reconstituting the 'mind file', into a computer medium. Kurzweil asks whether we implicate 'consciousness' in such an entity and in distinction from an actant that simulates consciousness. In either case according to Bostrom (2003):

Transhumanism does not require us to say that we should favour post-human beings over human beings, but that the right way of favoring human beings is by enabling us to realize our ideals better and that some of our ideals may well be located outsides the spaces of modes of being that are accessible to us with our current biological constitution.

(p. 495)

Bruno Latour (1999) identifies two versions of the cyborgian/transhuman quest – that which is technophilic, disembodied and masculinist and the alternative incarnational (often feminist) version concerned with embodiment and its zones, shiftings and make up. The distance between the two versions creates a map, a front line for a 'war zone' which induces such questions as 'what it is to have a democratic body? . . . what sort of bodies do we wish to have? What sort of bodies is it worth having?' (Latour, 1999, p. 2). How do we delimit sentiency and is there such a thing as human essence? Fukuyama (2002) additionally identifies three key areas of developments within technoscience that are likely to produce that which is called 'post-human', namely neuropharmacology, cloning and genetic engineering. Whilst these developments are dispersed amongst scientists and researchers acting in a seemingly disconnected way from other developers of prototypes there is also a growing movement of networks of association amongst philosophers, transhuman apologists, hi-tech cybernetic research companies and individuals willing to 'live out'[8] (experiment with) transhuman transitions. In the following section, I aim to provide a brief sketch of developments as they apply to our broader exploration of sifting through the consequences of transhumanism for the production of disability.

Simon Cooper (2002), in an essay reviewing Francis Fukuyama's (2002) book *Our PostHuman Future*, correctly poses the central ontological, political and conceptual dilemma that has arisen when grappling with the cultural context and impacts of contemporary developments in technosciences, namely 'how many times can we resolve problems through the technological simulation of embodied processes and still remain human?' (Cooper, 2002, p. 35). Engaging with this enquiry from the trajectory of studies in ableism, it is cogent to ask about the reception of technologies and their relationship to ableist norms. Not just by looking at processes of acclimatising and habituating a culture to a technology but conversely exploring how scientists response to public demands expand modes of being, in tandem with any existential anxieties to undergo constant self-improvement. The role of Hollywood movies in the form of techno-entertainment blurs the line between sci-fi (futurist fantasies) and contemporary clinical realities. Technological imperatives bolster up an ideology of *immanent preparedness* within the context of a risk culture. Indeed this quandary represents not a mere philosophical abstraction or a voyage into the world of sci-fi fantasy; rather the matter of representing the ambiguous technocratic 'body' has already arrived.

Body realignment is not new news but is yesterday's news. In post-war United States massive cultural transformation resulted in the development and widespread use of new medical technologies. Plastic surgery, wonder drugs, artificial organs and prosthetics inspired Americans to believe in a new age of modern medical miracles. The stigma associated with war-produced facial injuries promoted cosmetic techniques that would facilitate normalisation, community and workforce integration (Ryan, 1918). Serlin (2004) argued that many Americans put tremendous faith in the power of medicine to rehabilitate and otherwise transform the lives and bodies of disabled and those considered abnormal.[9] These medical technologies and procedures were used to advance the politics of conformity during the 1950s. In fact, being precise, this body arrived in graphic visual form in the February 1989 issue of *Life* magazine containing an image titled *Replaceable You* – a catalogue of mechanical and prosthetic replacement body parts. James Hughes (1995) showcased an uploadable brain chip developed by the INTER Consortium. Such a chip is made up of matrices into which nerves can grow, and may permit two-way communication between neurons and computers (Agnew & McCreery, 1990; Compston, 1994; Hughes, 1995).Theodore W. Berger from School of Engineering at the University of Southern California is developing biominetic models of hippocampus to serve as neural prostheses (see Handelman, 2007).

This small sample of techno-scientific developments raises a myriad of questions and challenges the foundations not only of the Judeo-Christian legacy of personhood as having a distinct and inviolable essence but also the Enlightenment concept of atomistic man whose self is transcendental: timeless and universal (Kyle, 1993; McGrath, 1994). Modernism, in the Latourian sense is ruptured; there has been a dramatic movement from the Kantian catchcry *sapere aude!* (have courage to use your own reason) to *Non sum qualis eram* (I'm not what I used to be). An exemplar of this orientation can be found in the writing of J.S. Mill (1975), who in *On Liberty* suggests,

Among the works of man [sic], which human life is rightly employed in perfecting and beautifying, the first in importance is man himself... Human nature is not a machine to be built after a model, and set to do exactly the work prescribed for it, but a tree, which requires to grow and develop itself on all sides, according to the tendency of the inward forces which make it a living thing.

(p. 73)

Although this transcendental belief fosters growth, the 'self' is essentially conceived as intact, in a state of finishedness, having a 'universality and necessity in the fundamental modes of human experience' (Solomon, 1988, p. 7). The reader justifiably might ask about what *degree* of implants or new body parts would constitute a changeover into a 'new' person or another form of species or quasi human? For instance, is the figure represented in *Life* magazine to be considered 'human' and what difference, if any, does it make if the 'foreign body' is machine or organic (human or animal origin)? Fukuyama whilst acknowledging the fluidity and variability of human behaviour concludes that 'it is not infinitely so; at a certain point deeply rooted *natural instincts* and patterns of behaviour reassert themselves' (Fukuyama, 2002, p. 14 – emphasis added). Yet a key platform of disability services is the developmental model of disability which articulates the view that all people are capable of change. Transhumanists argue that our psyches are not finished projects and technological initiatives are aimed at changing the constraints of Self (Hopkins, 2008).

A search on the World Wide Web using the keyword 'post-human' uncovers a large array of frontier organisations which could be regarded, if only cursorily considered, as fringe groups celebrating the virtues of post-humanism and transhumanism (both words are often used interchangeably). Whilst purporting a global membership most organisations originate in the United States. The oldest is the *Extropy Institute* (Marina del Rey, California) founded by Dr Max More in 1988. A number of prominent technologists such as Dr Marvin Minsky (1988) (Toshiba Professor of Media Arts & Sciences MIT and Ray Kurzweil (1999a, 2005) have been engaged as its advisors. The Institute produces a journal *Extropy*, discussion papers and publishes the *Extropian Principles 3.0, A Transhumanism Declaration* (More, 1999). According to this document extropianism is

A transhumanist philosophy. The Extropian Principles define a specific version or 'brand' of transhumanist thinking. Like humanists, transhumanists favour reason, progress, and values centred on our well being rather than on an external religious authority. Transhumanists take humanism further by challenging human limits by means of science and technology combined with critical and creative thinking. We challenge the inevitability of aging and death, and we seek continuing enhancements to our intellectual abilities, our physical capacities, and our emotional development. We see humanity as a transitory stage in the evolutionary development of intelligence. We advocate using science to accelerate our move from human to a transhuman or post human condition. As physicist Freeman Dyson has said: 'Humanity looks to me like a magnificent beginning but not the final word.' These Principles are not presented as absolute truths or universal values. The Principles codify and express those attitudes and approaches affirmed by those who describe themselves as 'Extropian'. Extropian thinking offers a basic framework for thinking about the human condition.

The Extropy Institute's 3.11 (2003) version of its principles adopts a seven-prong principle philosophy: Perpetual Progress, Self-Transformation, Practical Optimism, Intelligent Technology, Open Society – information and democracy, Self-Direction and Rational Thinking. Another similar (competing?) body is the *World Transhumanism Organisation* (WTA) who aim to promote 'discussion of the possibilities for radical improvement of human capacities using genetic, cybernetic and nano-technologies' (World Transhumanism Organisation, 2002). The WTA was established in 1998 by Yale University philosopher Nick Bostrom (2002) to initially produce an international document: *The Transhumanist Declaration*. This declaration whilst purporting to be at the cutting edge of transforming the world is in reality firmly entrenched within an arcane liberal humanist framework – definitely a philosophy of 'this' world! Reading like a tract on humanism the WTA declaration argues from a base of possessive individualism (i.e. classic liberalism) to support the notion that the individual has a moral right to use 'enhancement' technologies. The declaration is silent about the potential changes to the (currently asymmetrical) relationship between human and machines and between categories of humans.

There is a raft of other fringe organisations such as David Pearce's *Hedonistic Imperative* web and the California-based *Foresight Institute* (*aka* Eric Drexler & Glen Reynolds) established to prepare (an assumed given) for nanotechnology. Whilst there are differences in the emphasis taken by these groups, one striking feature uniting them all is an uncritical belief in a *teleological views* of progress (e.g. Principle 1: Perpetual Progress. *Extropian Institute Principles 3.0*) and a Darwinian orientation (Bendle, 2002; Kurzweil, 1999a, 1999b). Whilst transhumanism purports to be a post-modern move, it is argued that in reality it is firmly embedded within an enlightenment, liberalist tradition. Indeed biophysicist and director of the Medicine, Technology and Society program (School of Medicine) at the University of California, Dr Gregory Stock (2002) asserts that it is the *duty* of all citizens to pursue biological enhancement. The theme of mitigation re-emerges – this time there is pressure to mitigate normalcy. No doubt there would be even more pressure on those 'disabled bodies' to make the grade. Transhumanism as boundless optimism is summed up well in a paper written by Stock (2000) for a BBC programme audience debating 'designer babies':

> The human species is moving out of its childhood. It is time to acknowledge our growing powers and begin to take responsibility for them. We have no choice in this, for we have begun to play god in so many intimate realms of life that we could not turn back if we tried. Some, of course, believe we should stop our audacious incursions into the very fabric of human biology – at least until we can summon up more wisdom. But the way to find wisdom about our newfound capabilities is not by trying to deny them (and thereby relegating their exploration to outlaw nations and scientific renegades), but by using them judiciously, by carefully feeling our way forward, and yes, by making mistakes and learning from them.

A meditation on transhumanism – what does it all mean?

Trans/Post-human literature takes an almost naïve approach to matters of social ordering and the further engendering of asymmetrical relations between humans, animals and machines. Indeed the social realm is kept at arm's length. It is assumed that a cooperative or consensual process will be evolved to work out any conflict or inequalities. Little attention is paid by tranhumanists to how transhumanism will become manifest within human practices. Miah (2003) argues that it is assumed practicalities that will be dealt with. Extropians, for instance, indicate there will be a free exchange of ideas where problems can be resolved in an open fashion (More, 1999). What is missing from much of the literature is a rigorous and sustained discussion of the contextualisation of developments towards transhumanism and the relationship of these developments to broader themes such as globalisation and the growth of asymmetrical relations between the first and third worlds. Transhumanism as an aspirational ethos matrixed to high technologies is very much a Western, first nation phenomenon. Other missing components of the debate relate to the very culturality of the transhuman entity and its linkage (if any) to certain kinds of racialised bodies. Advocates of tranhumanism respond to the distributive justice argument with the strategies that governments should be responsible for subsidising technological access (See Bostrom, 2003; Chatterjee, 2007). A recent development spearheaded by Max More as part of the Extropy Institute Summit in 2004 is the development of a Proactionary principle which involves 'not only anticipating *before* acting, but learning *by* acting. When technological progress is halted, people lose an essential freedom and the accompanying opportunities to learn through diverse experiments' (More, 2005).

However, the road to the transhuman has some significant implications – as the degree of change required is of an epochal nature. As Sloterdijk puts it, these changes inaugurate a new 'era of species-political decisions' (Sloterdijk, cited Bendle, 2002, p. 49). James Hughes (secretary of the WTA) is more explicit about the radical envisioning of the polity by the introduction *inter alia* of cryonics and nanotechnologies arguing that: 'sentience and personhood will become the basis of moral concern; regardless of its media ... rights will become independent of being a breathing human being' (Hughes, 2001). Hughes correctly identifies that the 'war zone' (to borrow Latour's expression) will be framed by two expressive and competing worldviews, namely biofundamentalism and transhumanism. Yet transhumanism feels like form of biofundamentalism in its rigid enactment of departures from the 'traditional' biological body. Hughes's recent work (2004) argues that the pursuit of enhancement must occur as part of a quest to radically strengthen democracy. There is little debate that the movement of transhuman technologies fundamentally disrupts deeply embedded notions central to Western philosophy (and indeed theology) related to human be-ingness and an essential essence.

The biofundamentalist camp's response to transhumanism has been to return (regress?) to a hard-wired approach to human nature ruled by biology and genetics (c.f. Fukuyama, 2002). A way out of this seeming deadlock would be to propose that the 'essence' of being human lies in our fundamental reliance on appendages, prosthesis and that which is 'outside' ourselves. New technologies, I propose, in fact bring to the foreground what to many was 'hidden': a *post ontology of impermanence*.

Humans become disembodied; only to be re-embodied into a sphere of assemblages and aggregates. This kind of way of thinking about human scaffolding is not all that new – not at least within the Eastern Philosophy of Buddhism wherein human be-ingness is constituted through a series of graded aggregates coming together to form a whole. (Jayasuriya, 1988; Thera, 1998). So what we have in the transhuman are humans that are a series of assemblages – viscous, machine and transboundary (virtual). The return to or re-direction of our attention to bodily attachments is what Latour (1999) nicely refers to as the *politics of incarnation*. It is the elevation of A.I (artificial intelligence) to the potential status of 'life itself' that pushes the envelope, which pressures the practices of purification by reconstituting 'established'[10] hierarchies of sentiency. Indeed much of the reasoning related to this question of the ordering of be-ingness has been influenced by the neo-utilitarian logic of ethicist Peter Singer (2000), who places 'consciousness' as the key criteria for the possession of civil rights and use-value.

Hughes has formulated a schema based on a Singerian rights framework that incorporates the post-human actant. This continuum and scaling of organic entities has major implications for shifting formulations of ableism and specifically the zoning of 'subhumanness'. Hughes (2001, see p. 9) argues that cognitively enhanced (post)humans and adult humans have mature personhood with full legal and civic entitlements. Whereas, children, adult apes, 'severely retarded' [sic] adults and some mammals whilst having personhood only have a right to life. Further down the consciousness chain, children, fish, late foetus' and severely demented adults having a sentient consciousness are entitled not to suffer, unnecessarily. Non-sentient beings (those unconscious, embryos, the brain dead, anencephalic newborns, headless clones and plants) have no civic status, they are deemed to be the property of their family. What is missing from the Hughes schema are the masses of other players, the traditionally regarded non-sentient actant – the machine. In her discussion on machine agency, Lucy Suchman (2000) notes that the relationship between humans and machines has been based on *asymmetrical* relations. A.Is are now moving into the matrix of being emergent subjects – in other words, the ontological positioning of artefacts is now 'up for grabs', an ontology or agency is produced as an *effect* of the morphology of relations of engagements. In other words, in contradistinction to Hughes (2001), consciousness and ontologies are not fixed (in a caste system) or hierarchical, rather they are network generated and are therefore more nebulous and dependent upon the ways in which other actors in the matrix coincide.

Consciousness, under Hughes' (2001) framework, becomes confused with sociability, whereas the real crux of the focus should be on unseating the sovereign body. Hughes' proposed new constitution is in reality an old one for it still proclaims, 'right in the West is the King's right' (Foucault, 1980, p. 94). In Hughes, the conditions for the iteration of selfhood (the mark of humanity) are still based on the qualities of rationality, autonomy, separation and self-mastery. Indeed as I have already noted self-ownership is viewed as a core ethos of transhumanism. The theory of singularity posits a hypothetical point in history where the rate of technological progress becomes so rapid that the world is radically transformed overnight. Machine intelligence is the tipping point that is likely to usher in the era (Bostrom, 2006). Returning to the ableist cartography proposed in Chapter 1, transhumanism would thoroughly rework the ableist landscapes of the normal and pathological and the processes of translation and purification. Pathology would be actively expansive, whilst the notion of normalcy would become obsolete. Limit pointed identities would process from the pathological or defective and move to the exceptional which becomes banal.

Leaving home – A new Deal for impairment?

> If we can make smart bombs, surely we can make smarter bombers. Imagine a soldier that is stronger, faster, more enduring, who learns more quickly, needs less sleep, and is not hampered by disturbing combat memories.
>
> (Chatterjee, 2004, p. 972)

At this point I am aware that there are many gaps and cracks in this conversation but I am mindful of not getting too carried away as the point of the task at hand is not to write a tome on the post-human, but rather to consider what these developments may mean for the lot of those humans considered 'impaired'. There is little debate about the potential merits of certain enhancement technologies in 'bettering' the lives of those individuals that in today's circumstances we consider 'impaired'. The science of physics would be a poorer discipline without Stephen Hawkins whose consciousness is mediated through a voice synthesiser. Yet, other forms of enhancement technologies – such as the mediated communication of a sign language interpreter – are not always considered desirable within an ableist polis.[11] In other words the language of enhancement efficacies are contextually matrixed and mediated by movements that conform to abstract archetypal norms.

In my discussion on internalised ableism in Chapter 2, I have already made mention of the numbers of disabled people standing in line to join the queue of the enhanced. These are the disabled people who live out their lives from an ableist standpoint where disability can only be viewed from the perspective of negative ontology. The anti-disabled disabled are at worst norm junkies and at best norm emulators. Jean Baudrillard rather discourteously in my opinion suggests that disabled people would make excellent candidates in the transhuman project:

> Such are the blind, and the handicapped; mutant figures because mutilated and hence close to commutation, closer to this telepathic, telecommunicational universe than we others: humans all-too-human, condemned by our lack of disabilities to conventional forms of work. By the force of circumstance the disabled person is a potential expert in the motor or sensorial domain. And it is not by chance that the social is aligning itself more and more with the handicapped, and their operational advancement they can become wonderful instruments because of their handicap. They may precede us on the path towards mutation and dehumanization.
>
> (Baudrillard, 1988 cited Overboe, 1999, p. 21)

This romanticisation of suffering bodies (endemic to certain kinds of Christian theology) has been replaced by a new Baudrillardian transhuman romanticism, where disabled people are likened in closer proximity to the twilight zone of mutation. Some disabled people with a mindfulness towards their impairment gravitate to transhumanism in order to gain supra-abilities. We have to cast our minds beyond the dust of a mere *instrumental* argument about the attraction of post-human technologies for disabled people and focus on the discursive shifts in the overall meaning and positioning of abnormality. My interest is in the 'lot' of those able-bodied people – who may become the 'new disabled', the new aberrancy, an oppositional sentiency produced by the transhuman.

My hunch is that whilst the movement towards transhumanism may bring gifts for the contemporary 'needy', the transhuman project, as it is founded on an unbridled form of ableism combined with an 'obsessive technological compulsion', will involve a meagre shuffling of the deckchairs – a rearranging of 'bums in seats'. The rankings remain the same (albeit with new labels that tell us and others who we are). Transhumanism reasserts systems of ranking bodies; vertical and horizontal rankings creating global raced divides. Its appetite is fed by the moral panic of a world awash with disorders, enveloped by dementia as the population ages (Chatterjee, 2007).

The schema of Hughes (2001) further diminishes the 'rights' of people with intellectual disability (only having the right to life) and bears with it an inference that enhancement technologies can do 'nothing' for those deemed severely retarded [sic]. Little is said within this new ranking about the creation or broadening of new kinds of 'intellectual' disability because of the emergence of cognitively enhanced post-humans and the stripping or delimitation of characteristics deemed to be cognitive. The point being that not all cognitive enhancements will be valued. There may be a division between those enhancements that transcend or favour disembodied virtues, rather than enhancements geared towards the senses or emotions. Within this world of the transhuman ableism as an ethos is undisputed. On first sight a transhumanist understanding of disability would appear to be progressive in its rejection of the disabled body as defective. However, since normalcy is under its logic quashed and the pathological is expanded, ALL human bodies are defective!

What do Extropian's and other transhumanists think about human impairment, anomalous bodies regarded as disabled? It is hard to tell – explicit discussion about disability concerns in the literature has been limited (for exceptions, see Bostrom, 2006; Wolbring, 2006a, 2007). However, my intuition is that disability as a form of legitimate sensibility would be frowned upon. Stock (2002), for instance, appears ambivalent – he notes that deaf people who want deaf children can utilise new reproductive technologies to make that selection. Yet when it comes to any ethical consideration of those choices, Stock's response is that these choices should be left to parents until those choices amount to child abuse or endanger society. Simplicity of the argument aside, Stock demonstrates little awareness of contested notions of child abuse and social endangerment especially when the parents concerned have non-traditional profiles (e.g. gay, lesbian or intellectually disabled). In an earlier online interview with BBC's online Horizon programme, an interviewer asked the following question to Stock:

[Interviewer]: Technology has positive connotations – people believe in its promise. Do you think that in the future when people can design their own babies, those who refuse it will be accused of not giving their offspring the best possible care?

...[Prof. Gregory Stock]: I think that when we have the ability to intervene in this realm, there will be a whole new area of law –

issues such as wrongful birth, where children sue their parents for not correcting some disease, and others who sue their parents for 'improvements' that were made. But my perspective is from the United States, where everyone sues everyone!

(BBC Horizon, 2000).

Gregor Wolbring has been at the vanguard of confronting the transhumanist movement's ableist orientation. He argues that NBICs (nano-bio-info-cogno technologies) inaugurate new models of health globally which refigure global agreements about the social determinants of health (Wolbring, 2006a, 2006c). He convincingly argues that a transhuman or enhanced concept of health means:

> The concept of health no longer has the endpoint that someone is healthy if the biological systems function within species-typical, normative frameworks. ... All homo sapien bodies' (and in the end all bodies of all species) – no matter how conventionally medically healthy – are defined as limited and defective. ... health in this model is the concept of having obtained maximum (at any given time) enhancement (improvement) of one's abilities, functioning and body structure. Disease, in this case, is identified in accordance with a negative self-perception of one's enhanced body.
>
> (2006b, p. 23)

The inference being that whilst the social is usually kept at arms length by transhumanists, choices made by parents and others maybe coerced by the prospect of future or predicted penalties. It is unclear whether there would be penalties by employers, towards individuals who choose not to engage in cosmetic neurology (Appel, 2008). Possibilities of posthumanism developed within the context of technologies of ableism may provide a 'new deal' for some – but on closer examination the tentacles of ableism reassert itself through the a dominant trend in the literature and research to propose a virile style of transhumanism that despises vulnerability. Other opportunities and emancipatory styles of transhumanism may emerge. Alternatives rejecting the conflation between use-value and the delimitation of humankind, an oppositional transhumanism that proposes cyborgs whose central qualities are those of relationality and the experience of growing.

What becomes clear throughout this chapter is that people with disability have complex relations with technologies and that these relations transmogrify disability subjectivities. Certainly in terms of ableism, specific technologies have been harnessed to shore up ableist notions of normalcy, whereas other technologies have unpredictably produced subversive and alternative ways of living an affirming disability life. It was Heidegger (1977), who concluded that technologies *per se* were neither intrinsically effective nor destructive, rather that technological engagements had the capacity to radically alter our way of thinking about human ontologies.

Part 2
Spectres of Ableism

5
The Deaf Trade: Selling the Cochlear Implant

> Cochlear implants remind me, more than anything else, of sex-change surgery. Are transsexuals really members of their chosen sex? Well, they look like that other sex, take on the roles of that other sex and so on, but they do not have all those internal workings of the other sex, and cannot create children in the organic fashion of members of the chosen sex. Cochlear implants do not allow you to hear, but rather to do something that looks like hearing. They give you a process that is (sometimes) rich in information and (usually) free of music. They make the hearing world easier, but they do not give you hearing. What they give you has value, so long as you know in advance what that is
>
> (Solomon, 1994, p. 14).

This chapter is about the power of rhetoric and representation, not only of marked bodies known to the hearing world as 'the Deaf,'[1] but about an artefact branded as a *Cochlear Implant* (CI). It is also a story – a story about the incubation and birth of an artefact that its designers argue creates or mimics 'sound'. Narratives of persuasion enabled the transmogrification of an experimental and rather novel 'hearing device' into a *bona fide* curative solution to the 'problem' of profound deafness. The CI additionally invokes a story of culture (wars); ostensibly about ontologies – those that are privileged and those outlawed and the ways competing notions of being-ness and rhetorical positioning are fashioned through either *etic* or *emic* lens (Clifton, 1968; Freire, 1970).

As part of the storytelling, I am interested in examining the *conditions* of the implant's production, the kinds of *commitments* invoked in product development and the processes of *bandwagoning* that led to the creation of a CI *black box* – a type of toolkit of knowledges, devices, plans and rationalisations. The selling of the CI was made possible through the creation of an actor network. A network develops by the way of a process of *translation* and consists of three major stages: problematisation (the defining and limiting of interests), interessmant (a process of convincing other actors and stakeholders to accept definition of the focal actor, in this case the manufacturers of the implant), and enrolment (Callon et al., 1986). This chapter will show that numerous actors have been involved in a different process of translation, each with its own level of engagement and outcomes. I conclude that the 'successful' normalisation of the CI is due, not just to the obtainment of inter-organisational networks of 'relevant' social groups but was made possible through a deferment to, and a harnessing of, negative ontologies of Deafness (and disability). Instead the deployment of the inherent preferability of 'hearing' as social capital was invoked. In this way, I argue that technologies of cochlear implantation, by being promoted as a technology of 'treatability', in effect produce agreements and foreclose discussion on the contestability of the concepts of deafness, hearingness, aberrancy and normalcy. The discussion is divided into two parts. The first part looks at the development of CI as *morphed* hearing. Part two moves to a discussion of critical ontological concerns that feature as subtexts in the rhetoric of deafness and cochlear implantation.

The epigram by Solomon (1994) that opens this chapter points to the ways technology has the capacity to mediate and destabilise forms on human subjectivity and ontologies of corporeal holism. The tale of the CI is primarily about ontological transitions and tussles over the locus of power. Biotechnologies enact, to use Hofmann's language, a *techné matriké* inaugurating a constitutional binary of 'this' and 'that', 'what is' and 'what isn't':

> Medical technology has become the measure of all things; a kind of *ars mensura*. It has become the *techné matriké* of the modern age, the measure of what is good and bad, what is to be treated and not, and hence, what is diseased and what is not. This can be entitled the *technological invention of disease*.
>
> (Hofmann, 2001, pp. 17–18)

From another angle, such versions of constitutionality shape and ultimately seek to enforce certain moral landscapes of reading difference and cultural ordering as well as contestable ethos of sound. Whilst the theme of this chapter may well be described in terms of ontological contestations, my analysis also points to sites of converging interests between apparatuses of medicine, law and commerce.

Working on a doable problem: the evolution and acceptance of the cochlear implant

CIs are touted by the popular press and the flashy brochures of manufacturers as providing the miracle of hearing, as resembling a 'bionic ear'. This is despite the fact that both audiologists and otologists alike regard children with CIs as remaining 'severely hearing impaired' [sic] (Boothroyd, 1993; Horn et al., 1991). This discussion examines how this rhetorical situation came to be and how the CI was transformed from a dubious experimental device to an established, celebrated developing technology. It was Jean-Marc Gaspard Itard (1774–1838), a doctor at the Paris Institute for the Deaf, who, in 1808, developed a *medical* formulation of deafness after the investigation of a 'mute' student named Lefebvre. Nicholas Mirzoeff (1995) sums up Itard's criteria for diagnosis:

> If the patient showed signs of improvement in understanding and intelligence, the disease was simply deafness; if not deafness compounded with idiocy. Diagnosis thus depended upon the results of treatment, not upon the invisible and immeasurable deficiency of hearing it was supposed to correct.
>
> (p. 56)

Now that a definition and diagnosis of deafness was possible, all that was needed was a cure. Itard was understood to have used injections, astringents, electricity and hot irons to 'unblock' deafness (Lane, 1992, pp. 212–213). The CI can be understood as a modern descendant of this search for a cure. The first direct stimulation of the auditory nerve was carried out by Lundberg in 1950 and improved by otologist Charles Eyries and medical physicist Djourno in Paris (1957) after a desperate request by a deaf man for some hearing (Clark & Tong, 2000; Djourno & Eyries, 1957). Stuart Blume (1997) provides a worthy synopsis of the history of CI development so I will only detail the key points of technological emergence. The period from the 1960s with the development of the multi-channel CI William House prototype until the late 1970s can be characterised as experimental, ambiguous and somewhat controversial (Blume, 1997; House, 1995).

It was only with the surgical implantation in 1978 by Australian otologist Graeme Clark and then throughout the 1980s that CIs were understood as a useful therapeutic artefact, thereby gaining credibility amongst otological peers (Clark & Tong, 2000; Epstein, 1989). Like Alexander Bell, Graeme Clark's motivation to develop a 'solution' to deafness was due in part to his experiences with a deaf father. Both Bell and Clarke conceptualised deafness as a world of silence and horrendous isolation (Clark, 2000; Mackay, 1997). Since the 1980s to the release of the *ESPrit 3G*™ in 2000 (a behind the ear processor), by Cochlear Limited, the development of 'morphed hearing' transplants has been multidirectional, alternating between single and multiple electrodes, invasive and non-invasive prototypes.

I now turn to the work of Clarke and Fujimura (1992), for assistance in identifying what needs to be studied to create a 'roadmap' for our inquiry. Their schema for studying scientific work of CI is instructive:

> *Everything in the situation*, broadly conceived: who is doing it and how is the work organized; what is constructed as necessary to do the work; who cares about the work (in the pragmatist and philosophical sense); sources of sponsorship and support both locally and elsewhere; what are the intended products, and for which consumers or users; what happens to the products after they are sent out of the door into the user workplaces; and last ... what interpretations do participating actors construct over the course of the work.
>
> (Clarke & Fujimura, 1992, p. 5)

Pinch and Bijker (1987) provide a slightly different, but complimentary process. Using modelling based on a Social Construction of Technology (SCOT) methodology, they formulate a multidirectional approach to technological development by mapping four key areas, namely: artefact, social group, problem and solution. Combining these two approaches not only provides a rich source of information but also will help in the mapping of broad networks of association across many social worlds.

One of the most striking features of the multidirectional development of CIs is the lack of artefact stabilisation, that is the switching from single to multi-channel electrodes and back, the regional diversification of key stakeholders and the non-linearity of product development. Nonetheless the project of building a 'hearing device' was viewed by scientists and technicians as doable from the start. According to Fujimura, 'the construction of a doable problem is the process of solving a problem from the beginning to the end. ... Doable problems are sociotechnical achievements' (1996, p. 10). Yet the doability inscribed to the scientific work, occurs *ex post facto*, after the 'solution' to describe and mask developmental problems.

Arguing from a different perspective, Hesslow (1993) suggests that technological treatability (in this case the CI) constitutes the 'disease', that is formulations of deafness and hearingness. He concludes, 'It is not really the presence of a disease that is crucial, but the fact that some medical intervention may be beneficial and that it is within the physician's power to help the patient' (1993, p. 7). In other words, technologies of 'treatability' engage in a circular logic with the agency of the artefact folding back onto the potential recipient who is then figured as diseased or deficient, that is the possibility of 'curing' deafness means that Deafness needs and therefore must be cured, for disability is always 'in waiting' and pre-emptively deficient even before diagnosis.

The CI as a product

About 400 Australians receive a CI each year with 33% of implantees being 18 years of age or younger. At a cost of AUD$ 25,070, less than 10% of people who could be candidates for a CI are able to access the device (Access, Economic, 2006, p. 50). This figure represents the 'tip of the iceberg' in terms of potential users, according to the annual reports of CI producers, who reiterate to stockholders that the market reach has been barely exhausted; arguing a significantly larger market exists that is yet to be captured.

A CI is a form of instrumentation that directly stimulates the cochlea and purports to 'elicit patterns of nerve activity that mimic those of a *normal* [sic] ear for a wide range of sounds…today's devices enable about *10 percent* of those implanted to communicate without lip reading and the vast majority to communicate fluently when sound is combined with lip reading' (Eddington & Pierschalla, 1994). The device is made up of five components: The electrode array (which is inserted into the inner ear); a receiver; a speech processor that is usually worn by the user; a transmitter coil and a microphone that are worn behind the ear.

The internal component of the cochlear implant

Lane et al. (1996) provides a precise description of the three to four hours surgery required to insert the implant:

> The surgeon cuts the skin behind the ear, raises the flap, and drills a hole in the bone. Then a wire carrying electrodes is pushed some

25 mm into the coiled inner ear. The tiny endings of the auditory nerve are destroyed and electrical fields from the wire stimulate the auditory nerve directly. A small receiver coil connected to the wire is sutured to the skull and the skin is sewn over it. A small microphone worn on an earpiece picks up sound and sends signals to a processor worn on a belt...the processor sends electrical signals back to the implanted receiver via a transmitter mounted behind the ear, and those signals stimulate the auditory nerve.

(p. 388)

What is rarely mentioned in literature produced by exponents of the CI is that creation of 'sound' occurs at the expense of any 'residual hearing' during the surgical implantation of long electrode CIs in the recipient (Bogies et al., 1989; Wrigley, 1996). The forces of scientific ableism produce a rather strange, if not perverted, logic that instrumentally proposes that it is efficacious to 'knock out' residual hearing in order to gain 'synthesized hearing'. This kind of destruction represents a point of significant divergence from traditional hearing aids. Given the surgical requirements and internal nature of the implant, implants are only removed for medical reasons; if a user chooses to stop using a CI, they can only remove the external component. There are no reports of total removal, academic or anecdotal, and only a minor number of anecdotal stories of people choosing to 'turn off' (Christiansen et al., 2002; Ray et al., 2006).

The nature of the artefact – 'what is it meant to do?'

Representations about the nature of CIs have not only shifted since the early prototypes of the 1950s, they reveal contestations over the 'purpose' and outputs of such devices and their reception within various socio-medical contexts. CIs have progressed from the initial Experimental notion through Established devices to a Developing Technology. So what professions are engaged in research and development and how has the work been organised? The key players have been otologists working in conjunction with biotechnology corporations. In addition, alongside these players are various fundraising/education bodies funded either by the corporations or in an adjunct relationship. As we will see later, a vast inter-organisational network of association has converged around this emergent technology in order to authenticate and entrench the CI's future. Whilst the work was originally (especially in the 'experimental' phase) conducted by various universities, today it is situated within the context of high technology specialised companies spanning various global networks and the precarious world of share trading markets.

The CI industry is dominated by two major players, the North American corporation, Advanced Bionics (AB), that manufactures the *Clarion* range of implants, and the Australian multinational Cochlear Limited (COH) that produces and markets the *Nucleus* implantation system. Advanced Bionics, founded in 1993 to manufacture and distribute the CLARION CI, evolved from two other highly successful companies that developed and marketed medical devices, such as pacemakers and micro-infusion systems (miniature drug delivery pumps used in the treatment of diabetes). The Clarion System was based on work of the research laboratory of the University of California, San Francisco, conducted by Alfred Mann. Mann entered into a licence agreement with the University in 1988 for the right to make, use and sell the inventions of the University developed over the previous 15 years. Thereafter, a small team of engineers and scientists began to develop the device in the Alfred Mann Foundation for Scientific Research, as well as MiniMed Technologies, Limited, the predecessor of Advanced Bionics.

Minor players include AllHear Inc, which manufacturers a single electrode CI in the tradition of the work of William House and an Innsbruck, Austria-based company MED-EL, which manufactures a 'thin' high speech multi-channel CI known as the *COMBI 40* system. AllHear Inc is a company that designs, manufactures and sellsCIs. The company was founded by Dr. William F. House who produced the first practical CI in 1984 in conjunction with the House Ear Institute and the 3M Corporation, and then bought out by the Envoy Medical Corporation in 2007. The CI of AllHear, Inc. is unique among the current crop of implants because it uses a short, single electrode that apparently does not destroy natural or residual hearing. AllHear's CIs at the time of writing were not yet approved by the FDA for general sale in the United States (House, 1995).

While most of the manufacturers of CIs appear to have adopted a relatively cautious approach to terminology describing the outputs of CI hardware, the rhetorical and fundraising arms of such ventures are not so restrained – they represent CIs as 'miracles of hearing' or machines that enable an adult or child 'to hear because of a bionic ear' (Bionic Ear Institute of Australia). Another variation to this theme is the expression that CIs produce 'useful hearing sensations' (Cochlear Implant Clinic, 2000).

Concomitantly, corporation logos provide interesting examples of imaging and iconic representation. The Cochlear Limited web page opens with the following logo *'Cochlear: Hear now. And Always'*(http://www.cochlear.com.au). The April 2002 edition of the Advanced Bionics web page advertised in graphic form the following jingo: *'More Sound Better Hearing. Imagine the Possibilities'*. Subsequent editions of this page, since October 2002, no longer include this representation. Are these shifts and changes merely a sign of regional and contextual variations or is something more rhetorically significant happening? I am in agreement with Blume who observes that there is a wide gulf between 'the extravagant claims by media [or marketing flyers and] the rather more modest claims made in professional periodicals' (1997, p. 44.) Our analysis needs to take Blume's observation's one step further and examine the kinds of constructions of CIs that are being used in order to justify, legitimate and carry out scientific research, product development and sales of CI. Whilst COH still speak of 'bring[ing] the gift of hearing to every child and adult who can benefit', in the same breath when referring to the device terms of functionality, the representation is discursively manoeuvred to become a 'stimulation' that is designed to allow individuals with severe to profound hearing loss to 'perceive sound' (Cochlear Limited, 2002). The other key aspect in the advertising of CIs is an emphasised return to 'normalcy' through CI use, and a return or reconnection to community life – 'Hear Life' being the key catchphrase of the MedEl CI, with other slogans on the webpage including 'I can enjoy conversation in restaurants again' and 'I can now talk to my husband on the telephone' (www.medel.com, 2008); Cochlear Limited also use the motto of 'Connecting thousands of people . . . delivering technology for a lifetime of new opportunities' (www.cochlear.com.au, 2005).

'Sound' is not a value-neutral or mere audiological concept; rather it is possible to speak of cultures of sound and hearing. Some sounds and hearing that are deemed pathological – *hearing voices* being a case in point, while other formulations such as *seeing sound* – invoke the strange and unknown. CI adherents could be accused of proposing a moral quality to sounds not unlike the ways that advertisers attempt to seduce customers with certain sounds identified as highly desirable and pleasurable. The subtext of this manoeuvre provides fertile ground for bigger philosophical battles over the nature and representation of 'sound', 'hearing' and by default 'deafness'. If 'hearing' became an explosive term – how is 'that' which is produced by the CI to be framed? Sound, of course, is the rejoinder, the discernment and perception of complex sounds (Cochlear Limited, 2000, p. 2; Wrigley, 1996, p. 208). So we may well ask whether sound and hearing aides are one and the same thing. According to House (1995):

Implants provide access to sound, do they not? To say no is to engage in a semantic dispute which begins in words and ends in words, and which has no pragmatic consequence. Come, let us admit the matter until we have some useful reason to deny it: implants provide access to sound... For those who would quibble, the phrase might be more accurately rendered as 'implants provide a stimulus which is interpreted as sound,' but my point is that a functionally significant difference has never been proven.

A more nuanced interpretation is provided by Timothy Reagan (2002, p. 55), who suggests that 'implants do not restore hearing; rather they create the perception of sound'. This perspective is supported by a group of CI users who articulate the outcome of CI in the following terms: '[CI's] do not provide normal hearing – they provide an improvement in the use of sound' (Cochlear Implant Association Inc, 1997). Nevertheless, what is meant by 'sound' and what are the conditions of its interpretation? Is what is being referred to a matter of degree (and quality) of audiological inputs, that is a strictly medical delineation or does 'sound' denote and elicit a more cultural nuance, a qualitative aspect of subjectivity that interfaces and mediates a world obsessed with oralist interactivity? For example, in 1880 the International Congress of Educators of the Deaf held in Milan marked a turning point in framing sound and its relationship to communication in narrow terms, by officially banning the use of sign language in schools. Does such a concept of 'cultural sound' provide space for a Deaf person to 'see a voice' (Ree, 1999). Certainly biomedical perspectives have shaped and dominated this limited debate to the exclusion of issues raised by the Deaf community (culturalists) and have made it 'safe' (at least within academic cohorts) to acknowledge the provisional dimension of CI 'sound'. As Arthur Boothroyd (1991) suggests,

> The immediate purpose of hearing aids, tactile aids, cochlear implants, and visual aids is to enhance sensory evidence. This point cannot be emphasized strongly enough. Prosthetic assistance does not directly change the perceiver's knowledge or skills. It may do so eventually, in combination with training, maturation, and experience, but its immediate effect is at the sensory level.

Similarly, Thomas Balkany acknowledges that such 'hear[ing] does not approximate that of normal subjects' (cited in Cherney, 1999, p. 29).

Overall, many questions remain unanswered about the benefits and efficacy of CIs, suffice to say that evaluations overall report poor performance and little understanding of sound variability across patients. Dr Robert Shannon of the House Ear Institute in Los Angeles has the last word on this matter:

> I think we are at the stage in cochlear implants at present which is analogous to getting a pair of glasses, except that, in the cochlear implants, we give everybody the same set of glasses. Although that works pretty well for some people; for others, those glasses aren't well suited for this kind of vision problem (1999).

For the public the representation of the 'success' of CIs is less provisional. CIs are touted as a technology of possibilities (... made real).

Networks of interest

For the CI to become viable in terms of market reach and credibility the product developers (otologists and corporations) needed and continue to need to enrol many allies to support their project. This kind of necessity means that scientific work is in essence heterogeneous, having a diverse group of actors and participants whose task is to '... create common understandings, to ensure reliability across domains and to gather information which retains its integrity across time, space and local contingencies' (Star & Griesemer, 1989, p. 385). These networks of interest in their connectivity enact, perform and configure ontologies of deafness and hearingness. The achievement of consensus about the merits and efficacy of CIs is necessary to make the project continually doable (especially as the target group for the device grows broader). Consensus is required amongst otologists about the reliability and design of the technology and further consensus is required about product justification, which is the necessity in the first place to 'cure' deafness thereby making the enterprise a form of ethically valid work.

The networks of interest for CIs have moved beyond the containment of the audiological industry and developers have actively solicited the interests of a broader cross-section of society who they have deemed may 'care' about the work. It is this elastic and broad enrolment that is the key to the rise of the hegemonic status of CI as a 'cure' for deafness. Other allies to care are obvious: educationalists, speech therapists and the 'cure' industry in general, whilst some actors such as multinational companies and governments emerged by necessity. In the case of companies, CIs are big business (more on that point later), while governments have been enrolled to potentially defuse concerns about cost containment and funding (Blume, 1997).

As competition beefs up amongst the two largest CI producers, the rhetoric underpinning these networks of interest increasingly takes on a nationalistic tone. This turn to nationalism reflects the changed context in which the discourses of science and technology are produced in a fluid market economy. As Cohen et al. (2001) points out, there is a view that:

> Sees the purpose of scientific endeavor as the generation of national prosperity and the improvement of quality of life . . . publicly funded research should take its lead from industry . . . to ensure that its work addresses real problems, thus benefiting industry and (by extension) the country as a whole.
>
> (p. 146)

Two news stories from 2002 support this assertion. The first relates to a report in March 2002 about a Deaf same-sex couple in the United States who used assisted conception to conceive a Deaf child (Anstey, 2002; Hays, 2002). The Australian press could not report this story without reference to the impact the choice of a Deaf donor would have on the shares of Cochlear Limited should Deaf Australians dare consider this option (Griffith, 2002a,b)! CIs have become seemingly integral to the Australian Gross National Product! The other story, also from the United States (July 2002), concerned the link between the use of CIs and the risks of contracting meningitis. COH went to great lengths to distance itself from the US story suggesting that consumers should buy the superior Australian product. For example, Cochlear Limited shares plummeted 7.5% ($27) when to story broke only to surge five days later (to $33.40) when its rival, Advanced Bionics, withdrew their product. Professor Graeme Clarke was reported as saying in one news story, 'I am concerned that what has been a wonderful thing for so many deaf people [has been] tarnished by a company that has actually designed something incorrectly' (Infolink, 2002). Many Deaf people report a hesitancy to criticise CIs because to do so would be to criticise the work of Professor Graeme Clarke and bear the allegation of being pronounced un-Australian and therefore a defective citizen (Baker & Campbell, 2006).

'Would the real deaf stand up?': Battles over target groups

It would not be possible given concerns about the efficacy of CIs for this device to be trumped as a technological miracle had the carriage of the CI not been accompanied by the trade in negative symbols of disability and deafness, emerging in particular from a conceptual schema of scientific ableism. Scientific ableism is not unlike its conceptual twin scientific racism, a coital union between law, medicine and ethics which uses science to argue for the facticity of impairment as deficiency, thus distorting if not obscuring the social and cultural production of disability and the privileging of certain bodily formations. An *etic* framework of deafness assumes a life of tragedy and silence. As Robert Crouch (1997) puts it:

> According to many among the hearing, the life of a deaf person is a priori an unfortunate and pitiful life, and is considered by some to be a full-scale tragedy. The hearing parents of the deaf child, themselves members of hearing society...will naturally turn to the medical community in the hope that their child's disability will be 'fixed'.
>
> (pp. 14–15)

In other words, the aim of CIs is to simulate (fabricate) 'hearing' in order to facilitate the assimilation of deaf individuals into the dominant hearing world, thereby ensuring the deafened become productive (ableist) citizens and, as Hughes (2000) puts it, 'aesthetically validated'. The original target population for CIs was post-lingually deafened adults aged 18 and over. The U.S. Food and Drug Administration (FDA) approved the first 3M/House device for adults in October 1984. However, the uptake from this group was slow. One explanation for this was that Deaf communities were not involved or consulted in the processes of product development. This is not surprising, as Blume (1997) indicates that the dynamic behind techno-medicine.

> Can be understood in terms of the articulation of [a] common interest between medical and surgical specialties on the one hand and their industrial suppliers on the other... patients are typically not seen as competent interlocutors in the innovation process.
>
> (p. 32)

'Hearing' designers simply assumed that Deaf adults would have nothing to contribute to the CI prototype or understanding of deafness and would willingly accept such technological gifts with open arms. Despite vehement opposition from a large number of otologists and neurophysiologists to implantation of pre-lingually deaf children over the decade of the 1980s, CIs steadily became normalised and thus accepted (Crouch, 1997; Lane & Grodin, 1997). This broadening acceptance and increased target group purview does not however mean that CI candidacy is an 'open affair'. Candidacy is for reasons that will become clear, strictly policed.

Although the dominant rhetoric invoked by manufacturers focuses on the scientific and outstanding capacities of CIs as a therapeutic artefact, when it comes to the actual usage of CIs this rhetoric 'thins out' and transmogrifies into an emphasis on the burden of 'success' of the technology falling squarely on the recipient. As similarly explored in the chapter on Clint Hallam (see Chapter 6), the recipient of the world's first forearm transplant, with the use of CIs, there is a shift in the burden of responsibility towards the patient (victim blaming) when the incorporation of such tentative technologies, 'fail' in any way. There is a reversal of the old rhetoric of virtuous suffering, where the impaired person gracefully accepts their limitations towards a compulsion of mitigation through prosthetic correction. Seymour confirms this view and argues that where there are 'endless possibilities for bodily manipulation ... If one can choose to alter one's body to reflect particular attitudes, one must accept blame for failing to act in accordance with broad social ideas about proper behavior, presentation, and practice' (1998, p. 183).

The CI can be squarely characterised as a technology of self, in a Foucauldian sense. Acceptance into a programme requires the candidate (and their families) to be motivated, productive and compliant with the therapeutic regime installed as part of the implantation package. As a device that morphs hearing, CI individuals are able to enact a 'number of operations on their own bodies and souls, thoughts, conduct and way of being, so as to transform themselves in order to attain a certain state of happiness, purity, wisdom, perfection or immortality' (Foucault, 1997a, p. 225). The promises of the CI are based on a process of continual deferment where the candidate foregoes immediate needs in exchange for the potential gains that technologies may hold out for the common good. Crouch (1997) points to the 'opportunity costs' of such a process and suggests that the burden of failure extends beyond the CI process itself. He argues that:

The child whose life is centered upon disability and the attempt to overcome it grows up in a context that continually reinforces this disability, despite his or her own best efforts to hear and to speak and despite the diligent work of the educators... These children are therefore always aware that they are outsiders, outsiders attempt to be on the inside.

(p. 18)

It is not surprising then that the CI recipient's relationship with the implant can be aptly spoken in terms of a *marital merge* – not just with the artefact but with the corporation. In fact manufacturers, to instil a sense of brand loyalty amongst their customers have used this 'lifetime therapy' with the corporation as a marketing tool. The branding and badging of implants has resulted in brand wars amongst recipients posting 'flames' (inflammatory internet arguments, often personal in nature) in defence of their brand in various Internet discussion forums. I will now move into part two of our discussion and consider critical ontological concerns that feature as subtexts in the rhetoric of deafness and cochlear implantation.

Ontology wars: Hearing vs. deafness

The hearing world in general *thinks-deafness in the audiological* and displays a limited awareness of Deaf culturalist paradigms. For some people a Deaf worldview is so foreign, so subaltern that the following statement by Karen Lloyd from the Australian Association of the Deaf may appear shocking. Lloyd (2001) states,

> To us [Deaf identified people], deafness is a natural part of life, it is something that has always been there and is an integral part of who we are. It is not something we have lost or that needs to be 'cured'. The Deaf community has a rich cultural heritage that revolves around its language, Auslan, and Deaf people who belong to this community enjoy a fulfilling and active social and cultural life.

This sub-section explores the silencing of Deaf sensibility and the subject of hearingness and the creation of the productive citizen by invoking and simulating 'hearing' as social capital.

The silencing of deaf sensibility

Like other forms of different bodies considered impaired, the life of Deaf people (because of deafness) has been considered one that is *inherently* negative – silent and pitiful. In this view deaf people are not just different but are evaluatively ranked and are considered 'at least in a physiological sense, inferior to hearing people' (Reagan, 2002, p. 45). It is easy then to appreciate that for many hearing parents with a deaf child, they would unquestionably assume that hearing is *objectively preferable* to being deaf. Whilst internationally there have been flourishing Deaf subcultures for centuries, it is only recently that the Deaf community has euphemistically 'come out of the closet'. Dolnick (1993) in *The Atlantic* remarks,

> Lately . . . the deaf community has begun to speak for itself. To the surprise and bewilderment of outsiders, its message is utterly contrary to the wisdom of centuries: deaf people, far from groaning under a heavy yoke, are not handicapped [sic] at all. Deafness is not a disability. Instead, many deaf people now proclaim, they are a subculture like any other. They are simply a linguistic minority ['speaking' sign language] and are no more in need of a cure than are Haitians or Hispanics.
>
> (p. 302)

Earlier I pointed to the highly developed networks of interest that have converged to legitimate CIs. The Deaf community's entrance into this terrain has been very late and therefore I would proffer that they have been on the back foot in challenging dominant perspectives. The D/deaf spectrum has been subjected to the politics of diagnostic enumeration; resulting in the placement of audiological impairments and identities, 'like' and 'unlike' in a single cluster. As Blume (1997, p. 51) has pointed out, unlike other marginalised groups, 'Deaf people have been required to harness allies with legitimated and privileged voices due their own lack of cultural and social capital (credibility)'. For the hearing (and often the hearing impaired) population, Deafness induces no social capital; is a profoundly foreign, alien land existing in the hidden backwaters of civilisation (Reagan, 1995). The adoption of counter rhetoric about the CI has been through engaging articulate academics to put forward alternate viewpoints as well as the use of television documentaries (Blume, 1994, 1997; Crouch, 1997; Reagan, 1995, 2002). Broader attempts have been made to showcase Deaf culture in the public domain by way of Deaf Festivals of the Arts, national weeks of celebration and Deaf culture expos.

Overall, the response by Deaf culturalists has been to view the CI as another emergent technology that represents a cultural invasion where the dominant hearing world seeks to impose their values on a smaller minority culture. In other words, while CI may be the newest gadget, as a technology, its construction is in keeping with historical genealogies of Deaf subjugation. Deaf activist Paddy Ladd described the implants in terms of 'Oralism's Final Solution!' (cited in Blume, 1997, p. 48). Equally strong language has been used to describe and deconstruct the technicians engaged in CI production. Invasive medical procedures have been described as a form of child abuse that has robbed the Deaf child of their priceless gift of deafness. George Montgomery accused the implants of being 'cheerful headchoppers in the Sir Lancelot mould, hell bent on curing deafness and thus committing casual genocide on the deaf community and its language' (cited Cherney, 1999, p. 28). Wrigley (1996), in rather an understated fashion, summarises the tension as a clash in *ways of being*, the exclusion of an alternative way of knowing and the meaning given to different kinds of personhood.

Telling about hearing

As with many forms of asymmetrical relations, much of the orientation of the CI/deafness debate has centred on the delimitation of deafness rather than on the deconstruction and problematisation of hearing, hearingness and hearingism. Ableist epistemological foundations that assume the preferability of 'hearingness' and the compulsory abolition of deafness have an unacknowledged centred location with bio-technological discourses. The inversion of this traditional, seemingly common-sense gaze enables an exploration of what the silencing of Deaf sensibility can tell us about hearingness. It is only then that the problematisation of the CI seems likely rhetorically.

In his work on the Deaf in sixteenth-century Turkey, Mirzoeff (1995) introduces the concept of the *silent screen* to denote the processes of interactivity between hearing and deaf persons that configures ontologies. In the interaction between hearing people looking at deafness, Mirzoeff proposes that Deaf people respond to such voyeurism by subverting or confirming the image produced. This screen/visualisation becomes a fabrication, a simulation that does not necessarily bear any resemblances to Deaf subjectivity or hearing subjectivities of deaf people. The conclusion reached by Mirzoeff it that the *silent screen* is a shifting construction that requires two people to see deafness. Mirzoeff (1995, pp. 62–64) also notes that in resisting appropriation of their culture, Deaf people have engaged in acts of mimicry, lampoon imagery and conceptualisations. While I agree, Mirzoeff neglects to mention that the *silent screen* also produces the *seeing of hearing* especially for the hearing subject who can make sense of their sensorial difference.

The literature supports this conclusion asserting that the delimitation of deafness could only be achieved within the context of the development of technologies that could visualise/see hearing/sound (Ree, 1999; Sterne, 2001).

I wish to conclude this chapter with a discussion about the productive citizen. In its documentation Cochlear Limited continually stress that CIs will reduce the economic cost of supporting a deaf child as 'benefits may translate into reduced educational costs and increased earnings' (Cochlear Limited, 2000, p. 12), even though there has been a paucity of research undertaking a cost-benefit analysis of competing options (Newell, 2000). What is often stressed in CI promotional material and by CI advocates is the possibility of an easier life for users if they can function in the wider community, emphasising broader and more numerous work and study opportunities if they can straddle both the hearing and Deaf communities through CI use. The underlying assumption of this view is that Deaf people are somehow deficient and as adults they do not contribute to civil society and are economically unproductive. Negative ontologies of deafness (understood as disability) make it possible to construe the lives of Deaf people in terms of burden (both economic and psychic). This is not the case. What is more worrying about this approach is that there is an implication that a proper citizen is a productive one, that the use value of personhood is conflated with restrictive notions of productivity.

An etical view of deafness cannot be other than assimilationist geared towards 'breeding the deaf out' or at the minimum pursuing the goal of making deafness acceptable (palatable). Making deafness acceptable through the use of morphing or simulative technologies enables deafness to bear some commodity/use value to hearing society (Crouch, 1997; Wrigley, 1996). The CI performs this role. No mention is made in the literature of the impact of corporeal transformations on CI users and the ways that such bodily reconfigurations maybe understood by oneself, others and the public framing of legal disability. One of the unintended consequences of the move (to use CIs) is the creation of hybrids, who are destined to exist in 'the twilight zone'[2] of the hearing and Deaf worlds. As previously discussed, CIs are only removed for medical reasons, in cases of infection or serious illness; there is no evidence, either academic or anecdotal of voluntary removal of the entire implant. In situations where implantees choose to stop using their implant, they can remove the external component of the implant and 'return' to being deaf. However, it has been reported that both implantation and voluntary non-use can lead to identity issues, with implantees existing in an undefined space between the hearing and Deaf worlds when using CIs, and then feeling only temporary belonging to the Deaf community when not using the CI; this has especially been noted in cases of adolescents who choose to stop using their implants (Christiansen et al., 2002, p. 313). The implantation of a CI leaves people in an indeterminate state, an ontologically problematic realm where they are *not*; neither entirely part of the hearing community, nor entirely part of the Deaf. Leaving aside matters of subjectivity, such hybridity in the public realm problematises the delimitation of legal disability. In other words, can CI users utilise disability protection laws when their impairment has been mitigated? (Campbell, 2001).

Conclusion

In this chapter I have attempted to show the impetus for the development of (disabled) technologies such as CIs as a case study. These developments occur within a purview of contestations over ontologies of deficiency and perfectibility. Negative ontologies of deafness that assume an ethics of compulsory correction towards hearingness and such ontologies were harnessed rhetorically to promote the efficacy of cochlear implantation technologies as well as the nullification of oppositional discourses of Deaf culturalists. Notions of 'deafness' and 'hearingness', phenomenologically and audiologically, reside and are formulated in an interdependent relationship. The examination of the technical developments of the CI within this chapter has foregrounded many disjunctures and disagreements amongst scientists and commentators over the representation of CI technological outputs – as morphed hearing, (real) hearing, sensing or simulation. A lesson from this study is that for marginalised communities to successfully claim narratological and rhetorical space, they need to enrol and engage with a broader range of networks of interest that are empathetic with culture-based arguments and have the social capital necessary to effectively transmit counter-rhetorical perspectives.

6
Print Media Representations of the 'Uncooperative' Disabled Patient: The Case of Clint Hallam

'The hegemonic location of biomedicalism among institutional forma-tions has meant our present capacity to experience the body directly, or theorize it indirectly, [has become] extricably medicalized' (Frank, 1990, p. 136). Freidson (1970) points out that this state of hegemonic biomed-icalism has meant that doctors have had a sanctioned monopoly to be able to define the continuum of health and illness and approaches to the treatment of illness. As one commentator put it, biomedicalism has resulted in the patientisation of the population (Taylor, 1979). In the case of disablement, biomedical epistemologies and the assumption that so-called 'abnormal' conditions are the principle obstacle to disabled people's integration into society have shaped social and technological practices as well as the formation of disabled subjectivities.

Disability is assumed to have an existence that is *factual, significant* and *objective*, altogether autonomous from any social context. Medi-cal practices, organised around the medical model, presume that the doctor's task is to diagnose diseases, to discover their causes and symp-toms, and design treatments. Any knowledge standpoint of the patient is sloughed off. The treatments are aimed at eliminating or minimising the symptoms of the impairment, or the cause of the disease, or the impairment itself. In this sense biomedicalism has encroached on the psychic life of the disabled individual because it asserts that disability is internal, inaugurating a crisis within the person's bodily or cerebral self, and as such is a state that warrants medical interventions and/or curative treatment wherever possible (Silvers, 1998a).

Discourses around medical research, new technologies and practices contain implicit narratives of disability as a *personal medical tragedy*. This theory regards the existence of impairment and the experience of disability to be tragic and this ontological negativity of the disabled body translates into the commonly held belief that nothing 'good' can be said about disability (Campbell, 2001). The medical model of disability is inflected in everyday understandings of disablement and feeds into unquestioned ableist assumptions. The explanatory power of biomedicalism is only possible because medical epistemologies appear not only to be 'common sense' (rational), but also gain credibility from the prestige of being connected to scientific-techno-medical apparatuses and corresponding notions of scientific objectivity. Whilst the neo-positivist tendencies of biomedicalism have been subject to countless critiques, from the perspective of the government of disability, biomedical models appear quite attractive especially in negotiating the 'needs' of partitioning and administering (non-productive) elements of the population.

One of the weaknesses of the medical model of disability is that it fixes upon the 'problem' of the individual (impairment inheres in the person) and ignores those aspects of impairment that are socially or biographically produced (Mishler, 1984; Todd, 1989). This focus has the effect of *redirecting* social policy towards medicalised and corrective services/solutions. Often what is ignored or forgotten is that barriers, seemingly due to impairment, may not be caused by the impairment *qua* impairment, but rather the way *an impairment is mediated within social structures* such as social planning and the design of space creating 'geographies of disability' (Gleeson, 1999 cited Freeman & Abou Jaoudé, 2007).

The Clint Hallam international surgical soap-opera played out in the electronic and print media during 1998–2000 is an apt example of the ways contemporary technological practices interface with both popular and technical formations of what it means to be 'dis-abled' and 'nearly-abled'. The case study is an instance where engagements with transplant technologies feed into *narratives of optimism* where the tragedy of amputation compels doctors to 'cure [or least perfect] at all costs' (Shakespeare, 1999, p. 675). This study is not just confined to an analysis of medical technologies, it specifically examines the ways print media uncritically re-mediates biomedicalism and narratives of disablement as tragedy. Hallam's saga is also a study of the way in which networks of ableism can be recuperated and thus remain reinforced and unchallenged. This chapter follows the travails of Clint Hallam and the (re)writing of Clint's 'hand' in media discourses. It analyses the convergence of the personal tragedy approach to 'disability' with the criminalised 'hand' (body). I conclude that far from considering new technologies as neutral isolated objects, the practices, coupling and effects of technologies reassert a new and vigorous bio-medicalisation of species-typical functioning and ultimately protect domains of ableism from critical review (see Chapter 4).

Disablement: Disability studies meets critical media studies

The biomedicalist conceptualisation of disablement has been sharply criticised by disability activist and disability studies scholars alike. The first-wave response to modernist discourses of medicalism is referred to as the *social model* of disability, making a theoretical distinction between disability and impairment in the same way that early feminist writing distinguished between gender and sex (Rubin, 1975). Today the social model acts as a litmus test for progressive disability politics and disability studies research within the Western academy. Such an approach understands disability to be socially produced, or a trope or neologism wrapping around and over impairment. Changes in the conceptualisation and delimitation of disability are consequences of changes in the economic and social organisation of society. Recently a second wave of challenging enlightenment discourses of scientism has emerged within disability studies based on a range of poststructuralist methodologies that map out postmodern terrains of disablement (Corker & Shakespeare, 2002). Rosemarie Garland-Thomson (2001) provides a pithy definition of a poststructuralist rendering of disability:

> disability is a fabricated narrative of the body, a system that produces subjects by differentiating and marking bodies...Disability is a broad term within which cluster ideological categories as varied as sick, deformed, ugly, old, maimed, afflicted, abnormal, or debilitated – all of which disadvantage people by devaluing bodies that do not conform to certain cultural standards.
>
> (pp. 1–2)

Based on this perspective, disability studies proceeds from a frame which figures disability as a *representational system* and not a medical problem primed with tragedy. It has been noted that there is a paucity of literature within media studies examining representations of disability (Goggin & Newell, 2000). Ross (2001) takes this criticism further and contends that mass media researchers have totally ignored disability as a thematic of interest, arguing that limited research has been content driven or positioned from the perspective of non-disabled people. There are however some notable exceptions examining such diverse aspects as newspaper disability terminology (Ann-Lewis, 1988; Auslander & Gold, 1999; Barnes, 1992), general media portrayals (Pointon & Davies, 1997, Meekosha & Dowse, 1997), fundraising imagery (Corbett & Ralph, 1994; Phillips, 2001) and radio (Ross, 1997, 2001).

Methodological approach

Whilst this case study redresses this paucity by drawing upon the methodological insights of content analysis and grounded theory (narrative analysis), this chapter's underlying argument is that existing cultural and media studies approaches to disability can be fruitfully extended by sociology of science and technology studies approaches situated within a poststructuralist disability studies framework. The study examined a sample of articles on Clint Hallam's transplant published in Australian and overseas newspapers (including internet versions). In utilising *content* and *narrative analysis*, I focused on those aspects of media reportage related to *appearance* (headlines, definitions), *intensity* (claims, argument style and evidence), *agendas* (presuppositions) and *status* (competence, credentials of the speaker) (May, 1998; Lee & Poynton, (2000).

Pinch and Bijker's (1987) work on *artefact stabilisation* and technological closures were deployed to enhance the discussion and analysis. *Artefact stabilisation* refers not only to the choice of technological apparatus (in this case a hand transplant donated by a deceased man) but also to the dominant 'meaning(s)' given to that artefact. Mechanisms of closure can be grouped into two kinds, namely *rhetorical closure* and *closure by re-definition of the problem*. The use of rhetorical closure in this case study drew attention to the existence of contestable meanings over the nature and purpose of a 'transplant' and any corresponding ethical dilemmas. For instance, is a transplant 'restorative' or merely a prosthetic enhancement? *Rhetorical closure* involves a cessation of controversy, with the dominant actors (the medical community and media) instituting a fixed meaning and 'disappearing' any problems. This process involves mobilising allies across networks of association to assist with inducing a particular thematic spin. As Pinch and Bijker remark, 'in technology, advertising [and media] can play an important role in shaping the meaning which a social group gives to an artifact' (1987, p. 427).

The second strategy of *closure by re-definition of the problem* is particularly pertinent in the story of Clint Hallam. In this instance, on the occasion of the first hand-forearm transplant, there were serious concerns about technological practices and artefacts. Instead of responding to perceived 'problems', the meaning of either the artefact (the limb) or its application was translated by the medical established mediated by media commentaries, to constitute a solution to *another* problem. The methodological approaches adopted for the case study assisted in foregrounding the way in which the body, psyche and voice of Clint Hallam have been put into speech. Additionally I document the formation of the *criminalised disabled* subject as a justificatory identity for the failure of the transplant.

The story

In September 1998, a radical hand transplant involving 13.5 hours of surgery was performed at the Edouard Herriot Hospital, Lyon, France, by an international team[1] of surgeons on the body of then 48-year-old New Zealander Clint Hallam. As a patient-subject, there were two features that become significant in media reportage about Hallam's surgical saga and the marking of his body. First, Clint Hallam had a criminal 'past', which becomes transmogrified over time into an all-embracing 'criminal mind' in opposition to the notion of the 'responsible citizen'. Second, Clint prior to the surgery lived for 14 years as a person with a physical impairment.[2] Despite this 'fact', absent from media narratives were any recognition of or explanations of Hallam's 'disabled life' due to the underlying assumption of tragedy. The translation or mixing of the 'criminal' and the 'disabled' body not only infuses the style of media reportage, but in many ways set the terms of the debate and the ways in which ableist-medical experts responded to criticisms over their technological practices.

According to media reports Clint Hallam lost his right hand in a circular saw accident in 1984 while serving a 2-year prison sentence for fraud in New Zealand. The UK newspaper *The Observer* notes a rather quirky aspect to this saga – hand transplant aside – Hallam 'is now the first person to have his right hand amputated three times' (McKie & Paton Walsh, 2001).[3] It was after the failed re-attachment that, according to one report, Clint developed his dream or obsession of 'a replacement human hand in full working order', as Clint states, 'I chose an artificial hand, believing that it would almost become humanoid...but I also thought that if they [the doctors] could do hearts and livers, one day they would be able to do limbs too' (Whittell, 2000, p. 5). Hallam pursued this quest and after meeting up with micro-surgeon Dr Earl Owen, set in place a chain of events that led to the world's first hand transplant.

Viability or freakish novelty – contestations over transplant plans

> To the doctors who performed the pioneering hand transplant surgery; it was a work of art that would cement their place in medical history. But for the man who has to live with the hand and forearm of a dead motorcyclist, it is a grotesque and useless appendage that has left him physically and socially damaged.
>
> (Middap, 2000)

From the start, Dr Earl Owen's plans to conduct a hand transplant were shrouded in controversy. The early media reports bear testimony to this context and it is only later (post-surgery and pre-re-amputation) that the contentious nature of the surgical experiment is erased and evaporates in media reports, replaced by the underlying theme of the marvels of medical discovery, 'gift-giving' (narratives of optimism) and Clint's ungrateful 'deviant' response. Owen initially made approaches to the British St. Mary's Hospital in Paddington. However according to *The Weekend Australian* (Whittell, 2000), British authorities baulked at letting the operation go ahead. Whittell lost the opportunity to engage in investigative reportage by exploring the problematical aspects of the technology; it is not clear why baulking was the response as no reason is given for this insinuation of hostility. An earlier piece in the *New Scientist* magazine headlined *Hands today, faces tomorrow* raising the spectre of the potential for creating a Frankensteinian monstrous body. Noting that the hand transplant was controversial, writer David Concar suggests in his opening sentence that the operation 'raises the prospect of something even *more macabre* – a human face transplant' (Concar, 1998). Aside from this rather glib and emotive statement, little analysis is provided to substantiate his concern. As if almost to allay any 'floodgate' type fears, Dr. John Williams, Vice President of the Royal College of Surgeons, is quoted in the same report as saying that the low incidence of severe injuries would call into question the 'worthwhileness' of such surgery. Within Concar's report the voice of Clint Hallam is silent.

Justine Ferrari's piece under the headline of *Hands-on Experience*, in an October 1998 edition of *The Weekend Australian*, remains one of the few articles that attempt any critical analysis of the Lyon corporeal-surgical intervention/corporeal violence (1998). While still being written from a biomedical perspective with its emphasis on immune-suppressant drugs, Ferrari does give Hallam a mediated[4] voice. Using the metaphor of 'bodily recycling' as well as a resurrection motif, she suggests that Clint Hallam might not be an ideal choice as a transplant patient: 'irrespective of his criminal charges... counting against the success of the operation is the length of time since Hallam lost his arm'. Ferrari is not referring to the possibility of conflict and turmoil that Clint may experience when renegotiating changes in subjectivity, which is from an 'amputee' to a 'transplant recipient'. Rather in an isolated frame, she is referring to the more mechanistic physical aspects of regeneration (coupling). It is Ferrari's exposition of the politics of immuno-suppressant drugs that raises significant questions about the ethics of normalising and perfecting technological practices. The problem of this technology, for Ferrari, is rhetorically closed off by limiting the discussion to the level of biological compatibility, rather than matters related to living with impairment at an ontological level.

The challenge of the surgery is that the impaired body has to be 'tricked' into accepting the colonising transplant. As many HIV/AIDS activists point out, life-long immuno-suppressant drugs have many significant and detrimental side effects (Paton, 1990). Most media reports are silent about this aspect of the transplant. There is an implicit assumption that a transplant is morally *preferable at all and any cost.* Later in this chapter I shall discuss what happens when an individual refuses to conform to and challenges this hegemonic ideal. But for now an important point should be made. Previously in this chapter, I mentioned the notion of 'disability' being posited as ontologically intolerable. The logical conclusion of this belief results in a bizarre and cruel bodily transmogrification, as Ferrari concludes, 'Hallam was previously a well man [with amputation] and now, under the influence of immune suppressive drugs, is a sick man'. The irony of Ferrari's conclusions is left hanging. This state of affairs is only possible through the existence of a rampant ableism and the ways this ethos is mediated by and in technological practices. As Campbell (2001) reminds us:

> ...We can argue that 'enhancing' and 'perfecting' technologies are really a form of assimilation by way of morphing ableism. A technological dynamic of morphing creates an illusion (appearance) of the 'disabled' body transmogrifying into the 'normal' resulting in a corporeal re-composition and re-formation of subjectivity.
>
> (p. 53)

In Ferrari's closing paragraph she points uncritically to the psychic dilemma of 'living with a stranger's hand'. Apart from the 'yuk effect', no real discussion takes place concerning the psychic or ethical implications of transplant practices. In a discursive manoeuvre that contrasts a face transplant, Ferrari (1998) rather glibly remarks, 'looking in the mirror and seeing a completely different person seems beyond the realm. But then, imagine living without a face'. In 1998, of course, this was merely a glib remark; over a decade on when facial transplants have and continue to be performed, this becomes a relevant and serious question, particularly given then inextricability of identity and face; ontologically speaking, what does the recipient 'become'? No longer looking like themselves, they will neither look like the donor – instead becoming a hybrid, composite construction.

Before moving on, Justine Ferrari's *Hands-on Experience* makes two additional points that are useful to keep in mind when examining the matter of techno-closure. The effects of immuno-suppressant drugs is discursively side-stepped by re-negotiating normative rules of clinical practice, what Joan Fujimura calls a 'gray box', of 'doable problems' in order to get the job done (1992, p. 176). So as Ferrari (1998) reports 'doctors who say they would not perform a hand transplant because of the side-effects of the immune-suppressant drugs are demonstrating a paternalistic attitude that is now outdated' (1998). The 'problem' then, is *not* one of technological practices; rather it has been discursively re-routed to a 'problem' of the individualised (backward) attitudes of certain (deviant) doctors who do not back these new narratives of optimism. The second point Ferrari (1998) makes relates to the trans-temporal media hype about the forthcoming hand transplant. She reports the 'event' was reported in a self-congratulatory manner weeks before the transplant even took place. Whilst Ferrari's piece provides some useful insights, in the end it skirts across issues of disability/normalcy by its lack of sustained attention to psychic matters of subjectivity and technologies of normalisation. Her piece ultimately lapses into a Cartesian dualism that privileges biologism or social organisation.

I conclude this section by considering two examples of more 'upbeat' media reportage about the proposed transplant. In particular I focus on the way science and media practices converge in order to convey a sense of 'consensus' and closure in the 'hand' transplantation debate. The work of Joan Fujimura around the politics of cancer research is instructive for our survey of the handling of rhetorical closure in the proposed transplant operation (Fujimura, 1996, 1992). Outsiders to science often believe that scientific procedures obtain agreement and objective verification before commencement. However, Fujimura shows us that procedural knowledge is constructed, by examining in her work practices of consensus building and the phenomena of 'bandwagons'. Fujimura's concept of 'standardised packages' enables the analysis of the achievement of agreement across various (often conflicting) social worlds in order to 'get the job done'. This is achieved through the narrowing of 'work space' and the range of possible practices. Such strategies create a standardised set of technologies that make it possible not only to enrol large numbers of players from multiple social worlds (e.g. media, financiers, government and the 'public') but also to construct new and stable definitions, for example 'disability', a 'transplant', 'cure', 'health' and 'disease'. The electronic and print media in its hype over the 'futurist- robotic man' is a significant player (actor). The two media pieces examined are a 1998 *Resoftlinks News* piece under the headline of *The first hand transplant in Lyon* and a later, retrospective piece (2001) by McKie and Paton Walsh in *The Observer* headlined *Trickster has transplant hand cut off*.

The 1998 piece in *Resoftlinks News* (1998) opens with the statement that surgeons are optimistic about the recently performed hand transplant. Optimistic that is, about Clint Hallam's body resisting rejection of the foreign parts. This spin is followed by that now familiar motif of salvific hope, an instituting of a 'bio-utopia' (c.f. Hindmarsh et al., 1998). Surgical team member Dr Jean-Michel Dubernard is reported as saying: 'The surgical breakthrough gives hope to millions of victims of workplace and domestic accidents, survivors of war or land mines and individuals born with hereditary deformities'. The reader is not provided with any substantiation of the 'logic' of this view of 'hope'. It is assumed (and probably rightly so) that the majority of readers hold to a deficit and tragic view of disability, a form of corporeality requiring correction. Instead of providing a critical reportage of the transplant event, this journalistic piece becomes an instrumental ally not only in the reinforcement of medical hegemony, but also of an uncritical ableism that posits the dis-ease of disability as intolerable and sickly.

The 2001 retrospective piece by Robin McKie and Nick Paton Walsh, *Trickster has transplant hand cut off*, in *The Observer* again takes up this theme of optimism and 'doctor as gift giver'. However, it contains traces of confusion and discontinuity related to the reading of the 'transplant event'. We are told that the operation was 'deemed a complete success', although no criteria or further explanation is provided to support this conclusion. Hallam's own 'voice' is allowed provisional entry. He says he woke up expecting 'to find life had returned to normal', yet Hallam's reaction to the immune-suppressant drugs resulted in him feeling 'more handicapped than before'. This moment of profound irony is just left hanging by the reporters – no comment is made about such an awkward juxtaposition. Instead the tried-and-tested strategy of victim blaming is deployed in order to draw attention away from the contestability of technological transplant practices. Concepts of normalcy and disability as pathology remain unexplored. Such *closure by re-definition of the problem* focuses on Hallam's deviancy and disruption of the gift giving. The reader is told that the problem is not the drugs but all '...the fault of Hallam, [who]...went without drugs for weeks'. Yet in a rather apologetic fashion, McKie and Walsh comment that the 'perennially cash-strapped Hallam...could not afford his £10,000-a-year drug bill'. Again another critical moment is missed: an opportunity to make critical connections between technologies, cost and matters of equity. Instead, the 'money problem' is recuperated in a rather perverse manner via the voice of surgical team member Dr Nadey Hakim:

> The longer the hand stayed on him, the longer it cost him money...He just said 'thank you' to me after the operation, and I felt he was being genuine. He is free of the burden of the last few years. That hand was something that he *could no longer afford to possess*.
>
> (McKie & Paton Walsh, 2001 – emphasis added)

Aside from the rather unfortunate monetarist imagery, Dr Hakim is given the last word in re-interpreting the potentially subversive 'voice' of Clint Hallam. Hallam is positioned as the rather ungrateful, untrustworthy and suspect actor/recipient of the surgical experiment. Just as the 'new hand' would be soon separated by way of amputation from Hallam's body, so too it is rendered ontologically separated/isolated in Hakim's speech. Indeed the 'hand' is allowed limited agency to be an actor, albeit a controlled one. 'The hand' has become a commodified object capable of being possessed and no doubt dispossessed and re-possessed.[5] This possession is contingent upon Clint Hallam's impaired body taking control of it, mastering its renegade forces. The catch is that such limbly possession is conditional upon acquiescence to the ethos and sacrifices of ableism; conditional upon the forces of economic monetarism capturing the uppity limb (the hybrid actant[6]) that refuses re-unification.

Who's tricking whom? – the criminalised body of Clint Hallam

> I mean this in the nicest way, but he [Clint Hallam] is a liar of extraordinary talent. He's an absolutely charming chap. He's clever enough to have fooled a great many people in his many careers.
>
> (Dr. Earl Owen cited Middap, 2000)

> Beyond admission, there must be confession, self-examination, explanation of oneself, revelation of what one is…'can one condemn to death a person one does not know?'
>
> (Foucault, 1978, p. 76)

Before the rather public 'outing' of Clint Hallam's difficulties with his new transplanted hand, typical commentary on the world's first hand transplant incorporated Clint's criminal escapades as a young man into the 'story'. This fascination is inserted to add some sizzling excitement to what might appear as another boring science story. As Reuven Frank, a producer and executive at NBC news (New York, NY) noted in 1963, 'every news story should…display the attributes of fiction, of drama. It should have structure and conflict, problem and denouement…these are not only the essentials of drama; they are the essentials of narrative' (Braun, 2007, p. 6). It is only later when Clint strays from being the perfect docile patient, becoming an un-cooperative patient that the criminality of Clint Hallam provides fodder for discounting/sabotaging his subversive speech and subjugated knowledge. Criminality, that is, innate deviancy, becomes the explanatory narrative for the un-cooperative patient. *New Zealand Herald* reporter Bruce Butler (1998), under the banner of *Hand Gained, Home Likely Lost*, plays with the theme of 'gain and loss'. The piece contains a series of one-liners about the career and travel circuit of 'convicted fraudster' Clint Hallam. Butler reports that the Western Australian police were considering refusing Hallam entry into Australia because of his criminal record. The piece closes with a nationalistic angle, reporting that New Zealander's can be refused entry into Australia if they have a criminal record, emphasising his New Zealand origin in juxtaposition to his assumed Australian identity.

A more alarming anonymously authored piece, reported 2 months later in the same newspaper, headlined *Hand at Risk as Hallam bails out* (*The New Zealand Herald*, 1999) draws upon the jail-bird iconography and contains a greater level of hysteria and judgmental overtones.

Building upon the criminal sensibilities of the headline, this reportage readily connects Clint Hallam's alleged lack of 'co-operation' with the medical establishment with his criminalised body. The context is that Hallam has broken contact with the transplant surgical team. Dr Jean-Michel Dubernard initially provided a psychological explanation for the actions of his defiant patient, suggesting he might be sick of doctors and then shifts gears in his suggestion that Hallam's problem may be related more to his problems in Australia with 'a marketing investment scam allegedly worth $NZ1.16 million'. It is not the operation that is the problem, rather Clint's *inescapable* criminality.

Ellen Connolly's (2000) piece in the *Sydney Morning Herald, Transplant man fled to avoid arrest*, is an interesting attempt to weave Hallam's criminal pursuits into an explanation of his actions in resisting hospital treatment. Although uncertain about Hallam's intentions, the headline infers to the reader that Hallam's disappearance is dubious. Although this journalistic piece reads like a 'rap sheet', it is reported that NSW police are uncertain as to whether Hallam's trip to the United States is to avoid arrest or seek new treatment to 'save' his hand. Furthermore, he is now being referred to as his deviant body, as a hybrid being, the 'transplant man'. The piece by McKie and Paton Walsh (2001) that I have already briefly discussed in the previous section, headlined *Trickster has transplant hand cut off*, was written after a very vigorous (if not one-sided) debate concerning the increasing rejection of the transplant by Clint Hallam's body and its eventual amputation. In terms of *intensity* this report adopts a moral tone of the normative voice of ableist reason, chastising a renegade, uncooperative and disruptive child (the impaired person). The voices of authority, the technicians of expertise, are doctors from the transplant team and the naughty patient is the criminal Clint Hallam. Hallam's criminal story is not just an adjunct to his life story, in this report it is infused in his very psyche, a core object of Hallam's being. Clint Hallam's body is criminalised – he is a 'trickster', a 'fraudster' and an opportunist not to be trusted. And as such the very legitimacy of Hallam's voice is not only totally discounted in this piece but is refused the 'right of reply'.

The space given to the doctor's 'gaze', his capacity to make powerful exhortations, as 'truth' are insightful. Michel Foucault suggests that the 'gaze' of the medical expertise is not confined to that of merely looking or observing, but rather the 'gaze' is calculating making possible the assessment of risk and chance (1975, p. 89). Dr Nadey Hakim can say without risk of criticism that his technological performance of amputation is conditional not only on the utter docility and compliance of

Hallam, but on the basis of a panoptical surveillance of his criminalised soul. The 'space' given by the media reports to the oppressive speech acts of the medical 'gaze' already condemns to 'death' a man named Clint Hallam whose re-constructed 'story' it *thinks* it knows. The ethically unsayable becomes legitimate in the 'voice' of the knowing expert:

> Hakim revealed he had carried out the amputation on the condition that his patient – *a convicted fraudster- agreed not to speak* to the press to earn money from his story. 'I asked for the telephone to be removed from his hospital room,' said Hakim.
> (McKie & Paton Walsh, 2001, emphasis added)

This statement is framed by the reporter's unsubstantiated comments that Hallam stopped taking the immune-suppressant drugs and being an unruly fellow, 'demanded' amputation. After Hakim's conditions, the piece, in order to reinforce the criminalised body, continues its foray into the alleged criminal activities of Hallam, both past and present. Although acknowledging that the 'cosmetic miracle ... had all the attraction of a Frankenstein reject', McKie and Paton Walsh still lay blame for the 'failure' of the transplant at the feet of Hallam himself. The last word is given to the transplant surgeons who argue, 'this unpleasant status was the fault of Hallam himself...'. The reporters agree, pointing out that another six transplants have taken place and '... all are *performing* perfectly' (emphasis added). Before closing this section I want to make some comments about the use of the metaphor 'trick' or 'trickster' that appears either in covert or in overt form in the print media coverage. Earlier in this chapter, I referred to the fact that the 'amputee body' has to be 'tricked' into accepting the colonising transplant; which is where immune-suppressant drugs take on the role of actors in this network of association. As part of the task of deconstructing the nexus between media reports, technological practices and biomedicine, I want to pause and look at this metaphor of the 'trick' more closely, albeit briefly. If the concept of 'informed choice' is critical, then it seems reasonable that critical discourse should not just focus on the 'miracle' of the transplant, but also on the other parts of the compulsory package – such as the anti-rejection drugs. Print media discussion should have focused on issues such as the side effects and management of life-long drug taking as well as matters of cost and the investment of the pharmaceutical industry as a dominant actor in this saga, particularly in relation to the functional necessity of the surgery. Furthermore, within this dialogue, technologies of transplant should not necessarily be seen as *inherently good*.

We could say that it was *Clint Hallam* and not 'the public', the doctors nor the media who were 'tricked'. Discourses that adopt the optimism of technology say little about the meaning/reality of 'cure', 'perfection' and 'restoration'. What is absent from discussion is a critical perspective about the 'good life' of being disabled, in distinction from being 'sick' and the preferability of ableism (or at least a morphed ableism). We could say that Hallam and others who submit to experimental and potentially dangerous, so-called 'restorative surgeries' have been 'tricked' by the power of ableism. Given that a need for surgeries like limb- and face-transplants cannot be medically established as heart or liver transplants can, the question remains of what it is that drives this need, what the fundamental goal of the surgery is. To alter a bodily appearance by surgical methods 'represents a threat to one's sense of personal identity...changes in physical appearance cause one to experience the body as unfamiliar and unrecognisable – as no longer one's own' (Kay Toombs, cited Leder, 1999, p. 236). As Freeman and Abou Jaoudé noted, 'disfigurement...is a social construct, so it must be asked whether "restorative surgeries" are merely [replacing] one disfigurement by another' (2007, p. 41). The media reportage in alliance with the medical surgical team suggests that it was Clint Hallam who acted in 'bad faith' – who became a 'trickster'. I would suggest otherwise, maybe we need to ask 'who's tricking whom'? Certainly the press has not provided the public with a balanced perspective on the ethics of technologies and their convergence with technologies of normalisation.

'Biting the hand that feeds you' – Clint rejects his 'gift'

It is longer than his other hand; a 30cm section sawn from a French motorcyclist that does not fit where it meets Hallam's arm. It is wider, attached to its host by a broad flange of scar tissue. The flesh is pink, whereas Hallam's is tanned. The outer layer of skin is flaking off; whereas Hallam's is hairy and healthy...There are leathery light-brown patches where there should be fingernails and ominous red dots where the hand is being rejected.

(Whittell, 2000, p. 4)

This section will examine the price of Clint Hallam's non-compliance with the techno-practices of 'new' transplant technologies and the way Hallam's refusal is mediated within media discourses through the usages of concepts such as 'harm' and 'blame'. The tenets of *biomedical realism* ensure that when assessing for morally heinous 'harms', the kinds of 'harms' spoken of are restricted to the purview of the biological and ensuing *medicalisation* of life. As such, surgical ventures and technological practices are geared towards 'fixing' the so-called 'biological problem', whilst ignoring the socio-environmental dimensions and potentially disastrous consequences of the 'fabricated' fix.

Two media articles report that Clint Hallam was forced to keep his 'new' hand covered at all times in a glove to avoid the stare of strangers and the terror and screams of children (Middap, 2000, p. 31; Whittell, 2000, p. 4). This reaction of repulsion towards Clint's hybridity is not restricted to strangers but also extended to his friends As a consequence, Clint speaks of becoming steadily 'mentally detached' and feeling 'more handicapped than before' (BBC News, 2001). Dominant media discourse did not take up the opportunity to consider the kinds of *ontological harm* that could occur, and in fact did occur, in the instance of Clint's hand transplant. The ontological harms, if stated, are more or less contained and de-legitimised. The *BBC News* provides testimony that Hallam's feelings were totally erased and overridden: '... [Hallam's] request [for an amputation] was turned down by the French doctor who led the team on the grounds that the body was inviolable under French law'. An interesting claim to make, Hallam's body was not deemed inviolable during the surgical process towards bodily normalisation, yet became inviolable when attempts were made to challenge this bodily ideal.

The physical body may be inviolable, but what then of the whole being, bodily, emotionally, psychologically, of Clint Hallam? One possible effect of external bodily transplants, with hand transplants and more the recent partial and whole facial transplants, which goes unquestioned under the permeating ableist attitude, is that of the assumed innate success of the transplant. While the recipients of any transplant may be seeking to become or regain their bodily 'normality', they may 'feel less normal than they did ... recipients will look neither like themselves nor like the donor: instead they will have a composite identity' (Freeman & Abou Jaoude, 2007, p. 77). What then of other 'harms'? Media commentary has given some space to what I term Hallam's *functional* 'harms'. The compulsory anti-rejection medication according to two surveyed media reports caused Clint Hallam significant physical and emotional injury: 'The drugs have side effects that include diabetes, chronic diarrhoea and a weakened immune system' (BBC News, 2001), and not putting too fine a point on it, Hallam says '[the] diarrhoea ... can make him shed 2 kg a day' (Middap, 2000). In terms of activities of daily living, Clint Hallam experienced burning pain and limited movement, making tasks typically performed by the hand difficult, if not impossible (Whittell, 2000).

Harms of an ontological or functional nature play second fiddle to the 'harm' experienced by the transplant team of surgeons. Two headlines capture this alleged harm well: *Clint hands gift back to doctors* (Smith, 2001: *Melbourne Herald Sun*) and *Hand Transplant surgeon say he was used* (AAP/Ninemsn, 2001). Hallam's troubles, many reports suggest, were due to Hallam's disregard of the proper treatment and not 'behav[ing] the way we [the surgical team] were hoping he would behave' (BBC News, 2001). French surgeon Dr Jean-Michel Dubernard was more harsh in his criticism, 'we were all used, the surgeons and psychiatrists...he (Hallam) played on our emotions' (AAP/Ninemsn, 2001). Giles Whittell (2000, p. 5) is the lone voice in suggesting that maybe the panic about the amputation was less about 'harm' to the doctors and more about 'preserv[ing] their entry in the annals of surgical history'. What I have been attempting to do in this section is to foreground the enduring hegemony of experts, in this case the medical apparatus and show the way media reportage has been mobilised to ensure the buoyancy of the medical-technocratic ableist dream. In the process of such one-sided reporting the experience and insights of Clint Hallam were not generally addressed and consistently erased.

'Wasted days and wasted nights'[7] – Is a hand handy to have?

> No need to hear your voice when I can talk about you better than you can speak about yourself. No need to hear your voice. Only tell me about your pain. I want to know your story. And then I will tell it back to you in a new way. Tell it back to you in such a way that it has become mine, my own. Re-writing you, I write myself anew. I am still author, authority. I am still the colonizer, the speaking subject, and you are now at the center of my talk.
>
> (Hooks 1990, p. 343)

This chapter is an attempt to document and understand the processes by which the saga of the world's first hand-forearm transplant was represented by the medical apparatus and mediated uncritically within print media discourses. I have discussed the ways that contestations over plans for a hand transplant have (not) been handled. In addition, I have tried to make connections between the criminalisation of Clint Hallam's body in accounts of the 'failure' of the transplant and the problematic concept of 'harm'. The text also points to ways *artefact stabilisation* occurs when various actors are mobilised to enact forms of closure and recuperation of techno-medical practices. The final portion of this chapter examines outstanding issues; in other words, what has been left unsaid.

The Clint Hallam saga presented the media with a clear opportunity to deconstruct not only the knowledge–power relations of the medicalisation of life, but also the practices and ethics of transplants *per se*. Nowhere is there any discussion of the meaning of a transplant strategy. Surely there is room to elicit a vigorous debate from a variety of actors in the community, including social science academics, transplant recipients, ethicists and disabled people in general. In an age of increasing geneticisation of human life and various enhancement technologies, the emerging 'transplant culture' already has a sacrosanct status. Any critique of this culture is usually consigned to the 'backward thinking' of religious conscientious objectors. It has been over a decade since Hallam became the first hand-transplant recipient. Since then there have been 39 hand transplants performed on 31 patients worldwide (http://www.handtransplant.com/news_release/071208.html). The first partial facial transplant was conducted in 2005, and the first full facial transplant was carried out in March of 2008. None of these transplants have received the attention Hallam attracted pre- or post-surgery, supporting the idea that these medically unnecessary external transplants have become as unquestionably accepted as life-preserving transplants such as kidneys or hearts. There needs to be serious ethical debates about the increased commodification of body parts. It was interesting to note as part of the research into Clint Hallam's story, the way the donor hand was put into speech. The hand was often talked about as an isolated object, with no agency or linkage, in any real sense with the donor as an expired human being. This conundrum meant that the question of who 'owned/possessed' the hand was left unresolved and bitterly contested. This is an issue deserving of even greater attention with facial transplants; surely issues of bodily ownership come into play more readily with facial transplants given the inextricable connection between face and identity.

At the level of formations about human subjectivity, a silent subtext never really addressed, except by Clint on the odd occasion, is the interface between technological practices and the production of 'nearly abled' persons. It became quite obvious in the various speech acts of the doctors and Clint that there is considerable ontological confusion about what Clint Hallam (and other recipients) ontologically become post-transplant. Are these people expected to have a self that adopts a normative subject position (able-bodied) or are they seen as not-quite-there-yet, 'nearly-abled', or a hybrid being – the 'transplant man' (or woman)? What does all this confusion suggests about the politics of ableism, and by default disability? Is disability such a personal tragedy that impaired people are morally obliged to adopt an uncertain morphing technological practice, because the normalised body is seen as the *most preferable option* regardless of cost? These kinds of questions are many and complex, the type that should be the substance of investigative reporting. At the end of the day Clint may well ponder the question, 'is a hand handy to have?' We can be less certain of his answer. In any case as Giles Whittell points out, 'Hallam's life does not depend on his hand, and even without it he water-skied and rode a motorbike... [Hallam warns]... of the dangers of pinning one's hopes on other people's limbs' (2000, p. 5).

7
Disability *Matters*: Embodiment, Teaching and Standpoint

Does it matter who teaches disability studies, whether that teacher has a disability or not? Maybe this might strike the reader as a peculiar question – to focus on the teacher's body or knowledge standpoint. There are certain theoretical and ontological implications in asking such questions. This chapter is an attempt to theorise about the way the bodies of teachers with disabilities are transmuted within the arena of teaching critical disability studies at colleges and universities. My exploration occurs through a theoretical enquiry drawn from the insights of critical disability studies (CDS). It examines the contribution that CDS can further make to thinking through the processes, formation and consequences of the teacher's(ing) body as well as the project of speaking otherwise about disability.[1] In particular, the presentation explores the ways teachers with disabled bodies can contribute to experiencing alterity outside of the frame of 'other' and the ways that the teacher with a disabled body, disabled teaching body, can displace the objectification of disability through pedagogical enactments of the lived experiences of disablement. In this way, this chapter refutes the assertion made by McWilliam and Taylor (1998) that the pedagogical inspiration of bodies should not be celebrated. Instead, the focus of this chapter is on working through points of difference between the way normative teacher's bodies and the disabled teaching body is mediated in the processes of subjectification, identifying points of convergence that can benefit dialogue across varied sites of scholarship.

Whilst disability is usually recognised as a form of somatic difference, this difference is deemed not to matter, or is superficial to the teaching body. In contrast, my argument is that the living of disablement imbued in the (disabled) teaching body shapes pedagogic performances in the teaching of CDS, provoking students to consider other modalities of the lived body in ways that are profoundly different from not-disabled teachers. First, I will provide a brief outline as to the insights of critical education studies regarding the 'disappeared' body of the teacher; second, the specific performativity of the disabled teacher's body will be addressed. The chapter then proceeds to a discussion of disputes concerned with embodiment and the teaching of disability studies and the role of positionality in pedagogical performances in CDS.

'A teacher is some body, who has a body who also teaches various bodies': Pedagogies return to the body

Studies in critical pedagogy have pointed to the disappearing body of the teacher in a range of pedagogic settings (McWilliam, 1996). Indeed any remnant of the teacher's body is at best ambiguous and restricted to being as unobtrusive as possible in teaching and learning processes. As early as 1989, Johnston realised the significance of studying bodies in education. Embodiment is infused with risk; a risk of the social, the subjective standpoint of personhood enveloping, and therefore disrupting the pursuit of attaining objective knowledges and cultivating the art of professional distance (another euphemism for professional, authorised disembodiment). A vigorous embodiment disrupts the neat compartmentalisation of mind and body, a division that traditionally has given more credence to cognition. Engagement in teaching and learning is, as Erica McWilliam rightly suggests, inherently playful, desiring and productive. Yet trends in the functionalisation and corporatisation of education, she argues, has neutered teachers 'rendering them functionaries without self-interest, without desire, without any "body" to teach (with)' (McWilliam, 1995, p. 4). Teaching performances are both visceral and somatic, becoming sites of 'evidence' in disciplinary inculcation. The act of performance is both personal and physical and as Ungar (1986) observes, 'a teacher who confesses or professes desire can no longer be scandalous except to those who still believe that the so-called life of the mind has nothing to do with the rest of the body' (p. 82).

Identities of teachers are formed in dialogue with their bodies. The work of teaching invokes simultaneously intellect, emotions, modalities of corporeality and negotiations with spatialities. The teacher's body rather than being a tolerated imperfection in the system instead is integral as 'the *site* and *sight* of authoritative display' (Angel, 1994, p. 63). The disabled teaching body then has the possibility to erode normative constructs of the authoritative and present an oppositional authoritativeness; oppositional, because authoritiveness and leadership are often conceived as oxymoronic to disability. Recognising that teaching and learning are a cultural process and the art of pedagogy is a cultural practice, the marking of normative bodily positions already demands the assimilation and containment of peripheral bodies (sex, race, age and disablement) in order to teach 'correctly' (Burbules & Bruce, 2001; Moje, 2000; Star Johnson, 2005), to have a disciplined body and becoming a disciplining body. The disabled body because it is deprived of normative validity, literary dys-appears from the bodies of teaching (and learning) subjects with disabilities. This kind of evaporation of subjectivity does not deny the fact that some people with disability experience oppressive forms of hyper visibility in the classroom (cited Erevelles, 2005, p. 428). An absent/presence, Snyder and Mitchell (2001), note leaves the possibility of two constraining 'options' – to endure 'the cultural slander heaped upon bodily difference' or the alternate to evade (disavow) the 'object of derision' (p. 368).

Phenomenological studies have long recognised the importance of focusing on the *experience* of the *lived body*, in recognition that 'we all inhabit bodies and live so fundamentally *through* them, that brings the consciousness of bodily harm home to us' (French, 1994, p. 72 – his emphasis). In short, we cannot 'know' existence without being rooted to our bodies. To this extent, it is problematic to speak of bodies in their materiality in a way that distinguishes between emotions and cognition. In rejecting Cartesian divisions between the mind (knowledge) and body (materiality and emotions) two dimensions of the body can be exposed:

> ... *der Leib and der Körper* [are] representing two dimensions of the human body. Whereas *Leib* refers to the animated living experiential body, *Körper* refers to the objective, exterior and institutionalized body.
>
> (Plessner, cited Turner 1992, p. 41).

Rather than merely focusing on *Körper*, as the discourse of education is inclined to do, Plessner's formulation can enable a rethinking of corporeal subjectivity. French (1994) argues that *Leib* can be configured as standing for the body-for-itself (a generative body), whilst *Körper* can be regarded as the body-in-itself (a biomedical body). The *Der leib* 'experiencing body' is not however pre-discursive, for 'experiences' are shaped by relations of power, complex histories and interpreted through a brico-lage of complex interwoven subjectivities. This approach to perceiving the body in terms of *geist* or animation has been applied by Deutsch (1994), who argues that it is the animated teacher's body that infuses the classroom discussion and animates the text. This reiteration of the idea of the animated teaching body could appear remarkable. Heideg-ger (1977) observes that the art of creating leaves an imprint on that which is produced. Such a bringing forth 'poeisis' results in aletheia, an 'unveiling' of the essence of technology, which is infused in the art of teaching and pedagogy in general. This personal imprinting in teach-ing performances is acknowledged by Coldron and Smith (1999) who conclude that:

> Every aspect of a teacher's work seems to have a personal dimen-sion...we want to say it is personal in the sense that other teachers do things differently....By using the term 'personal', we intend to invoke some relative independence from socially given resources. We contend that teachers generate additional resources through aesthetic response to professional experience.
>
> (p. 718)

The particularities of embodiment mean that animation of the teacher's body is imbued with racialised, sexed and disabilised performances. Lin-ton (1998b, p. 530) points out that the 'kinaesthetic, proprioceptive, sensory and cognitive experiences' of disabled people as they go about their daily life has received limited attention. This is not surprising as Nancy Mairs notes a *disability gaze* is imbricated in every aspect of action, perception, occurrence and knowing:

> Unless you've got a bad back, you're probably reading this sitting down. Look up from the page. Look around. Imagine that this is your angle of vision not just until you decide to get up and walk around...but forever. It's not a bad angle of vision, mind you...but it is a definite one, and the world you see from it is definitely differ-ent from the one you see when your standing. This is my perpetual view, from the height of an erect adult's waist. And the difference has consequences.
>
> (1996 p. 16)

In order to return bodies back to teachers, a re-conceptualisation of knowing (episteme) is paramount. Only this knowledge is of a carnal kind, where thinking, sensing and understanding mutually enfold. Acknowledging differences in corporeal modalities produce varied teaching performances; the next section will look at a kind of unruly (teaching) body which constitutes a dangerous juxtaposition: educator + disabled: educator + freak.

The performativity of disabled teaching

Impairment for me is exhausting. After 11 years paralysed and using a wheelchair and another 17 subsequent years being vertically challenged, dragging my feet along the ground to keep up with my head, I have recently been diagnosed with Diabetes. This not meant to be a sob story, rather a preface to argue that for a disabled teacher, in many instances, when we turn the light switch off and leave the office, we do not leave the corporeal implantation of disability behind. Like the poem *Hound of Heaven* (Thompson, 1917) disability is in heavy pursuit, the disabled teaching body lives, breaths and exudes impairment – for all its glory and despair!

Traditional teaching about disability within special education, nursing and rehabilitation studies has in many ways failed to comprehend that pedagogy is intrinsically embodied (Shapiro, 1994). Further, the interdisciplinary teaching of disability studies, which seeks to shift the pedagogical gaze from anchoring disabled bodies as objects to subjects of research, whilst recognising that a *body* is teaching other student (bodies) a myriad of disability perspectives, has failed to retrieve the corporeal implications of disablement by still teaching from the perspective of the disembodied 'Other' or by not taking seriously the significance of knowledge standpoint. I have already made mention of the evaporative dys-appearance of the '*disabledness*' of the disabled body. The disabled body becomes opaque by being re-spatialised into an anomalous zone. According to Razack (1998) these anomalous zones are spaces that tolerate departures from norms and therefore are places where there is the possibility of norm subversion. The overwhelming positing of disability conceptually and the disabled body more particularly, as *inherently negative* disallows the pedagogical imagination to consider disabled teachers as knowers (Campbell, 2001). When the teacher is disabled there is a radical de-coupling of embodiment and the pedagogic project assumes that the craft of teaching is unrelated to disability. To repeat Nancy Mairs's claim, difference (disability) has consequences. CDS insists that rather than viewing the disabled body as etiologically self-evident where medical deviations call for socio-medical solutions, disability should be understood as a fabricated narrative.

There is a tendency within cultural studies to denote bodies in terms of their performative corporeality; to reconfigure the body as an inscriptive surface of shifting performative norms and subjectivities. Erevelles (2005) argues that the disabled body, and in this instance the disabled teaching body, marks the limits of performativity. Argument based on performative reiteration breaks down when faced with the 'radical alterity of the disabled body ... the liminal state that marks the discursive edges of humanity' (p. 424). Whilst I am not entirely convinced by this argument, insofar as *even* bodies at the abject edge engage in performances, what is clear is that there is a difference that the disabled teacher's body makes to pedagogic enactments. McWilliam and Taylor (1998, p. 7) resort to citing Barthes about the difficulties of civilising the body in contrast to the control of utterances, as a sign that teachers confront the limits of their bodies in pedagogic events. Such 'peculiar' constraints for many disabled teacher are normative – business as usual – and induce other ways of engaging with one's body in and across space. Hansen (2001) refers to the notion of a body style which includes the habits, body language, tones of voices and movements that the teachers body brings to teaching, No doubt, as heterogeneous as the bodies designated by the neologism 'disability' are, body styles of disabled teachers are as variable as they are interpenetrating. Exposure to the material shifts and 'muck' of the disabled teaching body seeks to seduce the student into the multiple realities of living with impairment within an ableist society.

In the United States, the debate over the nature of one's disability status and its relationship to teaching disability studies has been intensive. Leonard Cassuto's piece *Whose Field is it anyway? Disability Studies and the Academy* for the Colloquy in *The Chronicle of Higher Education* (Cassuto, 1999) has become a canonical piece around the 'knowledge standpoint' debate.[2] The lead professional association in the United States, the Society for Disability Studies (SDS), also made the standpoint and teaching debate a theme at their 2004 annual conference 'Dissent and Dialogue: Re-envisioning Academic and Activist Landscapes'. In other countries, the matter of situated knowledges and the teacher's body has not (at least publicly) been subjected to vigorous scholastic debate. And whilst many CDS teachers still do not recognise corporeality and disability status as a vital issue, I argue that the question of situated knowledges has nonetheless a lurking omnipresence within the teacher's body and pedagogic practices. Although unstated, it has

clear implications for the competitive academic job market, to say nothing about affirmative action employment strategies, the future of a
vital leadership made up of disabled people and the ways the complexities and variabilities of the disability experience is marked and
represented. Breckenridge points out that whilst the education system
has paid increased attention to the well-being of the disabled child, this
concern has not been extended to promoting equal access for teachers
with disabilities (Breckenridge & Vogler, 2001).

The aberrant gaze – teaching with Grotesque materialism

> ... Every encounter with the Other, every performance and citation
> of the order, makes Foucault's 'biopower' system momentarily visible
> and inserts the sliver of difference into the safe spaces of 'normality'
> (Kuppers, 2003, p. 6).

An alternate title for this chapter could have been 'Having *a Career
in Disability Studies without even becoming Disabled!'* The theme intentionally conjures up matters of differential investment in the teaching
and research enterprise and the subjectifying forces of the disability/not-
disability experience. I argue that contrary to the neo-liberalist 'spin'
of empathising 'personhood first and disability second', disability cannot be subordinated or detached; it is part of the (disabled) person – it
enfolds us (rather like sex and race). The processes of identity formation cannot be separated from the person who is brought into being
through those very subjectifying processes of ableism that view disability as inherently negative (Campbell, 2008). Even though at a personal
level disabled people may refute ableism and take steps to undo our
own internalised ableism (disability self-hatred), the processes of being
clothed in disability always contains a mnemic trace which recalls
memory, history and is incorporated into beingness.

Whilst many disabled people enfold disability into our shifting selves
(to say nothing about other aspects of our profile: gender, race, sexual
orientation, religion) in varied ways, I argue that the disabled experience
*does c*reate difference – a valuable difference – a different perspectivism
or mind style of living in the world. This is not to say such experiences
induce some kind of epistemic privilege because of their purity. Several
writers argue that no experience is pre-theoretical and therefore experiences are always in need of ongoing deconstruction and interpretation.
Joan Scott (1992) reminds us of the problematics of an experience-based
paradigm:

[It is] not individuals who have experience, but subjects who are constituted through experience. Experience in this definition then becomes not the origin of our explanation, not the authoritative (because seen or felt) evidence that grounds what is known, but rather that which we seek to explain, that about which knowledge is produced.

(p. 26)

Scott's analysis makes it quite clear – although we should be cautious about the notion of an 'uncontaminated' experience, it is important to examine tacit knowledges that flow out of experience. So what does all this mean for the effects of different kinds of performances of differently situated teaching bodies? Although there is not an automatic correlation between social location and standpoint, it is important for teachers that are positioned differentially through dialogue, to establish common narratives. Indeed, subjectivity, which is a complex matrix of resources of language, experience and culture, is forever in process, in a state of becoming, being deployed as a strategic and delimited practice. The teaching position of the disabled body has 'seductive power' which is unhinged from the force of institutional authority. Nonetheless, a disabled person teaching disability studies is both the subject and the object of their curricula and research and it is in this 'space' of merging between the subject and the object that the sliver of difference (as the Kuppers, 2003 epigram suggests) can be revealed.

Taking into account the problematical associations with experience-based arguments, it is clear that people with disabilities *do* possess privileged knowledges when it comes to an immediate familiarity with the daily experience of being a disabled person, negotiating the specter of ableism in its various nuances. Our experience cultivates an inferential insight into the dynamics of ableism in a way that is *distinct* from those whose lives are not infused with impairment. As Narayan observes, insider knowledge is mindful of 'all the details in which their oppression ... affects the major and minor details of their social and psychic lives' (1988, p. 36). So the question of disability status within the context of an acknowledgment that knowledges are situated or positioned is *not* a question as to whether someone 'is disabled or not', but rather a *call* to foreground the ways one's own positionality resonates with disablement. It is important at this point to warn that although it is critical to acknowledge that teachers are differently situated, at the same time it is imperative that pedagogy not *preform* the teacher's body to a particular 'class' of bodies before embarking on the pedagogical relationship (Gabel, 2002, p. 181). As Calabro (1999) correctly observes,

> The point is that every researcher [or academic] has a 'disability status'. What maybe lacking, and seems curious is the resistance to awareness of one's own disability status. Self-awareness and reflection should always be part of the scholarly enterprise.

Indeed not to do so, I argue, is to succumb to a form of ableist passing, where in the hiddenness of the life-force of disability, the teacher and scholarly community in general fails to ask about difference and in doing so enforces the illusion that it is possible to see disability from nowhere (and everywhere). Deborah Marks, in her quest to resist teaching disability studies from the perspective of the colonising 'Other', also recognises the importance of reflecting upon her own position in relation to disability, especially her dis-ease about holding an academic post that exists as consequence of the exclusion of disabled people from universities and teaching more generally. She discloses,

> While I do not wish to engage in narcissistic confession regarding my interests in learning disability, it is certainly worth noting that I have learnt, only gradually, through critical engagement in studies of disability, that I have a number of personal investments in understanding the experience of stupidity and exclusion. This is likely to be true for many academics, who are attracted to a particular subject in order to work out unresolved issues.
>
> (1996, p. 71)

For my own part, I like many enduring disability activists, see my investment in teaching disability studies along the lines of an extension of a lifetime of personal and professional activism. Other disabled scholars, who have embraced the slogan 'nothing about us without us', share a similar sentiment. The decision to render one's subject position visible is to open oneself up to vulnerability. Rosemarie Garland-Thomson articulates this dilemma well: 'It was a little scary. I felt vulnerable. I felt exposed. It was difficult for me to talk about an issue that I had imagined as being very personal, perhaps even embarrassing, sort of shameful' (cited Monaghan, 1998, p. A16). One 'danger' of disclosing disablement is that such an 'outing' may result in the academic's teaching and research perspectives being seen solely through the lens of the disability experience to the exclusion of other positionalities (Roman,

2009). This typecasting, by way of increased visibility can, rather paradoxically, lead to increased marginalisation. The teacher with disability, like the student with disability, is situated differently to the content of a course, irrespective of impairment, in ways that are fundamentally different for students and teachers that identify as referentially 'not-disabled'. In spite of some of these dilemmas, the standpointness of the teaching body of CDS and the impact that different differences has on working with students needs to be acknowledged, for as Moje (2000) states in another context:

> Teachers should examine how their embodied relations shape the research and teaching they do in classrooms. Relationships are always coded with difference – difference that is more complex and layered than just one institutionally based difference such as the university-classroom divide implies.
>
> (p. 39)

There always remains an unresolved tension within standpoint theory between the situated knowledges of the 'individual' and 'the group' (Stoetzler & Yuval-Davis, 2002). The teaching of disability studies to students with disability who until a particular point in the teaching semester have not self-identified as disabled (distinct from publicly 'coming out') presents an interesting challenge, especially when they recognise themselves in the narrative and teaching script. Suddenly the disabled body is made visible; the designation 'them' transmogrifies into 'me':

> This is the paradox of visibility, another of disability culture's great concerns: *now you see us; now you don't.* Many of us 'pass' for able-bodied – we appear before you unclearly marked, fuzzily apparent, our disabilities *not* handing out all over the place. We are sitting next to you. No, we *are* you.
>
> (Bruegemann et al., 2001, p. 369)

It can be a lonely place in crip land – Leadership, visibility and mentoring

> Before every action, there is a pause … and a beginning again. The pause is for description, for mulling over the requirements of balance, for comparing the proposed action with movements that are familiar, and for explaining to myself why I can or cannot do what is at

hand... In the course of daily living, the thinking is not observable; the behavior just happens, part of what this person does naturally. The physiology of 'a slight limp' is part of the unmediated expression of what my 'I' is.

(Kalekin-Fishman, 2001, p. 136)

Being a teacher with disability, without similarly situated peers, can be a lonely place. The passion to insert the absent, *speaking otherwise*, disabled voice back into disability discourse is as rewarding as it is draining. The presence of a disability studies teacher and researcher with impairment disrupts the traditional invisibility and exclusion from the school and the academy and from positions of competence or leadership. For many, the notion of disabled leadership is an oxymoron and the actualisation of such a possibility is unfamiliar territory. At the level of representation alone, it is good to experience leadership in action. Anecdotally, students with disabilities (and those without) are open to the opportunity to be confronted with the strangeness, the embodiment of a person with an excluded body, whose speaking position flows from the 'us' of disability. Visibility in this respect connotes possibility, a belief that says, 'if you can then I could too'. The disabled teaching body in its performance of disability, in the teaching and learning of CDS, invokes a process of self-emptying, an interior *kenosis* on the part of the teacher with disability. Self-emptying, the radical disclosure of disablement occurs through the imparting of gesture, psychic presence, and differential reference points and in the utterance of passionate emphasis during the pedagogic event. Kenosis however tries to capture more; to capture a depth of self-transference that takes place within the spaces of imparting content about the subject/object of disability studies, namely disabled people. A self-consciously aware CDS scholar with impairment has the possibility to disrobe themselves in ways profoundly different from the bystander. In the next section of this chapter, I explore the contribution that referentially not-disabled teachers can make to CDS.

Not-disabled positionings

Throughout this chapter I have argued that the question of situated knowledges has a lurking omnipresence, for whilst there maybe a level of silence about this matter, the vexed question of a CDS academic's 'disability status' and the specific modality of their teaching body remains, albeit with a repressed presence. I have also reiterated that a focus on 'disability status' is not as commonly articulated as an impairment test.

Rather the question of status is a call to reflect upon and *publicly acknowl-edge* the ways one's own positionality intersects with disablement and the impact this may have on teaching and research. What is not being called for is a reactive response to disability apartheid; a call for all able-bodied people to give up their CDS positions to disabled teachers. Even if this perspective was desirable, the reality is that, at least in the Aus-tralian context, the exclusion of disabled people from higher education means that there probably would not be a sufficient pool of scholars with disabilities to fill the vacant positions!

The forces of marginalisation has meant that academics, as public intellectuals are often called upon to 'speak for others', whether that be about refugees, survivors of domestic violence or people with disabil-ities. Linda Alcoff (1991) points out some of the dilemmas of speaking for and with others. For many academics engaged in the justice enter-prise, there will come a time when we will be called upon to speak for or about 'Others'. In disability studies there are challenges in speaking of disabled people as 'not-Other'. Our everyday teaching, learning and research lives involve acts of representation. We are often called to relate to people who do not have a 'voice', are not 'listened' to, people whose 'knowledge' has been excluded, minimised, has been disqualified or has been considered marginal. Surely it would be better, you might say, for those of us who have 'experienced' instances of marginality (in this case, disability) to speak. This kind of reasoning has resulted in a 'crisis of representation' for how can we speak of others, especially subordinated peoples in non-oppressive ways. Again, Alcoff (1991) neatly sums up this dilemma:

> When we sit down to write, or get up to speak, we experience our-selves as making choices. We may experience hesitation from fear of being criticized or from fear of exacerbating a problem we would like to remedy, or we may experience a resolve to speak despite existing obstacles. But in many cases we experience having the possibility to speak or not to speak.
>
> (p. 11)

As privileged speakers, what responsibilities do we as academics have to speak out about injustice and powerlessness and create spaces for resis-tance? Do we refrain from speaking and 'let' them speak? What if, for whatever reason, there is silence? There are some who argue that they cannot speak because 'they have not been there'. Throwing down the gauntlet, Spivak says in response: 'why not develop a certain degree of *rage* against the history that has written such an abject script for you that you are silenced?' (1990, p. 62 ~ emphasis added). Whilst both Alcoff and Spivak did not necessarily have the question of disability status in mind, it is my contention that the exploration of differentials in situated knowledges of those teaching disability studies can only contribute to gaining greater clarity to these questions.

The silence of the disability status conundrum, in tandem with the rise in the disability community's advocacy of a social constructionist approach to disablement, has meant that some referentially able-bodied teachers who have become uncertain about their role and constituencies of accountability unconsciously seek shelter in diagnosticism (reducing impairment to medicalised disability classifications). They have made their 'home' within disability groups they perceive have a limited voice, in contradistinction to groups they feel have increased vocalisation (and privilege). These hierarchies of suffering have been detrimental and can result in the othering of Othered disabled people – people who appear to have 'made it' in the system are not like those other 'real' disabled people who are excluded. The danger of this decline into diagnosticism is that it disperses the collective interests of disabled people and reduces physical and sensory forms of impairment to mere functional problems, thus diminishing the psychic manifestations of devaluation and oppression. For the academic, the inability to deal with and reflect upon their 'disability status' means that they do not confront their 'privileged status' nor feel the need to engage productively in dialogue with disability scholars with impairment. A vigorous and creative approach to disability studies depends upon *all* academics irrespective of their situated knowledges to actively engage in dialogue and not opt out. In the final section of this chapter, I extend this discussion by focusing on power and exclusion.

'Nothing about us without us': Power and exclusion from the academy

When I read [Cassuto's piece in the *The Chronicle*], I immediately turned to the index of positions available in the same issue, then checked the index for the following four issues. In each case, there was a listing for 'Disabled student services.' There were no listings for 'Disability studies.' One of the issues connected with this question is that of employment and a paycheck, which every faculty member in academia enjoys. The unemployment rate among people with disabilities exceeds 80%, so that the majority of people with disabilities exist on the fringes of society, experiencing discrimination in all aspects of daily life. I can assure you that no able-bodied person, even those who travel with me and experience the discrimination I face first-hand, have any idea of what it's like to live as a person with a disability. I am currently employed, and have the luxury of being able to subscribe to *The Chronicle;* however, my present contract expires in just over a year, and I am beginning to look at what is available to me in the job market. If the field of disability studies is beginning to take root in academia, I question why faculty positions should not at the very least be open preferentially to those of us who, with academic qualifications in hand, should not be interviewed and considered before those who do not understand disability from the inside out.

(Bishop, 1999)

The struggles of Helen Bishop are unfortunately not uncommon or restricted to searching for jobs in US institutions. The tussle for a presence in the academy and schools starts at the point of access to undergraduate study. Australia has a contemptible reputation in regards to access and equity to tertiary education for people with a disability. The equity data for the State of Queensland (Australia) in 2004 indicates that only 3.25% commencing students identify as having disability (DEST, 2004). There are few undergraduate scholarships available and intensive resource support by universities is patchy. Investment by the Australian Government in the long-term education of disabled people, especially those people with severe disabilities, has been a low priority. Many 'training' schemes have been of a short-term or remedial nature. The game of chance features more significantly when a student moves through to graduate studies especially with the reduced completion times for doctoral studies. The question needs to be asked is whether there exists a 'glass ceiling' for the disabled scholar and prospective teacher who wish to obtain a continuing position in disability studies. In many instances the disabled student's educational career has taken longer than their able-bodied peers. The student teacher may need more flexible working hours due to the nature of their impairment. Alternatively, they may experience that 'chilly feeling' in the academy, in the field of disability studies where the vast number of scholars in Australia (at least) are able-bodied and have not fully confronted the vexed question I referred to earlier of 'disability status'?

The welcoming of disabled scholars into the academic and school community is one matter, but recognition of the 'special position' of the scholar with a disability and the particular contribution that we can make to the study of disability is another. The slogan *Nothing About Us without Us* is not just about the insertion of the disabled voice(s) into existing courses, the catch cry is about power (imbalances) and the steps that are necessary to recognise contemporary and historical power differentials between disabled people and universities. Redressing power imbalances is not just about assimilating 'outsider' voices, it is fundamentally about bringing those 'outsider' voices into the inside, into the font of CDS, by taking steps to ensure that suitably qualified disabled scholars are offered affirmative action opportunities. This should not be perceived as a threat but as an opportunity to create a rich and accountable discipline, where there is an ongoing dialogue between theory and praxis and where the subject of disability status is enlivening and fruitful.

Conclusion – Emptying the disabled teaching body

Summing up, I have attempted in this chapter to problematise the vexed question of 'disability status' as raised by Cassuto (1999) and highlight the necessity to engage in a process of dialogue between teachers with differentially situated knowledges. The recognition that knowledges are situated or positioned means that the matter of 'disability status' is not just a coded impairment test, rather it is a call for the recognition of the necessity to reflect upon and publicly declare the way that one's positionality intersects with disablement. Disability status is not solely a personal and therefore private issue. Drawing upon the insights of critical pedagogy and an understanding of the curriculum as a normalising text (Erevelles, 2005), this piece is a timely reminder of the necessity for the disabled teaching body to be present within classroom settings in order for students to fully grasp the complex distilling of disability and the differences that different bodies make to the learning enterprise. I have also drawn attention to the critical issue of contemporary and historical power imbalances between teaching and learning communities and disabled people and have argued that in order to redress those imbalances, the disability studies project needs to address and explore meaningful ways of promoting disabled people to teaching positions. Finally, yes you can have a career in disability studies without ever becoming disabled, but who would want to miss out on all the fun!

8
Pathological Femaleness: Disability Jurisprudence and Ontological Envelopment

Aristotle once described women as mutilated males. Pregnancy has been suggested as a class of disability under law and premenstrual 'syndrome' has been lauded as a defence to murder. This chapter continues in the discussion of how law imagines disability (the disabled existence) and negotiates some of the torturous questions related to ontology and volition. It explores how the *woman question* and the *disability question* can best be resolved through the prism of studies in ableism. As an exemplar the chapter interrogates the legal cartographies of premenstrual syndrome and disability parking, concluding that the notion of ontological envelopment can be engaged either as an instrument of disability resistance or as a force for the rearticulating and (re)pathologisation of femaleness.

Law, as we have seen, is preoccupied with matters of ordering, disorder and constitutional compartmentalisation between the 'normal' and 'pathological' and ways that stories about wholeness, health, enhancement and perfection are told. Women's bodies are messy and female corporeality's are dis/ordered not in the sense of pathology, but the female body is anti-order; it is difficult to contain. Western histories of ideas have attempted to grapple with the leaky body through a notion of women's recidivistic carnal nature (various theological arguments about *imago deo*), medico-pathological pronouncements and feminist liberal projects that disembody by emphasising reason over biology. Through a critical disability studies lens, there has been a failure to address the contingency of the material gendered body and the complexities of ontological envelopment and animation. Much of the feminist project of inclusion has been built for a performative passion for sameness relying on difference disavowal, lest difference be construed as deficiency. The fabrication of gendered performance disregards the reality of many women's lives, which are governed by the materiality of their existence. Such fabrications reinforce ableist norms of particularised bodies. This chapter offers a brief encounter with the lineage of women as pathological followed by an examination of certain ontological themes of disability in law and then engages these theoretical debates in the treatment of the two thematic case studies.

A disability lens

Compulsory ableness and its conviction to and seduction of sameness as the basis to equality claims results in a resistance to consider ontologically peripheral lives as distinct ways of being human lest they produce a heightened devaluation. It is argued, ableist norms produce a belief in femaleness as pathological. Women in this sense do not come up to scratch; 'we' actually fall short of the ableist ideal.

Ableism's casting of 'woman' out to the margins is veiled. So how is this ambivalence towards women contained? Where are the points of seepage in biomedical and legal discourses that reveal the hiddeness of an assumed female *portentum*? What is the threatening or disquieting significance of woman and how can critical studies in ableism help us think these matters through? The performances of disability in law produce subjectifying discourses where disabled subjects are brought into being, not just for themselves, for the rest of us inaugurating what can be said and what is unsayable about disability. It is important not just to look at what is confessed with discourse, in this case, the trial process, but also a need to interrogate the silences. The silences are spaces where law's investments in the maintenance of ableist delimitations of impairment are framed; setting the ontological parameters of disablement in contradistinction from illness and normal 'difference'. In debates over women's reproduction in general it is useful to ask what cannot be said about the pregnant or menstruating body. What are silences that surround the messiness of pregnancy and the impact of menstruation in women's lives as we go about our business?

In contrast with biomedicalism, contemporary disability studies scholarship argues that the neologism disability is a relational signifier emerging out of interactivity between impairment and modes of socio-economic organisation framed by epistemologies of corporeal perfection. The pregnant body is paradoxical; reproduction is a necessity yet there is a devaluation of generativity. Some scholars extend this analysis, disputing the binary between observable axiomatic impairment on one hand and the social construction of disablement on the other, arguing that impairment *qua* impairment is a particular kind of body characterisation shaped, extended and moulded in the social. The metaphor of the möbius strip is apt to characterise the epistemological and ontological figuring of bodies known as disabled (see Grosz, 1994); for like the möbius strip, there is no 'inside' and 'outside' of impairment. Recent case law and philosophical enquiry has attempted to unravel the chain of being between impairment and relations of ontology. The first position suggests that disability is an addendum to ontological being, acting as an inconvenience incidental to the key attributes of self-ness. The other perspective suggests that the lived, experiencing body of the disabled person is inextricably connected to ontology, ethics and action. Frug (1989) reminds us, lawyering engages in a contestable understanding of law and the nature of social organisation. Legal reasoning invokes an ableist norm that contains an already assumed 'scaling of bodies' wherein the weak form the 'benchmark body's' ontological exterior. The notion of impairment or labouring under a 'special disability' is based on the spurious belief that (a) there is an axiomatic 'weakness' that inheres in certain kinds of bodies and (b) should that weakness 'exist' its attributes *automatically* connote an overriding deficiency which is ontologically invasive.

Law has two, not necessarily coherent, orientations towards disability. The first is a fixed axiomatic condition that relates externally to the world in the form of either an overcomer or a victim of disability. At law alternative discursive realities are erased by being in-validated in the processes of translating the everyday experiences of disabled people into legal knowledges. This approach aligns itself with moves by disabled people to act in a strategically essentialised way to adopt the postures of ableist norms or refuse them (risking invalidation or outlaw disability status). Disabled peoples' interactions with law necessitate that disabled performativity and its ensuing subjectivities are iterated with discourses mediated within a norm of ableism.

As a result of this orientation, the litigant with disability, if wishing to present an alternative approach to living with impairment – an affirmative approach, coloured with a mixture of joy and despair held in simultaneous tension, a representation diametrically opposed to the dominant cultural narratives of disablement as catastrophic – will find enormous difficulty for the 'law constraints make it impossible for [those] stories 'to be heard and recognised' (Rovner, 2001, p. 277). Legal discourses through the performance and enactment of disability subjectivities play a critical role in maintaining these structures of purification between those designated as 'sick', 'well', 'deserving' and 'undeserving'.

The second orientation involves ascertaining the limits of disablement, the boundaries and edges of disability in the form of a *constituting subjectivity*. I have invoked the notion of 'ontological envelopment' to challenge the belief that disability is an independent and seemingly unrelated variable to the formation of subjectivity. Of course like any construct that is potentially transgressive, the concept runs the risk of being recuperated into a kind of ontological predeterminism whereby disability envelops the person to the extent it is all 'I am' and all that 'you see' – hence the neologism as a noun 'the disabled'. This notion is typified by Charles Gaspard De la Rive's description of the madman whose '...mind is almost entirely absorbed by the action of the ideas produced by the deranged state of his brain' (cited Foucault, 1961, p. 130). The more nuanced approach to ontological envelopment understands that disability or impairment (constructed figurations or the 'real deal') come together, circulating as discursive assemblages where psychic gestures of impairment are exchanged, relayed, overlaid and counter laid by the forces of normalcy that interpolate how the disabled persons is meant to be. An enduring question corresponding with internal ambivalence experienced by many disabled people is, if disability is me, what parts of 'it' are me? Like gender and race, does disability constitute the animated body – or as normate ideology would have it, is disability incidental to animation?

Women as pathological

What is the stereotype of the premenstrual women? She is portrayed in popular culture as a frenzied, raging beast, a menstrual monster, prone to rapid mood swings and crying spells, bloated and swollen from water retention, out of control, craving chocolate, and likely at any moment to turn violent.

(Chrisler et al., 2006, p. 375)

It is not possible to fully explore the ways women's bodies have been positioned as sites of dangerousness and disease; as an arena of monstrosity. Needless to say the abject woman provokes a sense of fear and dread. Western philosophy and jurisprudence has a long history of viewing women as intrinsically deficient, as mutations of males; profoundly disabled. Such detailing of women's pathology was both bodily and psychological. Women *qua* women are deformed. In *Generation of Animals* Aristotle has the following insight into women: 'just as the young of mutilated parents are sometimes born mutilated and sometimes not, so also the young born a female are sometimes female and sometimes male instead. For the female is, as it were, a mutilated male' (Aristotle, 1998, 2.3, 737a26-27). The monstrosity of the female sexed body was considered by Aristotle as a natural *anomalia*[1] not as an aberration. This *disabled* and recalcitrant body was a necessary deficiency, subordinated to ensure ongoing human reproduction Women were prone to being norm-defective hence irritable, dispirited and over-wrought. The theme of hysteria was appended to women whose behaviour was deemed unacceptable to the prevailing genders norms throughout the centuries (Code, 1991; Ussher, 2006). Rodin (1992) proposes three stages in a genealogy of hysteria. In ancient times hysteria was seen as a disease of the wandering uterus, a 'logical consequence of an organic imbalance' (p. 50). In Christian times, there was a shift to viewing hysteria not just as a moral malady, but as a moral failing. Certainly 'The Hammer of Witches' (*Malleus Maleficarum*) of 1494 designated women as defective and therefore enveloped by deceit (see Winzer, 1997). This very marking of bodies contributed to the distinction within Western philosophy between 'essential' and 'inessential' corporeality. Due to their 'more delicate constitutions, because they lead a softer life...and not [accustomed] to suffering' women were seen to be prone to greater risk than men to states of derangement (Foucault, 1961, p. 149). The onset of menstruation was also regarded as increasing women's predisposition to mental disorder, manifesting itself in uncontrollable, malicious and troublesome conduct:

> To act hysterically had long meant to act as a woman.... It served too, to reinforce its deep rooted and multifaceted association with women and the worst of womanliness, an association manifest most literally in the terms, etymology (from the Greek *hysterikos*, or womb).
>
> (Lunbeck, 1994, p. 209)

Indeed women's generative organs were viewed to be the controlling organs of the female body (Showalter, 1987; Thomson, 1997). In medieval marriage law, women were defined as disabled therefore requiring protection (Lochrie, 1999). Through its discourse on hormones nineteenth-century biomedicalism contributed to the view that women experienced corporeal debilitation demanding surveillance and regulation. Women's engagement in work and unnecessary education was seen to cause disability. Modern day lineages of this approach exist, in the high levels of medical interventions, in the 'illness' of pregnancy. The intersection between the sexed and disabled body, resulting in the denial of women's deliberative capacity resurfaces in the nineteenth century through the figuring of sexed differences as disability in law (Silvers, 1998b, pp. 92–93). It is not surprising then that much of feminist thought has been orientated towards resisting any argument along the lines of biology is destiny, that is destiny being based on deficiency. Yet there is a precarious holding to delineating aspects of embodiment. Uncritical feminist thought, potentially, has an uneasy relationship with the condition of impairment.

The unencumbered, gender-neutral appearing employee has replaced the rhetoric of the main breadwinner. The 'unencumbered' worker:

> Is an employee who behaves in the workplace as if he or she has a wife at home full time, performing all the unpaid care work that families require. This 'gold standard' worker is an employee who works full time, year round, is available to work overtime as requires by the employer, and takes no time off for child bearing or rearing. (Appelbaum et al., 2002, p. 8)

Changes in gender relations re-factor the basis of the productive body in public life. The gendering of social care (child rearing, care of aging family) produces women's bodies as inherently encumbered and therefore deficient – emerging as a quasi class of disability.[2] Pregnant women and disabled people requiring attendant care breach that carefully constructed divide between the public and the private realm by bringing multi-subjectivity, outside of the workplace, inside. As Fursman (2001, p. 5) notes, 'women do not fit the mold...they occasionally exhibit bodily needs that cannot be mechanically routinized'.

Case study 1: Premenstrual syndrome

Premenstrual Syndrome (PMS) is one of those denotations that have consistently reappeared in both medical and legal literature since the syndrome was coined in by Frank in 1931.[3] Rittenhouse (1991, p. 416) notes that 'whilst PMS appeared consistent in the medical literature between 1931 and 1980 it was not considered a major problem for the bulk of women'. As Halbbreich (2006) notes, the social history of PMS is entangled with a history of gender relations. This can be expanded to suggest that more than gender is at work here. Reliance on the pathological of corporeal difference, PMS cannot be understood outside of an imaginary of ableist relations that positions normative and anomalous states. The stereotype of uncontrollable femaleness lurks beneath the surface of research agendas revealing anxieties about women's bodies, including the unpredictability of woman and unarticulated beliefs about normalcy (Gurevich, 1995). It is not my wish to restate the existing literature on the topic but to draw out themes as they relate to deliberate or implied gendered disability argument. Research trajectories around PMS have been motivated and shaped by the evidentiary requirements in criminal law proceedings, so it is no accident that there is an abundance of literature in the decade of the 1980s which reduces to a trickle through the 1990s largely as a consequence of the case of US State of Virginia trial *Commonwealth v. Richter*[4] (1991). Although the bulk of the literature since the 1980s has been on the identification of a fixed diagnostic criteria for PMS (Ussher, 2003), in the early period from 2002 onwards, there appeared a shift towards more ethnographic research directed to exploring women's own experiences of menstruation and their perception of the concept of PMS (Chrisler et al., 2006; Figert, 2005; Henshaw, 2007; Lee, 2002; Perz & Ussher, 2006; Sveindóttir et al., 2002; Taylor, 2006; Ussher, 2003).

In 1981, the medical hypothesis PMS was first recognised in UK criminal law as a partial defence of diminished responsibility in *R. v. Craddock*[5] (1981). Sandie Craddock, who killed a co-worker, had the charge of murder successfully reduced to manslaughter on the basis of diminished responsibility due to PMS. A condition of sentencing to deal with Smith's so-called 'raging hormones' was regular progesterone injections. Craddock, who changed her name to 'Smith', came before the courts again when she threatened to kill a police officer with a knife. Smith's progesterone dose had been reduced and so she was able to successfully plead mitigation and was released on probation (*R v. Smith*[6] (1982)).

PMS was used as a factor in sentencing *R v. English*[7] (1981). These 1980s British trials generated a flurry in both academic and popular literature that bordered on hysteria and moral panic (Laws, 1983; Rittenhouse, 1991; Zita, 1988). Zita (1988) documents an emerging literature suggesting that high rates of workplace accidents were due to women's monthly cycle. During this time there had been several attempts in the United States to have PMS recognised (*People v. Santos*[8] (1982), *Re Lovato v. Irvin*[9] (1983)). In *Irvin*, PMS was specifically rejected due to the absence of substantive scientific support for the defence.[10] *Irvin* related to the non-payment of a debt whilst *Santos* concerned an injury to a child. What is significant is that in both these cases PMS was used to argue 'non-responsibility'; that 'the defendant asserts she was out of control or could not formulate criminal intent because of this disabling condition' (Holtzman, 1984, p. 3). In *Richter* (1991), the PMS defence was accepted for the first time in the United States as a mitigating factor to explain erratic driving rather than intoxication. Although Dr. Richter was not under treatment for PMS at the time of the offence, the fact that she was in the PMS phase of her cycle was enough to cast 'reasonable doubt' as to her guilt (*Extract of Proceedings*, cited in Hosp, 1992, p. 436).

The role of medical expert is to mark, contain and map the PMS structure. Dr. Katharina Dalton, expert witness in both *Craddock* and *Smith*, argues that a feature of PMS is that behaviour is 'spontaneous, irrational, and accompanied by loss of insight, confusion, amnesia, or loss of control' (1986, p. 152). Whilst spontaneity is the essence of the so-called PMS crimes, Dalton argues that these crimes occurred each premenstruum: 'it is not unusual for a PMS arsonist to stay at the site of the fire and tell the police exactly how it started, or for the PMS prank telephone caller to wait in the phone booth to be arrested' (Dalton, 1980, cited in Dalton, 1986, p. 152).

McSherry (1993) asserts that Dalton has raised a series of open-ended clusters of symptoms to a fixed discourse of PMS as 'disease' or illness. Discourses of PMS are based on the assumption that PMS is a real, identifiable disease (Gurevich, 1995). The theme of women's (occupational) disruption occurred during a time large numbers of women were entering the workforce in the late 1970s and 1980s 'and were proving themselves to be quite capable within this context' (Rittenhouse, 1991, p. 420). But even as early as the 1950s, when the post-war economy was concerned with reintegrating returned soldiers into the workforce, Dalton, amongst others, promoted the dangers and liabilities of menstruation to the workplace (Figert, 2005; Gurevich, 1995). 'It is one thing to say that women experience cyclical changes centered around menstruation but quite another thing to say that certain changes are symptomatic of a pathological syndrome which can lead women to violence' (McSherry, 1993, p. 295). This would be to argue that women's bodies are in essence pathological and normally disordered.

How is the PMS argument explained in law? One approach is to consider women with PMS 'insane', morally excused for their behaviour and therefore not criminally responsible. The other perspective asserts that PMS should be used as a mitigating factor on the basis that such women lack 'specific intent or requisite state of mind for a certain crime' (Hosp, 1992, p. 439). The stumbling block for the acceptance of a PMS defence is the lack of consensus about the existence and the origin of the 'condition'. Is PMS an aberration of the female condition or a normal part of it? PMS literature suggests a fluctuating prevalence between 5 and 95% (Hosp, 1992, p. 441) and that women potentially have to negotiate over 150 symptoms of PMS (Gurevich, 1995; Hosp, 1992).

Silencing of women's voice outside of the pathology of ableism

Existence of rhetoric of PMS can lead to a *defensive othering* where women learn to see their experiences of menstruation by articulating that their symptoms are not as bad as those experienced by other women. Such evaluative ranking is also typical of biomedicalism. Research by Chrisler et al. (2006) has shown that women tend to believe in the stereotype of extreme uncontrollability. Feminist disability studies has pointed to the difficulty for disabled women in talking about some of the challenges of their impairments (pain, fatigue, incontinence) without that complaint or harm being reinterpreted in a bio-medicalised and pathological way. Social constructionist approaches to disability were a reaction to embodiment being not only viewed medically, but as a deficiency that inhered in the person awaiting repair. Feminists have shown that bodies do indeed matter and even if PMS is a fabrication – if women and men define PMS as 'real' – then there are 'real' outcomes (Figert, 2005). To a certain degree disability studies still adhere to a social model of disablement but has shifted emphasis to a cultural analysis by seeking to bring the body back into consideration.

Women's silence over PMS needs to be acknowledged, 'parts of our experience maybe expressed whilst others may not, and to question the kinds of self-expression being offered' (Laws, 1983, p. 20). Ussher (2003) reports that women may mitigate their PMS by avoiding social relations with others. Women are taught to describe their experience of the menstrual cycle in medicalised ways and through the lens of illness or disease (Laws, 1983; Ussher, 2003; Zita, 1988). A recent ethnographic study from Iceland indicated that women were unhappy with the presentation of PMS by media, men and other women (Sveindóttir et al., 2002). There was concern that PMS was adopted as a 'catch–all' concept to explain away or validate 'unacceptable' behaviour. Ableism's dominant ethos which pathologises women's experiences in effect 'turns women's experiences against them' (Sveindóttir et al., 2002, p. 417). The study revealed a common notion with regards to disability embodiment; a discursive silence about particularised (in this case gendered) bodily functions and processes. Biomedicalism is often engaged as women often feel that their issues around PMS and sexed bodies are not taken seriously unless there is a biomedical explanation (Lee, 2002, p. 31). Instead of reading emotions of anger and irritation as a logical response to bearing stress and high levels of responsibilities, Ussher's study found that these emotions were viewed by women in the study as a 'sign of pathology' (Ussher, 2003, p. 396).

According to Zita (1988) women are taught to segment off and contain 'unacceptable' behaviour that is expressed as being ontologically alien. Women who normally experience certain behaviours or emotions are spoken of in terms of 'not acting themselves' or being out of control. This results in a kind of ontological split – where pathological envelopment acts as a kind of gap-filler. Are there multiple selves and interiors – who is the 'real' woman? PMS not only becomes characterological, the medical discourse which divides the menstrual cycle into discrete phases where women experience a kind of episodic impairment, that due to its 'on' and 'off' predilection, needs to be compartmentalised. The respacialisation of PMS occurs in its relational aspects. Sveindóttir et al., 2002, found that when women referred to their own experiences they were grounded in the physical realm, whereas when they spoke of other women, perhaps friends, the PMS experiences were in the mental realm. If we adopt the French rendering of disability – as '*handicap de situation*' – a conceptualisation that disability is produced relationality to the environment, whereby ontological and corporealities are either geoaffirmed or geodismissed, then PMS can be circumscribed as a culture-specific disorder (see Johnson, 1987). Taking this further it is possible to assert that PMS is about women's negotiation of space and temporality, her movement and connectedness with public/private realms, industrialisation and urban living. In keeping with this understanding of disability within an overall framework of ableism, cartography of PMS blends well with Ussher's proposition that PMS is a relational issue. Ussher (2003) asserts,

> When women in this study were asked to describe their 'PMS', they did not talk about the experience or impact of the symptoms at an individual level, but referred to 'PMS' as an emotion or behaviour experienced and expressed in relation to others.
>
> (p. 390)

The pervasiveness of the disease or illness construct positing PMS to be ontologically negative makes it difficult to dissociate mental and somatic experience from a negative outlook. A positive menstrual imaginary is not something that many women speak of at their own initiative

(Sveindóttir et al., 2002). A Canadian study by Lee (2002) validates this assertion. Where women did have a positive outlook about PMS, they had to work on a transformed sense of 'unwantedness' to 'wantedness'. Although inconvenience was a significant issue, any ambivalence was turned towards positive aspects such as menstruation as a time of cleansing, slowing down or self-care (Lee, 2002).

Case study 2: Disabled car parking for pregnant women

An alternative reading of PMS sees the 'syndrome' as an articulation of psychological distress in women's lives. The female body is a signifier of volatility and is in need of containment. The leakiness grounded in sexual difference necessitates control through regularity mechanisms in order to close off unruly bodies (Keywood, 2000). Ambivalent performances can present possibility rather than invoke crisis. As Butler puts it: '[the]...persistence of unintelligible gender identities provide opportunity to explore the limits and regulatory aims of the domain of intelligibility and open up rival and subversive matrices of gender disorder' (1990, p. 17). In the debate over access to disability designated parking spaces and placards, the pregnant woman is unintelligible – is she like a disabled person, or different (a mere woman) – and in her material change (pregnancy) can she be conceived of as onto-corporeally new?

> The sense of disgust associated with fecund corporeality is also her – dark nipples, thin skin, nausea, bad breath, sweat, breasts left like flaps; the body excretions and reminders of mortality which underpin the positioning of the female body as abject. Who would be pregnant, or indeed, a woman, if this is what it entails?
>
> (Ussher, 2006, p. 87)

The matter of disability parking might seem an absurd study by which to consider pathologisation of women; however, as Miller (2003) notes, the moral high ground is passionately played out in disputes over the usage of car parking spaces and suggests the limitation that law plays in maintaining social order. Cresswell (2005) proposes a 'moral geography' whereby certain people, things, in certain landscapes are embraced and not others. Socio-spatial order invites a moral reading 'to examine the contextual thinking of moral concepts in the particular (local) circumstances of differentiated human being[s]' (Smith, 1997, p. 587). The 'cripping' of the landscape is only possible when anomalous zones are instituted. Disability parking is an example of an exceptional space where 'sized' zones exist alongside assumptions about reasonable allocation and positioning. Here I wish to investigate social order(ing) and the kinds of demarcations we make between disabled people and pregnant women, suggesting that disabled parking acts as a moral landscape. As Rose and Gregson argue, 'spaces do not preexist their performances; rather specific performances bring them into being' (2000, p. 441). Hence the turf war about the territorialisation of harm and the production of dis-ease and empathy. In June 2004, U.S. State of California Republican Assembly member, Tony Strickland introduced *Bill AB 1947*[11] which aimed to extend disability parking entitlements to women in their third trimester of pregnancy. Strickland withdrew the Bill when he was met with an avalanche of protests over associating pregnancy with disability. A similar, unsuccessful Bill (*AB 1940*)[12] was introduced in February 2008 by Republican Assembly member Charles DeVore. Specifically section 2(B) proposed an amendment to the *Vehicle Code* that defines,

> ... 'temporary disability' includes the last trimester of a woman's pregnancy through her first two months after giving birth. For the purposes of this subparagraph, the department shall require that the certificate be signed by a physician and surgeon, a nurse practitioner, a certified nurse midwife, or a physician.

Maintained in this proposed Bill are the technicians of certification who ensure eligibility is still grounded in bio-medicalism thus reinforcing the medicalisation of need. Argument in support and opposition to the Bill highlights some of the ontological concerns raised in this chapter and the constricted ways law negotiates and constrains the complexity of disability and (gendered) difference. The principal opponents of the Bill were the American College of Obstetricians and Gynecologists (ACOG) and the advocacy body National Organization for Women (NOW).

Central to the discussion was the notion of 'naturalness' (of pregnancy) juxtaposed with anomaly (in this case disability), and whether each of these corporeal differences necessitated the making of accommodations. The NOW argued strenuously that pregnancy was a 'natural function' and therefore should not be framed by the abnormal: 'It's very much a normal part of a women's life – we have children ... we've always been troubled by framing pregnancy as a disability' (Helen Grieco, cited in Sanders, 2008a). It is understandable that a woman's advocacy organisation would resist any inference that pregnancy be considered at best an illness or at worst a bodily aberrancy. Of significance is the debate in some jurisdictions to limit the purview of legal disability; that disability is normatively off-limits to the general population. Disabled people as a minority group are then delineated from the population as a whole. The exclusivity and containment approach restricts reserved 'disabled parking' spaces and placards to a discreet minority needing protection so that such needs-based provision remains an exceptional gift rather than a regularised social provision. This normalisation of special accommodations in the form of dedicated disability parking spaces becomes another reason to oppose the Bill.

The limits of accommodation are revealed in the ongoing concerns about extending access to these spaces to a broader group and matters of a shortage of disability parking. Creating an impression of 'false allegiance', Charlotte Newhart of NOW suggests that 'we[13] are creating an issue for the disability community without offering a solution' (Newhart, cited in Sanders, 2008a). ACOG invokes a moral discourse in their argument that disregards the materiality of the pregnant body and diminishes gender over disability 'suffering': 'there is no reason why a physically capable pregnant woman should be using the limited number handicapped parking spaces when there are people who truly need them' (Nursing Health Policy, ND). Interestingly, some sections of the disability sector took a more pragmatic option of suggesting that if the Bill passes there should be an increase in parking. Other disability groups wanted to hold onto their specialness and coveted spaces arguing for a form of disability protectionism, missing the opportunity to see what is potentially a commonality of an experience beyond the particularities of a 'disability' designation.

DeVore countered the argument that 'naturalness' in contrast with exceptionality or specialness discounts the making of particularised and differentiating provisions for certain sections of the population in use in certain times. Continuing to debunk the naturalness argument, DeVore asks, 'Could you say that somebody who was born blind, it's a natural function, so we shouldn't let them have a white cane with special traffic privileges' (Charles DeVore, cited Sanders, 2008a). The second prong of Griero's comments (cited in Sanders, 2008a) turns to troubled disability framing. Here is an example where the depathologisation of femaleness only appears possible by trading on binaries of the normative and disability as a deficient state of exception.

Ableistnormativity is veiled when presented by Shannon Smith-Crowley, legislative advocate for the California Chapter (District IX) of the ACOG who argued that pregnant women should be moving and walking (Sanders, 2008a, 2008b). Whilst that may be so, the compulsion to walk at all costs not only 'smacks of paternalism' (Wenzel, 2008), but closes down dialogue about the kinds of mobility needs that pregnant women and mothers might have. Some of the corporeal difference discourse is captured in a blog by Maughan (2008) 'Nett':

> There are some women that are not too tremendously happy while Pregnant. I am one of them. I love my children but I get very sick. I don't want to go out much let alone attempt to use a special parking space. So in a lot of ways, I do feel handicapped. I cannot do the things I want to do. Pregnancy is tough on the body no matter how fit you are. PG [pregnant] women SHOULD be treated differently and they should (treat) themselves differently. PG is not the normal state. It is a natural state but a temporary and uncomfortable state. I try to walk when I am PG but I have no ACL in my right knee and the extra weight is very painful. Try standing on a train 8 months PG while some other woman or man sits and does not offer to trade places. I dare say ANY PG women would be annoyed. So really, what is the difference?

Both Vic Finkelstein and Michael Oliver long ago recognised the walking at all costs argument. Rehabilitation aims to assist the individual be as 'normal as possible' resulting in endless soul-destroying hours at hospital attempting to approximate able-bodied standards by 'walking' with callipers and crutches (Finkelstein, quoted in Oliver, 1993, pp. 16–17). In critiquing the description of walking as a mere biological/functional act, Oliver suggests that 'walking' acts as symbolic capital associated with (real) life (Oliver, 1996). The privileging of walking over other modes of mobility has resulted in large numbers of people submitting themselves to regimes of medical torture – to be surgically modified and re-sculptured. As Oliver (1993) puts it:

> Walking is rule-following behaviour; not walking is rule ignoring, rule-flouting or even rule-threatening behaviour. Not-walking can be tolerated when individuals are prepared to undergo rehabilitation in order to nearly walk or come to terms with their non-walking. Not-walking or rejecting nearly-walking as a personal choice is something different however; it threatens the power of professionals, it exposes the ideology of normality and challenges the whole rehabilitation enterprise.
>
> (p. 104)

In terms of women, a moral discourse is invoked for fear that pregnant women, for reasons of comfort and efficiency, opt for the 'preferential option for disability rights' and disregard the performance of gender. Assemblyman Devore, recognising the struggles of many pregnant women, argues for 'practical logistics...It goes way beyond a strict definition of medical necessity'[!]' (DeVore, cited Sanders, 2008b). One wonders why the creation of spatial accommodations for pregnant women is so rule-threatening. There is a discursive silence, a non-disclosure about the impact of bodily changes and functions on women's life especially when those changes are not commensurate with existing spatial and temporal structures. The resistance to foreground biology lest it be recuperated as disability means that it is problematic to discuss economic, time loss and compromised performance in the workplace associated with menstruation (Borenstein, 2005; Côte, 2002).

The 'specialness-as-disabled' argument is deployed and linked to the pregnant woman's body in the school system to reconfigure teen pregnancy in order to provide supports. Pillow (2004) documents attempts in the US school system to define teen pregnancy as a disability or disease with the 'uniqueness' of pregnancy being recuperated and transmogrified as 'specialness' – requiring special needs. The discourses of pregnancy as a disability result in the contortion of the teen pregnancy experience to access bodily accommodations that diverge from the 'benchmark student'. As Pillow puts it, 'the pregnant/mothering...is only afforded the right to any special needs by first being identified as somehow disabled, untouchable, and deficient by virtue of being a teen mother' (2004, p. 101).

Drawing together

These case studies point to important issues about the way gendered ontological differences are negotiated and spoken of and how these differences intersect with ontologies of disability that inform social policy and law. Disabled people in the city have an ambivalent relationship to space given the histories of exclusion. The main mechanism of disability inclusion has been through a norm of exception – disabled people are a discreet class deserving of and being reserved special accommodations. Disability studies questions the formation of the productive body based on the atomistic possessive individual. Disabled people's bodies and mentalities are figured as burdened, troubling and requiring government. Despite appearances to the contrary, the benchmarking of the corporeal citizen is not static but is driven by the compulsion to enhance, mitigate and re-normalise. Horney captures the notion that women are essentially disabled compellingly:

> ... The menstruating woman is seen as basically 'mad or bad' ... prone to 'lunacy'. This implies that women might spend one sixth of their reproductive lives suffering from a disabling illness which makes them unfit for many types of work.
>
> (Horney, cited in McSherry, 1994, p. 147)

Ableism forces a game of disassociation, obstructing consideration of gender and disability in terms of sameness by deploying a politics of fixed difference; in the case of disability an ethos that affirms disabled people as an insular minority and in the case of women, a dangerous presumption that women's bodies *per se* have a predilection towards monstrosity and uncontrollability.

9
Disability Harm and Wrongful Life Torts

Wrongful life and wrongful birth case law is plagued by folk demons and moral panics in the same way that increasing knowledge of human genetics brings with it inchoate fears of eugenic excess and monstrosity.

(Mackenzie, 1999, p. 178)

...the good advocate grasps at complex confused reality and constructs a simple clear-cut account of it...a case is very much an edited version [and] it is not just edited into a minimal account – a microcosm of the incident – it is an account edited with vested interests in mind...The good advocate is not concerned with reproducing incidents but producing cases, not with truth but with persuasion.

(McBarnet, 1983, p. 17)

It is understandable that a parent desires to have not only a healthy, but also a beautiful and intelligent baby: the best and the happiest baby in the world. At the same time, however, nobody can be sure that a healthy child will be a happy person, nor that a disabled person will necessarily be an unhappy person.

(Marzano-Parisoli, 2001, p. 659)

Impairment, in particular those that are multiple and of a severe nature, requires extensive resources in order for the person concerned (and often, their families) to have full equalisation of opportunities and a reasonable quality of life. Support and financial assistance provided by governments though welfare systems are becoming less available and when available involve considerable time delays. As a last resort, many disabled people look to the court system by way of case law for remedies that provide financial solutions. The opening epigrams of the chapter invoke notions of persuasion.

The use of the law of torts is one area of civil law increasingly being tested in Europe, North America and Australia. This chapter focuses specifically on a specialised area of tort known as 'wrongful pregnancy, birth or life' actions, and what these actions signify in terms of ableism and ableist constructions. In this chapter, I argue that what is objectionable about the use of these tort categories is not the quest for compensation or financial support by families of disabled people and themselves, rather the objection relates to the processes of accessing law. The plaintiff and their legal team are required to 'trade' in symbols, in particular, trading specifically in negative ontologies of disability and ableist constructions in order to argue wrongdoing and claim compensation. This chapter begins with an outline of the fundamentals of torts, in particular wrongful birth/life actions, and then moves onto a consideration of legal reactions overseas and in Australia. The final part of this chapter looks at the broader philosophical and social policy impacts of using this particular area of tort law.

The basis of torts

Torts are civil 'wrongs' recognised by law as grounds for a legal action. These 'wrongs' result in an injury or 'harm' constituting the basis for a claim by the injured party. Whilst some torts have criminal penalties attached, the primary focus of tort law is to provide remedies for the damages incurred and deter others from committing similar 'harms'. The injured person may sue for an injunction to prevent the continuation of the tortuous conduct or for financial compensation (damages). Among the types of damages the plaintiff may recover are loss of earning capacity, pain and suffering, and medical expenses deemed 'reasonable'. The assessment of damages includes both present and future expected losses. A number of elements need to be satisfied in order to test the validity of bringing a tort action:

a. the existence of a duty of care owed by the defendant to the plaintiff;
b. a breach of that duty;
c. a proximate chain of causation between the misfeasance of the defendant and the 'harm' suffered by the plaintiff; and
d. damages (Hersch, 1983, p. 134; Ossorio, 2000, p. 309).

Fundamentals of wrongful birth and life actions

Two concepts that have gained a level of notoriety under common law legal systems are the torts of 'wrongful birth' and 'wrongful life'. For simplicity's sake, 'wrongful birth' (hereafter referred to as WB) involves cases where the plaintiffs, the parents of the impaired child, sue for wrongful birth on the basis of misdiagnosis or a failure to detect a so-called 'genetic defect'.[1] In this kind of action the 'wrong' or 'harm' is that the child itself constitutes a damage; in other words, the birth of the child is a form of physical injury (Somerville, 1983). In the United States, some State courts (24 in total) have recognised a WB action whilst other States, notably Michigan and Georgia, have ruled them invalid. Claims for WB actions are fairly established in Canadian jurisdictions (Nelson & Robertson, 2001, p. 103), with the lead case being *Arndt v. Smith*.[2] In Australia, WB torts have been recognised by some State courts in a limited way (see *Veivers v Connolly 1994*[3] in QLD and *CES v Superclinics (Aust) Pty Ltd 1995*[4] in NSW).

The concept of 'wrongful life' (hereafter referred to as WL), however, involves an action brought by a person experiencing impairment on the basis that they were born with an 'impairment' due to the actions or omissions of a doctor or another party who owes or owed a duty of care to that person. Hersch (1983, p. 133) argues for a further division of WL actions by proposing two classes, namely pre-conception ('but for the doctors negligence the plaintiff would not have been born') and post-conception ('but for the doctors negligence the plaintiff would not have been born impaired, or would have been terminated if the "impairment" had been detected').

Few jurisdictions in the United States recognise WL as a basis for action. In fact 23 State courts have rejected WL claims, whilst eight state legislatures have prohibited WL claims by statute. The lead case claiming a 'wrongful life' action is *Curlender v. Bioscience Laboratories*.[5] While the English courts specifically rejected this basis for action in *McKay v. Essex Area Health Authority and Anor* (1982),[6] the Italian Court of Verona[7] recognised this right in a limited way, as has the Cour de Cassation in France.[8] In the Australian context, courts have rejected WL actions following the English precedent established in *McKay* (1982). *McKay* was applied in (NSW) *Bannerman v Mill (1991)*[9] and (QLD) *Veivers v Connolly (1994)*.[10] In March 2002, the law firm Maurice, Blackburn, Cashman unsuccessfully attempted to test a WL action on behalf of three plaintiffs with impairments in the Supreme Court of NSW. Elizabeth Collins (1983–1984, p. 701) provides a summary of the fact situations characteristic of WL claims in the United States:

a. Dissatisfied life;
b. Incorrect sterilisation procedures;
c. Unsuccessful abortions;
d. In cases of pre-conception negligence, parents are denied information on the possibilities giving birth to a child with impairment; and
e. Due to the post-conception negligence of a health professional, parents are denied the option of 'avoiding' a child's birth.

The differences in legal reasoning between the two concepts are significant, with WB actions claiming that the birth *per se* is wrongful (not the 'disability'), whilst WL actions invite the suggestion that life with an 'impairment' is inherently harmful – in other words, courts are asked to rule on whether life with an 'impairment' is preferable to the non-existence of life itself (Botkin, 1988; Butler, 1992).

Legal reactions – the United States

In the United States of America, Wrongful Birth/Life cause of actions are mainly negligence torts and as such are jurisdictionally the responsibility of state common law. In other words, the argument presented and relevant precedent followed in tort differs from state to state. In this section, I make no attempt to review tort law on a state-by-state basis, rather I wish to track and discuss key themes in legal reasoning by the courts. The earliest attempt to bring about a WL cause of action (not on the basis of impairment) occurred in 1963 in the case of *Zepeda v. Zepeda*,[11] subsequently denied by the US Supreme Court in 1964. Since that date a number of attempts, some successful, have been made to have WL cause of actions recognised by various State courts. It is worthwhile to examine, albeit briefly, some of the arguments introduced by plaintiffs to support their claim of WB/WL and the response to these claims by the courts.

In 1967, the New Jersey Supreme Court heard the first WL case based on 'impairment' as an injury or harm. In *Gleitman v. Cosgrove*,[12] the WL cause of action was claimed in conjunction with a WB action by the parents. The plaintiffs sued Mrs. Gleitman's doctor for failing to inform her that the rubella she contracted in the early stages of her pregnancy would in all probability lead to foetal impairment thus denying her the obtaining of an abortion. The mother, Sandra, sued for the 'emotional distress caused by her son's birth defects'; Irwin Gleitman, the father, sued for the costs that would be incurred in caring for their child, whilst the child Jeffrey Gleitman sued for his 'birth defects'. The Court's reasoning was based on the presupposition that every child has the right to be born a whole, functioning human being, and because of the alleged actions of the doctor this right was being denied. On the basis of such reasoning, the Court proceeded to argue that since this right has been infringed and the plaintiff subsequently born impaired, that the harm was (an impaired) life itself, which would have been resolved by the intervention of a termination, but for the negligence of the doctor:

> The infant plaintiff is therefore required to say not that he should have been born without defects but that he should not have been born at all...but for the negligence of the defendants, he would not have been born to suffer with an impaired body. In other words, he claims that the conduct of defendants prevented his mother from obtaining an abortion which would have terminated his existence, and that his very life is wrongful...Ultimately, the infant's complaint is that he would be better off not to have been born.
>
> (Gleitman, at 692)

Adding insult to injury, it becomes clear that the Court in *Gleitmen v. Cosgrove* held to a belief in the inherent intolerability of impairment and acted as a de facto mediator of the experience of the impaired person from an ableist perspective:

> It is basic to the human condition to seek life and hold on to it however heavily burdened. If Jeffrey could have been asked as to whether his life should be snuffed out before his full term of gestation could run its course, our felt intuition of human nature tells us that he would almost surely choose life with defects against no life at all.
>
> (Gleitman, at 693)

Despite this argument, the Court rejected the cause of action brought by the plaintiffs on the grounds that the sanctity of human life in the end prevailed and on the basis of another argument, namely the difficulty in measuring damages:

> The normal measure of damages in tort action is compensatory. Damages are measured by comparing the condition the plaintiff would have been in, had the defendant not been negligent, with plaintiff's impaired condition as a result of negligence. The infant plaintiff would have us measure the difference between his life with defects, against the utter void of non-existence, but it is impossible to make

such a determination. This Court cannot weigh the value of life with impairments against the non-existence of life itself. By asserting he should have not been born, the infant plaintiff makes it logically impossible for a court to measure his alleged damages because of the impossibility of making the comparison required by compensatory remedies.[13]

(Gleitman, at 692)

The Californian case of *Curlender v. Bioscience Laboratories* (1980)[14] provides an early example of support for a WL cause of action by the courts. The plaintiff was born with Tay-Saches disease. There was no suggestion in this case the defendant caused the disease. Rather the plaintiff argued that the laboratory that incorrectly processed her parent's genetic tests were in part responsible for bringing her into the world (Chwang, 1997). The plaintiff argued and the court accepted that the she was seeking damages for her existence in an 'impaired' state rather than for her birth. The court recognised being born in an impaired state was cognisable at law:

We construe the 'wrongful life' cause of action by the defective child as the right of such a child to recover damages for the pain and suffering to be endured during the limited life span available to such a child and any pecuniary loss resulting from the impaired condition.

(Curlender, at 489)

Despite the precedent decision in *Curlender*, Brenda McGivern (2002, p. 57) points out two other cases[15] during the same time frame that provide a significant US authority supporting a contrary view to the reasoning given in *Curlender*. The states of New Jersey, California and Washington,[16] whilst denying a plaintiff a WL cause of action based on the comparing an impairment existence to non–existence, have recognised the cause of action in a more limited and prescribed way, namely the costs of medical and other support services. As Butler (1992, p. 884) argues these factors are 'easily calculated and therefore should be awarded to the child who can prove these damages'. In *Procanik by Procanik v Cillo*[17] (1984) the New Jersey court held:

Our decision to allow the recovery of extraordinary medical expenses is not premised on the concept that non-life is preferable to an impaired life, but is predicated on the needs of the living. We seek only to respond to the call of the living for help in *bearing the burden* of their affliction.

(Procanik, at 763 – my emphasis)

Wrongful life suits continue to be presented to various State courts with mixed success. Even when courts have recognised the high costs of rearing and providing medical care to children/adults with disabilities they have concluded that legislation (and not the courts) is the best mechanism to bring about policy change.[18]

Legal reactions – Australia

In cases where no Australian precedent exists, the courts in Australia have turned to the decisions made by courts in the United Kingdom. Increasingly, though being weaker in authority, decisions made in higher courts in the United States have had a persuasive influence in the absence of domestic cases. There has been a dearth of cases related to either WB or WL in either Australian state or commonwealth courts. The lead case in terms of a WL cause of action can be found in the English case of *McKay v. Essex Area Health Authority and Anor* (1982).[19] Because of Australian Courts reliance on *McKay* for the development of domestic judgments I will provide an outline of significant point of reasoning. But before doing so, I want to refer back 10 years to an earlier case heard in the Supreme Court in Victoria, *Watt v Rama* (1972).[20] Traditionally negligence law has deemed that a foetus has no separate existence (until it is born) apart from its mother and therefore is not legal person to whom a duty of care is owed (Hersch, 1983, p. 134). In *Rama*, Justices Winneke and Pape held that on the child's birth, the child experienced an injury such that *ex post facto* a duty of care was owed by the defendant (at 360). This judgment opened up the possibility for a cause of action to be brought on the basis of an injury suffered by a foetus *in utero* as a result of the negligence of a health care professional. In both Australian and English law the decision in *McKay* represents the most significant expression of judicial opinion of the matter of wrongful life causes of action. In *McKay* the appellant was a child who was born partially deaf and blind and experienced a range of other impairments as a consequence of her mother contracting rubella in the early stages of pregnancy.

As in the US case of *Gleitman*, the mother had been tested for rubella and had been told that on the basis that her tests results were negative she could safely continue her pregnancy. The child sued the health authority arguing that the doctor was negligent for failing to advise the mother to have an abortion. Put another way, the doctor was negligent for allowing her to be born. The plaintiff argued that her impaired life was injurious and therefore sought damages. The Court rejected this cause of action; Ackner LJ summarises the Court's reasoning:

> I cannot accept that the common law duty of care to a person can involve, without specific legislation to achieve this end, the legal obligation to that person, whether or not in utero, to terminate his existence, such a proposition runs wholly contrary to the concept of the sanctity of life.
>
> (McKay, All ER at 787)

Public policy considerations feature sharply in the underlying reasoning behind the judgment, particularly the discourse of 'the sanctity of human life' asserting the primacy of foetal rights over procreative rights. It was on this basis that the plaintiff was unable to access damages when in order to do so involved an 'evaluation between non-existence and life even in a flawed [sic] condition' (at 155). Whilst public policy considerations related to the sanctity of life were elevated in the judgment, this elevation also extends to valuing impaired living. The *obiter dicta*[21] of Lord Justice Stephenson, who delivered the lead judgment, reveals a concern with the possibility of endorsing negative ontologies of disability by giving assent to WL claims. To sanction a WL cause of action would be to accede to the assumption 'that a child has a right to be born whole and perfect or not at all' (Stephenson, at 1181). The implication being that such reasoning might suggest that impaired life is less valuable than a 'normal' child and therefore not worth preserving (at 1180).[22]

A final comment on a possible duty by a doctor that acceptance of WL cause of action might imply. Both LJ Ackner (at 1187) and Stephenson (at 1181) are concerned that endorsement of a wrongful life action would impose an 'intolerable burden' on doctors 'to advise abortions in doubtful cases' and raise the possibility of children suing their mothers for failing to abort them. Instead of focusing on the fear of doctors being sued, Robin Mackenzie argues that the framework of reasoning in *McKay* is flawed: 'the duty in *McKay* could have been framed in terms of a duty to inform the mother of likely handicap in order that she might make a decision whether to continue with the pregnancy' (Mackenzie, 1999, p. 181). This may well be an alternative approach, however I argue that the concern in *McKay* is still valid – for there is a real possibility of increased litigation by extending the basis of actions of negligence, to say nothing of the rise in medical negligence indemnity insurances. The *ratio decidendi* in McKay was applied in the New South Wales case of *Bannerman v Mill* (1991).[23] The facts of the case are similar to *McKay* and involve the plaintiff whose mother contracted rubella early in pregnancy. Master Greenwood in applying *McKay* argued that a WL action was 'not known at common law [and it is not] possible to assess damages in monetary terms'. (Bannerman, at 88) dismissed the claim.

The case of *Veivers v Connolly 1994*,[24] whilst strictly a WB action, can be included in this discussion of WL actions. Susan Veivers, who had contracted rubella and had not been tested by her doctor when she presented with symptoms, brought a WB action. Veivers argued that had she known of the existence of rubella she would have terminated the pregnancy. Her daughter Kylie, who experienced intellectual and physical disabilities, initially brought a WL claim. The plaintiff at the court hearing abandoned this cause of action as 'it was conceded that, in Australia, there was no legal authority for such an action'. The Court relied on an English decision, *McKay v Essex Area Health Authority*.(Fitzgerald, 1995, p. 194).

Three children who were born with 'severe' impairments brought about a WL cause of action in the NSW Supreme Court on 11 March 2002.[25] Alexia Harriton, 20, was born after her mother contracted rubella. Keeden Waller, a 17-month-old IVF baby, inherited a clotting disorder that could have been detected with screening, and Chelsea Edwards, 2, was born after a failed vasectomy. David Hirsch, a solicitor from law firm Maurice Blackburn Cashman representing plaintiffs Edwards and Harriton, said the complaint was about 'having to suffer the disabilities arising from being born' (Crichton, 2001). A key theme running through the submissions on behalf of the plaintiff prepared by Hirsch (2002) is that is that the terminology of WL is misleading. Argument by counsel relied extensively on the judgment of the Maryland Court of Appeal in *Reed v Comapgnolo* (1993)[26] that objected to the use of the terms WB and WL:

> These labels are not instructive. Any 'wrongfulness' lies not in the life, the birth, the conception, or the pregnancy, but in the negligence of the physician. The harm, if any, is not the birth itself but the effect of the defendant's negligence on the [parents] resulting from the denial to the parent's of their right, as the case may be, to decide whether to bear a child or whether to bear child with a genetic or other defect.
>
> (*Reed*, at 237)

Lawyers in the case prefer the concept of 'wrongful suffering' as this concept does not imply that no life is preferable to an impaired one (Crichton, 2001). Furthermore, proponents of WB torts argue that with the increasing success of WB claims, greater financial support will be provided to the families to assist with the extra costs of impairment. Hirsch argues that a better way is to accede to WL actions because the money is given to the child directly: it is, after all, the child who suffers the 'life with disabilities' and has need created by this (2002, p. 25).

On 12 June 2002, Justice Timothy Studdert of the New South Wales Supreme Court delivered his judgment on the wrongful life cause of action brought in *Edwards v Blomeley*,[27] *Harriton v Stephens* and *Waller v James*. After undertaking a comprehensive review of case law to date both in Australia and in other relevant common law jurisdictions, Studdert determined that to award damages on the basis of WL would erode the value of human life, and harm the self-esteem of disabled people. In reviewing the argument that non-existence was preferable to impaired existence, the legal reasoning of the judgment provides solace:

> There are many disabled members of society who lead valuable and fulfilling lives notwithstanding their significant physical handicaps [sic] ... To all such persons the notion that non existence may be considered preferable to living within disabilities would surely be perceived to be offensive.
>
> (*Edwards*, at para 75)

The judgment concluded with a summary of three public policy considerations for the inadvisability of WL claims that concur with the argument I have presented in this chapter; namely, the sanctity of human life and the impact that WL claims would have on the self-worth of disabled people and 'their perceived worthiness by other members of society' (at para 119[ii]). Finally, the Court argued that recognition of this category of tort would expose treating doctors and mothers who decided to continue with a pregnancy to liability for a tortuous legal action.

Summary of grounds for rejection of wrongful life actions

In drawing together the subsections related to legal reactions, a number of grounds can be identified that contribute to court's becoming apprehensive about granting a WL cause of action:

a) The sanctity of life in any form is preferable to non-existence, that is not having been born at all.
b) There is a difficulty measuring damages by way of a comparison to a party in a position where the injury had not occurred, that is comparison in terms could have been before existence.
c) Any WL cause because of its significant social policy concerns should be left to the legislature.
d) There is a limitation in using 'rights discourses' in arguing for a right not to be born or the right to be born 'normal'
e) Extending torts to WL could result in an increase in claims from people with 'less severe' impairments or other bodily differences.
f) The medical profession would be subjected to 'litigation frenzy' and an overwhelming rise in insurance premiums.

Ontological outputs, philosophical and legal implications

In this final section, focus is broadly on ontological, ethical, legal and social policy implications of some of the cases and commentary discussed in this study of WL torts.

Ontology

Elizabeth Collins (1983–1984, pp. 690–691) points out that claims for wrongful pregnancy, conception, birth and life are substantially claims about the 'wrongful formation' of the human person. Even though the right to determine the form of a child has not been established by the courts, Collins (1983–1984, pp. 691, 704) argues that this right is often implied in instances when 'impairment' is created – that is the 'choice' to continue to carry or terminate a foetus with impairment. Interestingly the right to 'choice' of form is rarely countenanced in instances where prospective parents 'choose' to create a child with a specific impairment such as Deafness (c.f. Griffith, 2002a, 2002b; McLellan, 2002).

Continuing the argument related to form, bioethicist George Smith advocates that notions of 'sanctity of life' be dispensed with and replaced with the notion that children have a 'right to a healthy and body' (Smith, 1981, p. 82). In the New York case of *Becker v. Schwartz*[28] (1978) the Court noted the difficulty of defining the standard of 'a perfect birth' (Becker, at 812). The whole basis of WB and WL ultimately rests on a comparison of the preferability of life with 'non-impairment' in relation to that constitutionally separated category of 'impairment' (see section 4.1).

Throughout many of the cases surveyed disability/impairment continues to be described in terms of 'bearing the burden of affliction', 'suffering' and an 'arduous responsibility'. It is my contention that the discourses of burden and negative ontology occur in both judgments that favour and dismiss WB and WL claims and that the continued use of negligence law in the terms of injury and harm will reinforce the negative associations of impairment. My conclusion is supported by some of the debate in the courts and commentaries about the terminology of WB and WL. In an attempt to escape the loop of 'birth and/or life' Robin Mackenzie (1999, p. 182) proposes that WL actions be reframed in terms of a 'diminished life' cause of action. Hirsch (2002) argued in the NSW Supreme Court (see *Edwards* 2002) that the concept of 'wrongful suffering' is more precise. Both these proposals, whilst attempting to reduce the stigma associated with WL and WB (and therefore impairment), really do not significantly alter the terrain of disability-talk, they simply replicate (and again reinforce) the idea of impairment as ontological intolerable and inherently negative.[29]

Ethical considerations

A number of WB cause of actions ruled in favour of the plaintiff by reasoning that it is important to curb negligent behaviour on the part of medical professionals especially in the usage and processing of diagnostic and genetic tests. These judgments encouraged the use and correct administration of tests in order to facilitate 'choice' on the part of parents and to reduce some of the costs of supporting impaired persons. As Faunce and Jefferys (2007) notes, regarding the *Harrington* case, to deny the existence of any medical duty of care 'practically amounts to the provision of exceptional and unwarrented immunity to health care professionals' (p. 473). Some of these arguments however conflate the use of prenatal tests with technologies of termination. It is assumed that a 'positive' result would lead to the choice of abortion and opposed to the exploration of other options.

I have already mentioned that in *McKay* there was concern over the potential for increased litigation when doctors did not advise abortion when a 'defect' is indicated. Such litigation 'phobia' could lead to instances where medical professionals are coerced into termination procedures as a first response, thereby acting out eugenics by proxy. The focus of WL actions has predominantly been in cases where the defendant is a member of the medical and allied health professions. It is seems to me that in time with the mounting pressure of costs and the increased use of rhetoric of 'mitigated disability' (see Chapter 3), an action will arise where a child/adult with impairment can sue their mother for acting negligently in not terminating their existence (*in utero*) after being made aware of a foetal 'defect'. Put more strongly, a woman who resists the 'desirability' of prenatal testing or the compulsion towards selective termination becomes a pariah, a carrier of a criminalised (negligent) womb (c.f. Karpin, 1994; Mason, 2000). Her decision to knowingly continue a 'defective' pregnancy would be characterised as a form of 'negligent foetal abuse' (Smith, 1981, p. 113). However, care has to be taken that this consideration does not turn into an opportunity for strictly anti-abortionist agendas – given the highly unlikelihood of a court concluding that a mother's decision to not undergo an abortion would constitute a breach of any duty of care owed to the foetus. Is it the role of the High Court to place encumbrances on the freedom of women to make choices about issues such as procreation or abortion, while at the same time denying the awarding of damages, leaving the burden of support and care 'to fall somewhat randomly on the (blameless) disabled person's family, on charity, or on the increasing uncertainties of social security' (Faunce, 2007, p. 474).

Law and social policy

One of the 'big picture' questions not addressed in the cases or commentaries concerns the relationship of these novel tort actions and broader concerns related to the welfare state and the relationship between common law cases and the legislature. The narratives of families and individuals with impairment point to the extreme difficulties of providing support and assistance to a family member with significant impairment, especially in terms of financial burdens. Any access of the validity of WB and WL claims needs to include also a discussion of the role of the State in providing assistance to those in need.

What is clear from the cases is that governments are falling short in this respect and families are left with little option but to pursue remedies within the uncertain and often costly setting of the courts. A number of the US courts have rejected WL claims arguing that such decisions are best made by the legislature. In the Australian context, these arguments I believe have merit. There needs to be a public debate about the costs of disability, the responsibility of governments (and communities) to provide for people with long-term high support needs. Finally, in what seems a light at the end of the tunnel, Brenda McGivern (2002) proposes that the focus of the claims, namely WB and WL, can be bypassed by 'avoiding the need to plead injury at all'. She argues,

> Actions for losses associated with negligent acts, but in the absence of injury, have long been recognized by Australian courts in claims for pure economic loss. In these cases, and in this instance, it has been argued that the protected legal interest . . . is financial security.
>
> (p. 59)

The good news is that a majority of jurisdictions have concluded that the disability life is still preferable to non-existence! Still there remains a belief in disability *qua* disability constitutes a harm. Can bodily integrity exist for the disabled person when they are conceived in terms of as an ontological harm?

10
Searching for Subjectivity: The Enigma of Devoteeism, Conjoinment and Transableism

Mentalities that shatter the illusion of the monster are particularly under fire as well as those scholars that have the audacity to propose the desirability of disability. Following the insights and shortcomings of postmodernist theorists, Elizabeth Grosz (1996) challenges researchers to raise the study of freakery beyond being an object of prurient speculation. This chapter explores the notion of *disability as a state of ambivalence*. It will look at the ways people with disability negotiate and experience internal ambivalence in their own lives as well as negotiate the ambivalence towards disability in society. How does the person with a disability negotiate the expectations and compulsions of ableism? In other words, do they choose to conform or hyperminic ableism or do they go it alone and explore alternative ways of being? People with impairments have impairment – mediated proprioceptive ways of experiencing being in the world. This draws upon the ideas developed in phenomenology of the animated or lived body and we can conclude then that people with disabilities and the development of self is remarkably and possibly radically different from people who have an ableist orientation. Is it possible to speak of a 'disabilities' orientation? What are the implications for the liberal project of inclusion rooted in sameness? Therefore this chapter explores the notion of a disability orientation – what are the different ways of seeing the world? The ancient Greek word for 'crisis' – *krisis* – denotes a moment of opportunity. In terms of performance of self, ambivalence may provoke a dialogical negotiation of opportunity. Some territories are so foreign that the traveller needs a translator to make sense of worlds ontologically different from our own. What is to be done about the realities of aberrant outlaw bodies (conjoined, inter-sexed, deaf-blind, transabled, devotees) that are so morphically dissonant from those in ableist homelands?

This chapter documents how the abled body is materialised through a set of practices and discourses. Under study are the juxtaposed stories of various conjoined twins who each provide counterpoints to the ableist project and the possibility of speaking otherwise about the human. We look at disability devoteeism to see what this orientation suggests about disability desire. We ask what do transabled people 'really' know about disability? All these people are in effect strangers in ableist homelands – who because of their strangeness have the possibility of a new vision or orientation.

Ableist Enigmas are Monstrous

> ...these diseases [were] partitioned into landscapes that obscurely gave them their style and their structure. On the one hand, a sodden, almost diluvian world, where main remained deaf, blind, and numb to all that was not his one terror: a world simplified in the extreme, and immoderately enlarged in a single one of its details. On the other a parched and desertic world, a panic world where all was flight, disorder, instantaneous gesture.
>
> (Foucault, 1971, p. 131)

The monster signifier can present both epistemological and ontological confusions. The 'monster' is a neologism for 'boundary – crossing', crossing boundaries of acceptability exposing the brute end of ableist sovereignty. We need to hold this rendering in distinction from the ascribing of the anomalous/noxious body as 'monstrous' or grotesque. Here 'monstrosity', as Foucault (1997a, p. 51) argues, 'combines the impossible and the forbidden' and as such not only disturbs juridical regularities but conjures up mystery, sublime, prodigy, awe as well as repulsion. There are practical aspects of this 'disturbance' that affront attempts at the codification of singularum: Guido of Mont Rocher in *Manipulus Curatorum Officio Sacerdotus* (1480) draws attention to this disturbance:

> But what if there is a single monster which has two bodies joined together: ought it to be baptized as one person or as two? I say that since baptism is made according to the soul and not according to the body, howsoever there be two bodies, if these is only one soul, then it ought to be baptized as one person. But if these are two souls, it ought to be baptized as two persons. But how is it to be known if there be one or two? I say that if there be two bodies, there are two

souls. But if there is one body, there is one soul. And for this reason it may be supposed that if there be two chests and two heads there are two souls If, however, there be one chest and one head, however much the other members be doubled, there is only one soul.

(Guido, cited in Friedman, 1981, p. 182)

Disability devotees, conjoined twins and transabled people all in their different ways reveal the limits of social integration and open a shutter onto *terra*-able landscapes of the forbidden. Each of these characters – everyday monsters – becomes undecidable and ambiguous resisting any enduring attempt at correction and therefore symbolises a transgression of law (scientific, religious and ontological). Foucault in *Abnormal, 22nd January 1975 College de France* lectures argues for the differentiation of disability and monstrosity. Whilst disability upsets the social order it is distinct because disability has a place at law. Foucault posits, monstrosity 'calls law into question and disables it' (Foucault, 2003, p. 64). This distinction by Foucault is incorrect. As I have shown in Chapters 3, 4 and 8, the disabled body upsets onto-classifications especially as to the leaky threshold of what counts as disability, normalcy and transient states. It is the disabled body's capacity to resist fixed categorisation that induces an ambivalent misrecognition. Baker and Campbell (2006) have shown this in the Australian case of *Purvis*[1] where there was confusion about the limits of intellectual disability and the ability of this impairment to be disengaged from other aspects of corporeality. The disabled body, contra Foucault is not readily readable and 'changes' according to context, not impairment, hence the division by Foucault into two groups is both arbitrary and artificial. I am convinced that the subject who defies ableist normativity comes to be figured in cultural terms as monstrous or alternatively in the language of medical-technics as 'mad' – pathological. Madness is preoccupied with mentalities:

The civilized person is refined in thought and action. He or she is deemed to live in a reasonable harmony with other, like minded human beings... the madman or madwoman rejects society, refusing (or being unable) to cooperate with others, to organize his behavior, or to adapt herself to prevailing norms.

(Sass, 1994, p. 83)

Madness according to Sass' script is not about mental illness rather can be equated with adaption and conformity with ableist norms. I have refined four propositions deduced from a study by Ingebretson (2001) of modern monsters that can test our confrontation with the abject subjectivities of conjoinment, disability devotees and the transabled:

- Monsters commit an 'offence' that is suggestively desirable;
- Monsters have a freedom we lack;
- The monster is a pedagogue – he or she teaches fear;
- The monster carries the emblem of civic disgrace.

Notes on autonomy and subjectivity

> An able-bodied and competent person is thus a body with a set of given functions, skills and properties, which are steered by a central command unit – the consciousness – which is situated in the head. Agency, mobility, the ability to communicate verbally, to make discretionary judgments make decisions and implement them – is thus located in the body and in the self residing in that body.
>
> (Moser, 2000, p. 205)

Citizenship is a status bestowed on those who are full members of a community. All who possess the status are equal with respect to the rights and duties with which the status is endowed. There is no universal principle that determines what those rights and duties shall be, but societies in which citizenship is a developing institution create an image of an ideal citizenship against which achievement can be measured and towards which aspirations can be directed (Marshall, 1963, p. 87). Probably one of the most influential figurings of enlightenment 'man' can be found in the 1784 tract by Immanuel Kant entitled *What is Enlightenment?* (Kant, 1996). Kant brought together an exposition of the relationship of full personhood to matters of reason and autonomy. For Kant the essence of the enlightenment spirit could be summed up in the slogan *Sapere aude*! 'Have courage to use your own reason!' This quality supposedly offers the resolution (justification) of conflicts between knowledge and power. As Jane Flax (1992, p. 447) puts it,

> ... reason both represents and embodies truth. It partakes of universality in two additional ways: it operates identically in each subject and it can grasp laws that are objectively true; that is, are equally knowable and binding on every person.

Such truths contain the instructions of comportment; how to act in the world or as Foucault would express it, encode 'technologies of self'. The bearer of reason, the disembodied and universalised he-man can arrive at a 'view from nowhere'; find authentic enlightenment by discerning the true nature of things. Hence, the mirage or illusion that people are highly individuated and expected to act autonomously. Matters of bodily locatedness and situated knowledges are easily sidestepped, reduced to the status of persona non-gratia. The human (adult) subject is assumed to be an independent centre of self-consciousness, who holds autonomy to be intrinsically valuable. Neo-liberalism's normative (autonomous) citizen in the words of C.B. Macpherson (1964, p. 3) is a nominal 'possessive individual':

> free in as much as he [sic] is proprietor of his person and capacities. *The human essence* is freedom from dependence *on the will of others, and freedom is a function of possession* . . . Society consists of relations of exchange *between proprietors* (emphasis added).

This imaging of the neo-liberal subject insists that all people fit Macpherson's regulatory ideal. It is probably more correct to say that the thrust of shaping identity is geared towards a 'best fit', normalising or morphed approach. In turn, philosophical formulations of autonomy are often associated with particular conceptions of freedom. For the moment though we can say that autonomy '. . . is said to consist of a capacity, or the exercise of certain competencies, that enables one to reflect on one's aims, aspirations, and motivations and choose one's ends and purposes through such a reflective process' (Barclay, 2000, p. 53). On this basis, autonomy as a form of self-rule becomes problematic in certain stances for persons whose state of being differs from the norm. John Law (1999) reminds us of the consequences and harshness of liberalism's formulation of legitimate personhood:

> . . . if a person measures up, or can be made to measure up, in these respects, then they become competent. If not, then they fail. All of which is, to put it mildly, a drastic divide. A divide, then, which resonates with the liberal concern with persons: but also operates as its dark side.

Within the contemporary Western, freedom is held to be an inalienable and inherent right of the atomistic individual citizen. Freedom is represented as autonomy, invokes the performance of a choosing, desiring and consuming subject. The 'free' citizen is one who can take charge of herself – to act as her own command centre. Such techniques of self are not usually imposed but rather sought, as we are all enrolled into the task of self-appropriation and designation. Such an ideal is an illusion as subjectivity that is always relational, human are bonded together as 'figurations' of people and as such these interdependent networks are not external to the person and diminish atomistic individuation (c.f. Elias, 1991). A drive towards self-mastery may mean that it is not possible for some disabled people to be truly 'free' within the confines of liberalism. These people may lose person status because they fail to meet certain criterion. Under liberalism, the production and governing of disability is facilitated, in part, through its taming into a mere logical and discrete etiological classification and ensuing ontological space. The performative acts of the 'logic of identity' reduce the disparity and difference of disabled bodies to a unity (see Foucault, 1980, p. 117). In law, we find this logic of identity expressed in the ideal of impartiality, which is predicated upon the benchmark legal subject.

The implications of classifying practices go even deeper than this sort of critique suggests. For the unruly, monstrous, and boundary-breaching qualities of disability must be tamed in ways that distinguish that category from other fluid and leaky categories (such as illness, poverty, and ageing) with which it is associated. Corporeal slippages of the disability kind need containment, in order to act as checks on which outlaw disabilities are permissible and assimilatable. Let us consider what the embeddedness of disability implies for understandings of that category and the ways in which disability figurations are mediated in law. The working model of inclusion is really only successful to the extent that people with disabilities are able to 'opt in', or be assimilated (normalised). This model of inclusion assumes that the people who cannot, do not, or otherwise refuse to, 'opt in', will developmentally progress towards autonomy over time.

The governing of liberal unfreedom responds to the problem of what should be done with 'governing the remainder', that is, those who are identified as 'less than fully autonomous' (Hindess, 2000). Hindess identifies three approaches taken to governing 'the remainder'. They are: (1) a clearing away; (2) the compulsion towards disciplinary techniques (e.g. through ableist conditioning) and (3) targeting external causes by creating welfare safety nets. In order to institute such 'dividing practices' of subjectivity, the aberrant subject may be extinguished (either before or after birth); be 're-appraised' (for instance, fabricated as a 'rehabilitated person'); become nearly able-bodied (via a morphed passing); or become benevolently transfigured into a 'deserving' welfare recipient *supra* the economy. Tendencies towards disability are put out by pathologising desire. It is this aspect to which we now turn.

Desiring disability – Towards an ethics of affirmation

> Desire: a kind of madness, an enchantment, exaltation, anguish... perhaps the foundation of a lifetime of happiness. Writing about desire: compulsive, a challenge, self-indulgence, anxiety... above all, a project that defies completion.
>
> (Belsey, 1994, p. 3)

It should be evident by now that people with impairments considered as disabled have had to live under the enormous weight of negative figurations of disablement. I hope that I have clearly demonstrated that this burden is not just a surface discomfort restricted to the arena of discrimination and prejudice. Rather, regimes of ableism have produced a depth of disability negation that reaches into the caverns of collective subjectivity to the extent that the notion of disability as inherently negative is seen as a 'naturalized' reaction to an aberration. Having said this, it is all the more extraordinary that disabled people have not yielded to this repression but have resisted docility and engaged in transgressive figurations of disability. Certain subjugated desires can, in their unfreedom, cultivate alternate kinds of liberty.

The placement of concepts such as 'desire' and 'disability' within a single context almost appears to be an oxymoron. We may well question whether a concept like desire, which has almost wholly been figured in heterosexual and ableist terms, can be harnessed so that it is capable of accommodating the very categories on whose exclusion it has made feasible? This discussion of desire is developed within a framework of some of Michel Foucault's early writings (1976, 1998). It will explore the relevance or otherwise of Foucaultian 'desire' in its consideration of 'disability' as oppositional ontology and engage in a project of alternative formulations. I open discussions by briefly surveying various philosophical treatments of the desire question in order to assess their usefulness to this undertaking. Next, I signal some of the quandaries that may emerge in applying desire and disability in the same context. The final section moves into an analysis of conflicting practices of *reading* desire and disability, in the form of the pathologisation of disability desire.

Our discussion engages the imagination by playing dangerously (yet cautiously) with matters of 'disability' 'desire', 'pride', 'culture' and a transgressive aesthetic. It is a vulnerable conversation, a *speaking otherwise* about 'disability'. By adopting the 'thought of the outside' (as expressed by Foucault, 1998) and repositioning our gaze it maybe possible to open up 'spaces' for oppositional technologies of self that posit disability as a positive erotic, grounds for subjugated celebratory experiences of disability.

Some philosophical treatments of the desire question

This does not mean that I proposed to write a history of the successive conceptions of desire, ... but rather to analyse the practices by which individuals were led to focus their attention on themselves, to decipher, recognize, and acknowledge themselves as subjects of desire, bringing into play between themselves and themselves a certain relationship that allows them to discover, in desire the truth of their being, be it natural or fallen.

(Foucault, 1976, p. 5)

The disabled body is a site of struggle over its signification and corresponding social meaning. As such, the task of discerning the relationship of desire and disability must be concerned with the conditions of the disabled body's referentiality. In other words, we need to keep reflecting on the prevailing conditions that not only make the disabled body intelligible but also enable us to refer to disability in a particular way. Instead of desire being a peripheral preoccupation within Western philosophy, Michel Foucault notes that in reality the desiring subject has performed as a central theme within the tradition, even in those philosophical strands that seemingly disassociate themselves from such concerns (Foucault, 1985, p. 5).

The treatment of the desiring subject however has not been uniform. Rather discussions of desire have oscillated between two frames of reference, either *desire as sex*, following Freud; or *desire as power*, following Hegel (and later Foucault). Indeed as Hugh Silverman remarks, 'these two models [still] dominate twentieth century continental philosophy ... [and can be] situated in the context of the whole history and text of Western metaphysics' (Silverman, 2000, p. 2). In this chapter, I am concerned with the latter, *desire as power*. Frederick Hegel's master/slave dialectic formulated in *The Phenomenology of Spirit* (1977) has in many works been allocated a pre-eminent position (Butler, 1987,

1995; Silverman, 2000). For Hegel desire was formulated in terms of lack, a type of longing that remains unsatisfied. This Hegelian desire Grosz explains has a 'peculiar object all of its own – its object is always another desire. The desire of the Other is thus the only appropriate object of desire' (1995, p. 176). We could consider the use of Hegelian desire theory as a means to reconnect desire with disability (as Other) and therefore close the gap between kinds of difference. Such a strategy may have limitations – the catch is that desire is figured on the basis of unsatisfactoriness that is hardly conducive to the development of an ethics of affirmation. Desire, understood in this way, may have the appearance of rupturing and subverting existing constitutional arrangements but in reality, Hegelian desire is predicated on the maintenance of bodily polarisations. Such polarisations may end up re-instilling the notion of disability as deficient.

Contrary to popular perceptions the enactment of desire is not a free-for-all, rather the substance of desire is always played out within a regime of power relations, where the so-called 'perversions' are a fixture of the game (Foucault, 1976, p. 48). The very imaginary of desire is mediated by the productivity of power. *Reading* 'disability' in a positive ontological light requires an *a priori* negotiation with what Foucault refers to as the instrumental effects of the 'implantation of perversions', the consolidation and fortification of tangential desiring:

> The implantation of perversions is an instrument – effect: it is through the isolation, intensification, and consolidation of peripheral sexualities that the relations of power to sex and pleasure branched out and multiplied, measured the body and penetrated modes of conduct.
>
> (Foucault, 1976, p. 48)

These peripheral desirings, the will-to-truth do not occur in isolation. Rather they are framed within a 'double bind' of individualisation and totalisation. Strategies of dispersal and division – 'dividing practices'[2] result not only in the phenomenon of *internalised ableism* but also in an ontological separation of the normal from the pathological. On this basis, Foucault's' hermeneutics of desire suggests that a desire towards emulation of the ableist subject mitigates against the development of desiring disability outside of the realms of the perverse. Indeed the very necessity to mark off 'matter out of place' requires the subjugation of tangential corporeal forms and behaviours. The insurrectionary challenge then is to take up these 'implantation of perversions' and map out new territories of desire, to develop as Foucault puts it, 'the thought of the outside', a thought at the margins of culture:

> A thought that stands outside subjectivity, setting its limits as though from within, articulating its end, making its dispersion shine forth, taking in only its invincible absence; and that, at the same time, stands at the threshold of all positivity, not in order to grasp its foundations or justification but in order to regain the space of its unfolding, the void serving as its site, the distance in which it is constituted and into which its immediate certainties slip the moment they are glimpsed – a thought that, in relation to the interiority of our philosophical reflection and the positivity of our knowledge, constitutes what in a phrase we might call 'the thought of the outside'.
>
> (1998, p. 150)

It is in between these conflictual traces of subjectivity that the perverse inkling of disability desire, an insurrected ontology, lurk. For Foucault, 'the thought of the outside' contains a double imperative: (negative) desire reaches into our (disabled) interiority, the emptiness, and the state of be-ing outside: 'the fact that one is irremediably outside the outside ... infinitely unfold[ing] outside any enclosure' (154). Whilst inaugurating a space for positivity to unfold, Foucault's later work on governmentality (1991, 1997b) extends his analysis of desire towards a conception of 'conduct of conduct'. The concept of government as 'conduct of conduct' provides a useful theoretical mechanism for examining devoteeism especially the techniques that form conduct by working on the devotees' desires and beliefs. Desire shapes how we behave and act on others and ourselves. In terms of our discussion what are we to make of these ideas and are they helpful? Foucault is correct that we can never really 'know' the outside, the liminal margins because its 'essence' remains inherently unknowable and ambiguous.

Desiring disability or disability and desire?

The influence of the 'personal tragedy theory' of disability, a position that formulates disability as *inherently* negative, cannot but have an impact on our negotiations concerning desire and disability. It is difficult, if not impossible in this present moment, to *speak of disability as desirous or desirable* given the overwhelming influence of such negative ontologies. Alain Giami has reached a similar conclusion in his research

on disability pornography. Giami (2003, p. 44) notes, 'la représenta-
tion visuelle de personnes handicapées dans des documents considérés
comme pornographiques apparaît *a priori* impensable'.[3] As Swain and
French (2000) point out one cannot assume that the so-called 'emancipatory models' of disability (such as the Social Model) are supportive of
an affirmative approach to impairment, or are underpinned by a non-
tragedy perspective. Certainly many practitioners and academics who
embrace contemporary disability studies theoretical paradigms draw
the line to different degrees on the notion of celebrating and indeed
enjoying disability.

When it comes to matters of 'desire' (and in a more narrow sense
'sex') the status of disability takes on an act of perversion. We may ask
whether it is possible or indeed advisable to break this circuit and envis-
age disability as a desirous, celebratory possibility. When disability and
desire are placed in close proximity, the question of 'what is excited
and incited?' needs to be invoked (see Figure 3). In the case of disability
pornography, is there a double edged focus on 'something more' and
'something less thus revealing the hiddeness of disability and the ambiguity of compassion? (Giami, 2003). Additionally the linking of desire
and disability confronts the performance of gender by problematising
the construction(s) of masculinity and femininity.

Two problems or concerns become apparent when tackling these matters. What does it mean to speak in terms of *desiring disability*? The
answer seems incumbent on the location of the speaking position of
the addressee. For a self-identified disabled person, the matter relates
directly to the formation of individual subjectification and ontological
positioning. Power not only forms the subject by naming the conditions
of its existence but also simultaneously inaugurates specific trajectories
of desire. To step outside of the normative trajectories of negativity, not
only destabilises the conception of disability, but also confuses and disrupts the processes of subjectification by confronting the 'goodness' of
disability. Such an act is subversion because to position the impaired
body as erotic is perverse – I posture that ontologically the disabled
body *qua* body is perverse. I want to be clear here, I am saying that
the impaired body outside of the subsets of sex – desire and pleasure
is of itself perverse. Hugh Hefner, editor of *Playboy* magazine, describes
the erotisation of disabled people as the 'dirty underbelly of human sexuality' (Waxman Fiduccia, 1999, p. 279). By *desiring disability* the subject
adopts an oppositional trajectory of desire, demanding to be represented
as one who delights in the state of be-ing disabled and re-cognising disability. If this is the case, what kinds of possibilities become imaginable

Figure 3   Embracing Life (1999) Photographer: Belinda Mason.

when 'disability' is re-cast (or inverted) in terms of 'desire'? Is it possible to carnally fantasise about 'disability'?

The matter of desiring disability becomes a different one, when the desirer's standpoint or speaking position is situated within the purview of being 'able-bodied', that is identifying as a non-disabled person (even if they are bodily impaired – to use that reductionist term!). Their gaze refracts the disabled person as Other (albeit as 'positive' Other). What if our different/missing/deviant bits/oozing fluids/states are the *very sources* of that desire/fetish? As Waxman points out [able-bodied] people who have sex with disabled people are stigmatised and are seen as sexual suspects. What 'crime' have they committed? Waxman proposes that pornographic imagery of men having sex with disabled women is especially viewed as perverted, lewd and contaminated because it is under girded by paedophilic imagery – a belief that the man is attracted to having sex with a (perpetual) child. She remarks, 'It [sex] blows the lids off one of the last taboos, sex with a cripple, which in both a moral and public policy sense, is analogous to paedophilia and incest' (Waxman Fiduccia, 1999, p. 280). In 1997 Dr Richard Bruno (1997) proposed the psychological concept of *Factitious Disability Disorder* to explain and medicalise the desires of people termed 'devotees', 'pretenders' and 'wannabees', that is people who desire disabilities or people with disabilities. How reasonable is the assumption that a desire for 'disabled' bodies automatically connotes pathologisation on the part of the admirer? Can 'disability' as a bodily signifier be 'queered'?

The second aspect of concern relates to the broader question of representations of desire and disability. People with disabilities have a long history of association with the carnivalesque and freak shows in particular (Cohen et al., 1996). One of the first modern portrayals of disability in the erotic can be found in the 1987 July edition of *Playboy* magazine featuring images of quadriplegic Ellen Stohl in a provocative pose on a bed. This tightly choreographed image concealed her paralysed legs. Waxman described the uproar that this early image caused from some feminists with disabilities that the images 'reproduced non-disabled values of sexual attractiveness... Stoll [sic] started a controversy which got the fledgling disabled feminists [sic] community talking' (Waxman Fiduccia, 1999, p. 279). Seven years later the controversy still had not died down – so provocative was the image of sexualised disabled women. In enacting the erotic, great care is necessary in order to ensure that representations do not end up reinscribing problematic images of abjection and alterity. Fascination with alternate images and the explorations of conversations about the erotic and disablement have come from another of those peripheral sexualities Foucault (1976) spoke of: queer sexualities. Gay fetish and S & M magazine *Drummer* issue 93 featured a photographic exhibition titled 'Maimed Beauty' by photographer George Dureau in conjunction with a commentary 'Different Bodies' by Max Verga (Dureau and Lucie-Smith, 1995; Verga, 2000). Unlike the typical images of disabled 'soft' porn that rarely deviate from traditional constructions of beauty, for example well-endowed, blonde-haired person and blue eyed (i.e. like Stohl), the men with disabilities photographed by Dureau were African-American and predominantly from local, poor neighbourhoods of New Orleans. Verga's descriptions of the works are instructive:

> Ragged edged black and white portraits with a lack of background detail that forces the viewer to focus attention on the subject, often portrayed naked. George presents disability without visual comment or apology. George's subjects had not been in any war other than the war that rages around poverty. Some of them had been in prison. Others would wind up there. Some were from middle-class backgrounds, with only disabilities thrusting them to the fringes of society.
>
> (Verga, 2000, p. 4)

Shifting the spotlight on those practices that lead us to focus on ourselves enables a recognition and acknowledgment of ourselves as *subjects of desire*. It is not only able-bodied people who experience the 'cringe – effect' when exposed to the sexual desire of disability – but also disabled people themselves also often feel an awkward 'strangeness' when confronted with mirroring imagery. The erotic photography of George Dureau presents an affirming image of the beauty of disability, not of docility and despair. They speak of desiring disability. I am in complete agreement with Verga's summation:

> It was not hard to be impressed by the beauty of George's photos and the desirability of his subjects... beautiful as they were, the photographs only hinted at the sexual power they depicted... Unlike the photos of Diane Arbus, which emphasize the grotesque qualities of her subjects... Dureau's photographs suggest nobility through the directness of the images.
>
> (Verga, 2000)

More and more groups of disabled people are deciphering desire on their/our terms. A website, Bent voices (www.bentvoices.org), has been established to share the stories of disabled gay men and in scholarly circles there is the emergence of queer/crip/disability literature (Luczak, 2007; McRuer, 2006; McRuer & Wilkerson, 2002). The Society for Disability Studies has a queer caucus. In this collaborative exchange, 'points of contact' are occurring between queer and disability cultures in developing the 'thought of the outside' (Crutchfield & Epstein, 2000). One source of potentially transgressive discourses on desiring disability has come from the unexpected quarter of disability devotees, conjoined twins and transabled people. These three quite different groups have in the past few years been developing a kind of sociology of peripheral beingness 'from below'.

Desiring togetherness: The enigma of conjoinment

> I don't hate being a conjoined twin. It's the stuff that comes with it.
> (Lori Schappell, in Conjoined twins 2000)

Conjoined twins challenge the normative citizen (the individual capable of enumeration) who occupies modern thought, institutions and practices built on and ordered around it. Conjoinment is perplexing for many reasons – one being the seismic rearrangement of self-in-relation. In the place of an autonomous, stable, singular and detached self wherein the body is often conceptually bypassed, conjoined twins posit ambiguous and shared bodily boundaries, negotiated selfhood and the possibility of being together in one. Two persistent questions arise in discourses about conjoinment: what does individuality mean in terms of conjoinment and how are sexual matrices of 'wrong' bodies to be understood? It was John Locke who in *An Essay Concerning Human Understanding* (1689) tried to grapple with the unspeakability and corporeal ambiguity of changelings: 'Shall the want of a Nose, or a Neck, make a Monster, and put such Issue out of the rank of Men; the want of Reason and Understanding, not?' (Locke, 1979: Bk 4, Ch 4, 571–572). Locke unwittingly concluded that physical borders which individuate human beings from each other were not necessarily indicative of the metaphysical boundaries of persons. In other words, the edges of the somatic are not necessarily equated with boundaries of subjectivity.

Like other disabled people, conjoined twins struggle with maintaining a specifically embodied subjectivity in tandem with the compulsion to emulate ableist normativity: 'Frankly we're fine you know. We lead regular, normal lives. We do everything every-body else does, you know' (Lori Schappel, in Conjoined twins 2000). This should come as no surprise given the discursive legacies of monstrosity which to this day feature in encounters and official records such as medical and law reports. There is no mistaking the fact that conjoined twins constitutes two persons, which in plain language is usually translated as two individuals. Certainly in today's environment conjoined twins represent an affront to scientific ableism which views human duality as pathological. The judgment in the English Court of Appeal case *Re A (Children) (Conjoined Twins: Surgical Separation)*[4] affronts the communality and intersubjectivity of conjoinment. Whilst the court recognised babies Jodie and Mary (real names: Gracie and Rosie Attard) as separate rights-bearers with legal status, their unified bodies were driven towards individualism, abstraction and posited as opposing forces. The rights-based agenda underlying the petition for surgical separation adopted a mode of antagonistic, hostile social relations. Mary became the aggressor figure, a parasite stealing life from Jodie:

Mary may have a right to life, but she has little right to be alive. She is alive because and only because, to put it bluntly, but none the less accurately, she sucks the lifeblood of Jodie and she sucks the lifeblood out of Jodie. She will survive only so long as Jodie survives. Jodie will not survive long because constitutionally she will not be able to cope. Mary's parasitic living will be the cause of Jodie's ceasing to live. If Jodie could speak, she would surely protest, 'Stop it, Mary, you're killing me'. Mary would have no answer to that.

(4 All ER 961, per Lord Justice Ward, at 1010)

Dreger (2004) proposes a 'sex and morality' thesis to explain the shift towards compulsory separation arguing that surgeon have been motivated mainly by disgust at the thought of adult twins becoming sexually active and intermingling. Despite the rhetoric to maintain a two agency approach, from the position of intersubjectivity it is clear that there is something more going on, indescribable beyond named language – heteroglossic subjectivities unified. This said, holding onto the body integrity of twins is critical for the biopolitical context could easy demand that one 'body' be marked as an organistic remnant or as a 'lost appendage' (c.f. Murray, 2001). Consider the remark of a surgeon tendered to the court in *Re A(Children)*:

This (permanent union) condemns a *potentially normal* Jodie to *carry her very abnormal* sister, Mary, throughout the life of both (emphasis added).

(4 All ER 961 at 976)

The surgeon's comments are loaded with fluid subjectivities to describe the girls. Jodie is potentially normal – does that mean 'nearly able-bodied'? And poor Mary is characterised as a 'burden', an 'abnormal' despite the fact that the twins are interconnected. Dreger (2004) asserts through her historical research on conjoinment that most twins preferred conjoinment to life as singletons: 'They seem to be as disinclined to be separated as singletons are to be joined' (Dreger, 1998, p. 10). The conjoined body(ies) disturbs ableist arrangements of the normal and normalcy is implicated in the decisions about the separation of twins founded on a belief in the *preferability* of singleton status, despite the production of additional impairment and even death for the twins. Suggested in the judgment of Lord Justice Walker is that Mary would acquire body integrity even in death, leading to the thought that Mary and Jodie did not have body integrity in their conjoinment. The twisted logic of ableism not only argues that conjoined twins are not normal but must be made to resemble the norm even if other impairments and non-life ensue:

If you look at it in terms of Mary dying, no, there is not a therapeutic benefit. If you look at it in terms of what Mary's life would be like attached forever to her sister, then it is not a benefit for her to remain attached to her sister: she will be much happier if she is separate.

([2000] 4 All ER 961 at 983, per Lord Justice Ward)

We have a reversal of the kind of legal reasoning found in wrongful life torts (see Chapter 9) where the disabled life is preferred to non-existence to the following commentary about what to do with Mary. Non-existence (death) *with bodily integrity* is preferable to disability/conjoinment and by association, non-bodily integrity:

The only *gain* I can see is that the operation would, if successful, give Mary the bodily integrity and dignity *which is the natural order for all of us*. But this is a wholly illusory goal because she will be dead before she can enjoy her independence and she will die because, when she is independent, she has no capacity for life.

([2000] 4 All ER 961 at 998, per Lord
Justice Ward), Emphasis added

Twins who have only known conjoinment psychically transform that confined denotation to conjure an existence that is bodily different and an integral part of their being:

> We just happen to be born at birth with the corner of our forehead and that side of us connected and that's it and that is where that ends. Even though its there all the time, its not there all the time for us. I mean we still lead normal productive, everyday lives. We're not solely conjoined twins. I get tired of everyone thinking about that that's all we are, are conjoined twins. I'm just conjoined to another human being.
>
> (Lori Schappell, in Conjoined twins 2000)

Sensing their bridge differently, Masha and Dasha Krivoshlyapova, despite being subjected to cruel medical experiments at the Moscow Pediatric Institute when they were children, would not agree to separation surgery:

> We just don't need it. Even when we were little we did not want that ... We're 50 now. We'll stay like this for the rest of our lives.
>
> (Dasha Krivoshlyapova, in Conjoined twins 2000)

Abigail and Brittany Hensel turned 18 years of age in 2008. On that occasion Abigail remarked, 'We don't know any other way of living and don't want to go through surgery. Even if it worked we wouldn't be able to do all the things we do now' (Telegraph News, 2008). Instead of seeing conjoinment in terms of deficiency the Hensels have been able to transcend such an ableist compulsion and see their soma-subjectivity in terms of affirming possibility. Heidegger (1962) pointed out that Dasein or beingness which appears closed around extends itself by extending boundaries and maintains its central orientation towards closeness. It is clear that for some conjoinment is the ultimate form of closeness and intercommunality:

The best thing about being a conjoin twin is that there is always someone to talk to, you are never alone.
(Abby and Brittany Hensel (together), in Extraordinary people: The twins who share a body, 2007)

We are a little collective. We share our grief and our tears.
(Masha Krivoshlyapova, in Conjoined twins, 2000)

Intersentiency is not just at the level of tactile and sensory inter-faces but extends to psychic discernment irrespective of differences in personality. The sharing reaches out to gaze at the world. Even the points of separation become problematic, as surgeons decipher-ing which 'bits' belong to which twin are literally constructing rather than separating the atomistic body. Expressions of dependency or independence are reliant upon the contingencies of complex material relations that have their textures and rhythms, producing very specific spatialities and affectations. Conjoined twins have forms of sentiency-in-negotiation, in taking turns, sometimes acting as signs of contrari-ness in one. Brittany Hensel describes the process of driving a motor vehicle:

Abby takes over the pedals and um the shifter [gear shift] and I take over Abby & Brittany come in together and speak: 'we both, we both steer'. and I take over the blinker, and the lights. We gotta go where we are going so we know whether we are going.
(Brittany Hensel, in Extraordinary people: The twins who share a body, 2007)

Biomedicalism is obsessed with carving up body bits and arranging them into their correct places, to clean up disorder and put matter *back in place*. What is lost in this quest is the exploration of the wonderful adaptive qualities of human functioning and the complex forms of psy-chic transmogrification that provide a well-spring of intelligence around intercommunality:

I think people need to look at Abby and Brittany as through the eyes of a child and accept them for what you see and quit trying to figure out how does this work, how does that work, how do you do this, how do you do that, and just know that it works because you can see that. We may never know how Abby and Brittany work but isn't it great that they can. Every part of their life is co-operating with each other to make it all go.

(Patty Hensel [mother], in Extraordinary people:
The twins who share a body, 2007)

Continuing our discussion of subjectivities that test the limits of ableist norms and offering points of transgression, the next section turns to people labelled disability (or sometimes amputee) devotees. These are people who have certain impaired bodyscapes as their points of desire, people who are not necessarily turned on by ableist sites of beauty.

Hot on disability: disability devoteeism as an affront to ableist norms?

As a matter of fact or beside the point, it doesn't matter, it's said as a common proverb in Italy that the person who hasn't slept with the cripple doesn't know Venus in her perfect sweetness. Luck, or some particular accident, put this saying in the mouth of the people long ago; and it's said of males as well as of females. For the Queen of the Amazons replied to the Scythian who invited her for love: 'the cripple does it best.' In this female republic, in order to get away from male domination, they maimed ('amputated' or 'mangled') during childhood, arms, legs, and other members which gave them an advantage over the women, and they used the men only for what we've used women in fact. I would have said that the swaying motion of the cripple might bring some new pleasure to the toil (of love) and some bit of sweetness to those who try it, but I've just learned that even ancient philosophy was decided in that; it says that since the legs and thighs of crippled women, because of their imperfection, don't get the nourishment that is due them, it follows that the genitals, which are right about them, are fuller, more nourished and more vigorous. Or that, this default prohibiting exercise, those who are tainted use less force and come more fully to the games of Venus.

(Michel De Montaigne (1588). *Essays*, Book III,
Chapter XI 'Of Cripples')

Disability 'devotees', so-called 'pretenders' and 'wannabees' have been engaging in peripheral sexual desires throughout history as attested to by the epigram written by Montaigne in 1588. This population however has only been medically delineated since the late 1880s. My exploration is interested in how the *processes* of ableism respond to the phenomena of attraction towards aspects of disability and the ways the devotee world has the potential to challenge the self-concept of people with disabilities and the formation of an affirmative ontology. I do not intend to present a psychological study concerned with 'causation' questions nor do I wish to propose any explanatory frameworks related to 'origin' fixations. Before proceeding any further, working definitions are necessary:

- *Devotees* are individuals (usually who identify as able-bodied) who are attracted to, fascinated by, or obsessed with, people with a physical disability and their orthosis and/or prostheses. Attraction to people with an amputation seems to be the most documented form; whereas
- *Pretenders* (a dreadful word really) refers to someone who, at times, likes to pretend they have an impairment usually by mimicking mannerisms, gestures, movement (they deem to be 'impaired') or using assistive devices like callipers. Individuals identifying with this group do not necessarily (beyond the fabrication) wish to become bodily 'impaired'; and finally
- *Transabled people* (sometimes known as *body dysphoria, body identity integrity disorder, wannabees*): Someone who has an intense and overpowering desire to have a physical or sensory impairment. Individuals experiencing this 'desire' argue that they feel 'abnormal' in their current bodies and incomplete without a particular body part missing or reshaped. The person needs to be physically or sensorily impaired to be 'whole'.

As is the case with any working definition these divisions are not clear-cut, some individuals oscillate between all three classifications. One of the central inquiries that emerged within discursive genealogies of disablement in the nineteenth century was the persistent question, 'Who are you?' In the case of people who desire persons with disabilities or the manifestation of impairment, this enduring question makes reappearance together with an obsession with matters of origin and causation, speculating about 'truth' in order to seek the resolution of a perceived 'problem'. This critical inquiry into devotees, pretenders and transabled (hereafter referred to as D-P-T) hinges around not only the basis of the pathology and meaning given to D-P-T but also the way pathologisation inscribes and marks out the terrain of disability and desire. It is for this reason that this study will be analysed in terms of the ways disability and the devotee are constituted. For as Butler (1997a, p. 41) reminds us:

The subject is constituted...in language through a selective process in which the terms of legible and intelligible subjecthood are regulated. The subject is called a name, but 'who' the subject is depends as much on the names that he or she is never called: the possibilities of linguistic life are both inaugurated and foreclosed through the name.

It is useful at this point to indicate the profile of devotees. The literature indicates that individuals categorised under this banner are overwhelmingly male, heterosexual and white. Whilst this maybe the case, this description may not be wholly accurate. For instance, in early studies of 'homosexual' behaviour and culture a similar characterisation was made. It was only as the canon of gay studies matured that female same-sex desire was acknowledged as just as prevalent, albeit hidden from the gaze of sexologists (Abelove et al., 1993; Greene et al., 1994).[5] I believe that this maybe the case regarding women identifying as D-P. On the basis of the devotee figured as male, Storrs (1996) indicates their ideal woman to be: '...blue-eyed, blonde, 29 years old, five foot five inches tall, 123 pounds, has one leg amputated above the knee and definitely is not wearing a prosthesis'. Surprisingly then a key study (see Bruno, 1997) of D-P-T uses as its sole case studies the accounts of two women. Due to the unusualness of D-P-T the quest to explain and understand their behaviour can also be understood in terms of a desire by 'experts' to erase ambivalence and ambiguity of D-P-T life and create certainty about human variation. The transabled e-lists are in contrast populated by a significant number of women. Three possibilities exist, one is to medicalise and pathologise D-P-T desire (the aim therefore is treatment or cure), another is to figure D-P-T desiring as another among the myriad of diversities and thirdly, to study D-P-T outside of a pathological frame (maybe sociological), with the D-P-T 'voice' as the centre of analysis. In spite of these methodological options, biomedicalism as a powerful explanatory framework has been the dominant response in trying to make sense of desiring disability.

A small study by Richard Bruno (1997) *has* taken on canonical status both within the devotee and disability communities, amongst those hostile or affirming of devotees. Bruno was not the first doctor to delineate D-P-T desire but he provides a study that summarises much of the psychiatric literature on this topic.[6] His review of psychological theories is used to propose *inter alia* the inclusion into the DSM of a new category of mental disorder termed *Factitious Disability Disorder*. Bruno

(1997, pp. 249–251) documents four kinds of explanations outlined here without comment on my part:[7]

1. The D-P-T has a preference for the disabled body because it is a less threatening and thus a more attainable 'love object';
2. D-P-T attraction is associated with unresolved disability related stimulus experiences;
3. D-P-T attraction falls into the bounds of the sexual 'perversions' of homosexuality, sadism and bondage; and finally
4. There is a high incidence of *body dysphoria* amongst D-P-T – i.e. a 'disabled person trapped within a nondisabled body'.

The personality characterisation painted by Bruno of devotees is that of an obsessive predator who is excessively solicitous towards people with disabilities. Whilst there have been reports of unsavoury behaviours (such as stalking) by some D-P-T these actions cannot be seen as behaviour definitive of the group as a whole. On the contrary, Child and King (1992) in the *Manifesto of OverGround*, an organisation whose constituency are people 'attracted to others with disabilities', reminds devotees of their obligation 'to give consideration to the rights and dignity of people with disabilities. *OverGround* wants devotees to be aware of the vulnerabilities of people with disabilities...'. After participation in an online forum of devotees disability activist and journalist Bob Storrs (1996) refutes Bruno's characterisation slur arguing for the *normalcy* of D-P-T:

> I was surprised to find them neither sick nor psychotic. The participants are computer analysts, doctors, engineers, and college educated professionals. There is much discussion of the guilt caused by their 'socially unacceptable attraction' and the fear that others will attack them for their 'dirty little secret' many describe a terrible frustration at their inability to find a disabled person to date....

Despite these observations, Bruno advocates deviancy making as the clinical response to D-P-T. Although Bruno points out that after a century of research clinicians have yet to determine the origin of D-P-T attraction he suggests that those with factitious physical disabilities (akin to Munchausen's syndrome) can be included with D-P-T to create a new diagnostic grouping *Factitious Disability Disorder* (FDD) as the ultimate explanatory model for this kind of 'implanted perversion'. His delineation is interesting in not only what it says of D-P-T but also what it implies about disabled people: '[The condition] in which dis-ability – real or pretended, one's own or that of another – provides an opportunity to be loved and attended to where no such opportunity has otherwise existed' (Bruno, 1997, p. 256). This classification would appear to institute the impossibility of communion between an 'abled bodied' person and a person with a disability where the attraction is in part disability orientated. A point of clarity is required here, many able-bodied people argue that they should not be considered devotees as such because their attraction is to the person in spite of their disability. This distancing/disavowal of the centrality of disability may remind the reader of the rationalisations adopted by some men in same-sex rela-tionships – 'I am not gay I am attracted to a wonderful person who just happens to be male'. The literature about devotees assumes that devotees et al. are able-bodied. It is profoundly silent about devotees who have disabilities being attracted to other people with impairment (either with the same impairment or different from their own). Given the overarching context of a biomedical explanatory framework and the figuration of disability as inherently negative, I want to shift our atten-tion to the self-perception of devotees how they read their bodies and desires and chart the relations between what is sayable and visible.

The narratives of devotees bear an uncanny resemblance to the nar-rative of the early homophile sub-cultures and identity politics of the gay community (Abelove et al., 1993). I have already mentioned that Foucault's (1997a) notion of governmentality may be a useful tool for analysis of shifts in devotee subjectivity. By honing in on that aspect of 'conduct of conduct', is it possible to see how devotees make sense of 'who' they 'are' by using prevalent discourses of desire and deviancy as filters of referentiality? Fraught with guilt and shame, devotees initially found a home in the world of psychiatry and psy-therapies. What they wanted was an explanation of the disease, a treatment and hopefully a 'cure'. Over time as individuals gathered, shared stories and engaged in the exchange of tacit knowledges, devotees began to resist the clutches of psychiatry and what was sayable about devoteeism and develop their own counter-discourse not just about their desire, but a counter dis-course of impairment. In the beginning the subversive response was a rather predictable return to immutability justifications and biologi-cal determinism. As Child and King (1992) articulate in the *OverGround Manifesto*: '... devotees and wannabees are not responsible for acquiring their interests. These phenomena are neither sick nor sinful *per se*, but different'. Building upon the biological argument 'Paul', a devotee in an academic styled article *Disability as a Symbol of the Ultimate Other*, posits that men are searching for symbols of femininity and D-P-T (whom he intentionally restricts his arguments to males) are attracted to female devotees (he is silent about other impairment attractions):

> ...because the absence of one or several limbs...is a symbol of this essential absence, which, of course, is everything but a void. So being an amputee would be a strong symbol of femininity. Therefore, my opinion is that the devotee is not attracted to the stump(s) in particular, but to the symbol of the absence it represents, reinforcing the difference, that is a women, as a whole, the exact one that he defined as fitted to be his partner.
>
> (Paul, 2002)

The difficultly with 'Paul's' argument is that it is predicated not just on the notion of *desire as absence* (or lack) but also on a belief in an Aristotelian notion (see Chapter 8) of woman as a mutilated male. The stump reads as a signifier of mutilation, a deficient void in need of filling. Recently some devotees have begun to reject psychiatric interpretations of desire as pathological and have employed discourses of normalisation to defend their position. 'Jeff', a devotee, explains disability desire as an attraction to a specific physical attribute along the lines of other attractions people are permitted to have; attraction towards blondes ('Jeff', quoted in Aguilera, 2000, p. 261). Likewise, 'J' sums up this normalcy:

> There's nothing bad about having feelings of attraction towards people with particular impairment. It doesn't mean you're sick or wicked. It just means you are attracted to people with particular impairments. Nothing to be ashamed of, nothing to be guilty about ('J', 2002).

It becomes clear that it is not enough to acknowledge that disability devotees exist but that the search for explanatory frameworks is critical for the formation of devotee subjectivity. The matter of 'managing' and governing their behaviours ensures that devotees after understanding the 'nature of problem' behave 'properly'. The devotee world is now a well-organised global network of interests with a range of social organisations, Internet sites and commercial enterprises (often run by amputee women). This networking has increased contact between other devotees and their visibility to the organised disability community. In response to the hostilities from some amputee organisations – devotees have been forced to articulate their desire in a more nuanced and refined fashion as part of the dialogical process with disability studies scholars and disability groups.

Re-orientating desire . . . and disability

Alison Kafer (2000) documents the trend within the rehabilitation context to encourage women amputees to cover (read: conceal) their stumps with clothing or cosmetic prosthesis in order to avoid the possibility of being 'somewhat unattractive and disturbing'. This kind of attitude has resulted in disabled women being embarrassed by their bodily differences and engaging in strategies that draw attention away from those anomalies. Such engagements in acts of concealment are fundamentally based on a belief in the *inherent* negativity of impairment and produce as an effect, disability self-hatred. This can be witnessed in the reasoning adopted by some members of the Amputee Coalition of America (ACA) whose hostility to devotees likens D-P-T desire to paedophilia. The 'troubles' of amputees towards devotees is that they focus on something that is understood by the women as a loss, as a deficiency. As Solvang (2002, p. 6) puts it, '. . . the last thing they find attractive is a special interest in the very part of the body signifying this sorrow [loss of limb]'.

Devotees point out that many disabled people find it hard to believe that their disability can enhance their attractiveness. Recent sociologically orientated literature has documented that once a women with an impairment 'gets her head' around the idea that a man is attracted to her (and her impairment) this realisation has contributed to a significant rise in self-esteem – pointing to the importance of being desired (Kafer, 2000; Solvang, 2002). One of the fundamental flaws of the predatorial and pathological argument espoused by Bruno (1997) and other clinicians is that much of the reasoning is premised on the belief that people with disabilities are passive, docile and therefore are in need of care and protection. Whilst this maybe the case in certain instances especially with individuals who are newly injured, such an assertion denies the deliberative agency of disabled people. It is assumed that people with disabilities are incapable of making choice about with whom to have sex or form a relationship. Aguilera's criticism of Bruno' study is along these lines: '. . . he] pathologises the attraction, and thus demeans disabled community [sic]. Not only are we unattractive, but we also are apparently unable to make our own decisions' (2000, p. 258). Erasure of agency and the accusation of exploitation are easy to make in sector known for its paternalism, patriarchalism and sex-aversion. Kafer (2000), whose study concerns amputees involved in the devotee community, argues that much of the literature by focusing almost exclusively on devotees perpetuates a belief in amputees being mere silent bystanders, victims of men's desire.[8]

Journey into disability: Transabled assaults on ableism

I've always gotten stares, you know the ones that people give you or avoid giving you; but once and awhile while weaving in and out of the crowds of people I'd catch someone looking at me and I'd see something else in their eyes, jealousy. They were jealous of me, jealous that I got to sit down and they didn't. Does that sound crazy to you? Carlos Brooks Director/Writer of *Quid, Pro Quo* (2008), Voice of Nick Stahl, paraplegic journalist.

...there is a simple, relentless logic to these people's request for amputation. 'I am suffering,' they tell me. 'I have no where else to turn'. They realise that life as an amputee will not be easy. They understand the problems they will have with mobility, with work, with their social lives; they realize they will have to make count-less adjustment just to get through the day. They are willing to pay their own way. Their bodies belong to them, they tell me. The choice should be theirs. What is worse: to live without a leg or to live with an obsession that controls your life? For at least some of them, the choice is clear – which is why that are talking about chainsaws and shot guns and railways tracks. And to be honest, haven't surgeons made the human body fair game? You can pay a surgeon to suck fat from your thighs, lengthen your penis, augment your breasts, redesign your labia, even (if you are a performance artist) implant silicone horns in your head or split your tongue like a lizard's. Why not amputate a limb? At least [Dr] Robert Smith's motivation was to relieve his patients' suffering.

(Elliot, 2000, p. 632)

In an era where both cosmetic surgery and cosmetic neurology are com-monplace, where humans have become surgically malleable entities, or in the language of Jordan (2004) made 'plastic bodies', why is it that the transabled or disability wannabees' quest for modification is seen as ontological, legally and morally repugnant even by supporters of gender reassignment surgery? I am not interested in explanations of transableness or apotemnophilia (be they psychiatric or neurochemi-cal) rather in the politics of *disability offence* and how certain kinds of transabledness radically disturbs, challenges and supports the notion of disability as harm. Before proceeding we need to get terminology out of the way to minimise confusion. Despite assertions to the contrary (see MacKenzie, 2008) the term 'transabled' was first coined by transabled activist Sean O'Connor in 2004. O'Connor operates a *Body Identity Integrity Disorder* information website (http://biid-info.org) and the *Transabled page* (http://transabled.org). The approach to transableness or BIID that I have adopted for this piece is that contained on the BIID information site:

> BIID, is a condition characterised by an overwhelming need to align one's physical body with one's body image. This body image includes an impairment (some say disability), most often an amputation of one or more limbs, or paralysis, deafness, blindness, or other conditions. In other words, people suffering from BIID don't feel complete unless they become amputees, paraplegic, deaf, blind or have other 'disabling' conditions.
>
> (http://biid-info.org/Transabled)

Transabled people wish to live in a body that conforms to their body image. They argue that something in their appearance (e.g. a limb, sensation, movement, or sound) should not be there. This is not a belief that the unwanted part is imperfect but that there is an incongruity or otherness to it. As Bridy (2004, p. 148) puts it, '...wholeness is experienced as incompletness, self is experienced as alien'. Bayne and Levy (2005) argue that the so-called 'healthy' limb or spine is out-of-place and therefore not healthy. Here's the inversion, through the acquisition of disability (the body modification) the transabled person is able to become 'able-bodied' fully functioning and complete. Plastic surgery already foregrounds the historicity and culturally contingency of beliefs about the integrity of the body and the notion of harm. (Jones, 2008). The assault on the transabled quest raises issues about the validity of the disabled body and the conflation of bodily integrity with ableness. The discourses engaged around this issues are deeply embedded with ableist notions, for instances the use of ' "self-mutilation" rather than self-modification' (Bridy, 2004, p. 152).

Because of the controversy in the literature and the disability community about disability devotees and the general absence of literature on the relationship between transabled people, disability attitudes and ableism I undertook a small online survey ($n = 17$) which is indicative of transabled perspectives. The promotion of the survey was through a number of e-lists and web information pages. Through my own participation in the 'Fighting–IT' list I was able to fully disclose my own disability status and the nature of my conceptual research and listen to the conversations. In keeping with the sentiments of this book, to preview the 'disability voice' and speak otherwise about impairment I have garnered transabled people's perspectives from a range of sources; email correspondence, interview transcripts, web blogs and an online survey. However, so as not to privilege any source, all names (and sometimes gender) have been replaced by a pseudonym.

Disagreeing with Bruno's (1997) assertions, I argue that the profile of transabled people appears to differ significantly from that of devotees. There are reasonable numbers of women who actively 'identify' as transabled. There is a significant presence on e-lists of both 'gay' and 'straight' sexualities and some individuals already have a physical or sensory impairment additional to their BIID desire. That 60% of survey respondents identified as having BIID might be an indication of the pervasiveness of the campaign among the transabled community to have BIID seen as a mental illness and the adoption of an explanatory framework to reconcile desire. As one survey respondent put it '[It's a] shame to have to call it a disease in order to legitimize treatment' (Imran, online survey). Eighty per cent of respondents either wished for an amputation or specific form of paralysis. It is often asserted that transabled people like disability devotees have an abstracted and isolated exposure to disability concerns. This belief appears unfounded. A few transabled individuals are employed in the disability services field and play significant roles in policy development, service delivery and research. Seventy-five per cent of survey respondents had contact with people with disability either through their friendship circle or in the workplace. Significantly, though 37.5% of respondents had limited contact with people with disabilities, whilst 44% were involved in informal advocacy and 31% are members of a disability organisation. In contrast to the rest of the population ignorance about disability amongst transabled people seems *less* likely:

Dr —— then goes on to state that many BIID sufferers are ignorant of disability issues. To be brutally honest, this is probably true. A lot of people, regardless of their background, are ignorant of disability issues. How many deaf people, for example, are fully versed in the issues faced by a wheelchair user, for example? There is ignorance on all sides; it's one of the problems caused by being human.

(Amber, 19/12/07, blog)

According to the online survey the main source of information which present an understanding of disability as an affirming life were BIID/Transabled e-lists (62.5%). Equally 56% of respondents held that the influence of their direct association with people with disability to gain disability perspectives was extremely important. Additional insight was gained from disability lifestyle websites (56%) and disability content films (31%). We know that transabled desires offend ableist notions of bodily integrity in a different way from the situation of conjoined twins. Unlike transexualism which is also about significant bodily modifications leading to gender regularisation, the object of desire (amputation, paralysis, etc.) offends cultural concepts of normativity (Sullivan, 2008).

On grappling with ableism

Transabled people believe that they have a 'wrong body' but the remedy is that they wish to obtain an equally 'wrong body', that is the disabled body! Hence many long time transabled people in order to move towards psycho-social integration (transabled subjectivity) have had to profoundly grapple with the forces of ableism and its internalisation:

> I know that disability is not supposed to be a desirable thing. When I realized that I wanted to be disabled then I went through a whole range of emotions starting with 'I must be stupid, nobody wants that' then on accepting that I really did want it I considered all the inconvenience.... I know that public opinion about disability is negative but I expect public opinion about an AB 'wanting' to become disabled would be even more negative. (Elizabeth, online survey); and

> I don't think about that, what other people think about me or other disabled persons. being disabled is not a negative thing for me (Steve, online survey).

In seeing the compulsion of ableism to rid society of its 'remainders' (c.f. Hindess, 2000), 'Barry' connects his situation with disability in general:

> I feel a lot of pressure to conform and be as normal as possible.... I see society as wanting to get rid of us one way or another so someone who is going to be voluntarily disabled isn't going to be taken kindly at all.
>
> (Barry, online survey)

'Howard' refutes the popular idea that transabled people like devotees desire to be 'noticed' and wish to trade on the misfortune of disability (c.f. Bruno, 1997). He refuses the belief that to 'choose' to be disabled is a choice to be dependent (MacKenzie & Cox, 2007):

> I wish I could just become or be who I am without notice. I don't want folks to feel sorry for me, as I sure as hell won't. I know that this will be a part of what people feel. I really don't know that on my part there is anything attractive or interesting about being an amputee. It is a need to be whole.... I don't plan on standing in front of a mirror and admiring my stump.
>
> (Howard, email, 3/2/98)

Like many people with disability there is a confrontation with the degree that one can pass as 'able bodied' and what such a gesture would mean to refuting ableist subjectivities. 'Michelle' in response to the accusation of 'fraud' because she would desire to use hearing aids to function in a hearing world and yet want to be deaf reports,

> I want to be deaf but I'd also use hearing aids to restore my hearing. Some people who have a desire to be amputees would use prosthetics. It seems paradoxical to want to lose hearing and then to use a device designed to AID hearing. Just like it seems paradoxical to want to lose a limb (or more!) and then use a prosthetic to 'replace' it.
>
> (Michele, 21/4/2007, blog)
> And again

> However, it's stupid to ignore the practicality of able-bodiedness and it's stupid to risk one's career to eliminate a double-life wherein one a person appears AB and in the other somehow not. I would rather go to work a hearing person (for now. Ask me in, say, 30 years.) and keep my job than get sacked for one day showing up with a more noticeable hearing problem! Practicality.
>
> (Michelle, 1/7/2007, blog)

Michelle's 'paradox' goes beyond transabledness and ties in closely with the argument presented in Chapter 3 about whether disability should be considered in its mitigated state. The stance also highlights the difference in ways that disabled people view technological objects beyond a self-contained apparatus to dis/tech's extension of disability ontology, where the device is in effect a love object (see Chapter 4).

On responses from the disability community
Unlike the kinds of debates that have taken place within disability studies about devoteeism, there has not been a substantive debate

from disability studies researcher about transabled claims. Most of the literature originates from ethics and cultural studies (Bayne & Levy, 2005; Bridy, 2004; Mackenzie, 2008; Mackenzie & Cox, 2007; Sullivan, 2008). It is unclear what the diversity of responses beyond sensationalism would be for the disability studies community. One 'hostile' blog suggests,

> You don't know what it is truly like to be disabled because when you have BIID you LIKE being disabled. None of us truly disabled like it. By like it, I say that because it seems to give those with BIID satisfaction. They feel whole and happy by pretending or actually being disabled.... We'd never lie about our disability and we'd never try to understand something we never could get. That is why I feel those with BIID simply cannot ever understand being disabled without a choice in the matter.
>
> (Tim, 2008, blog)

'Tim's' perspective is interesting because it draws on the ableist assumption that people with disability do not 'like' being disabled (impaired), in contrast with being fed up with the implications for the social context of impairment. There is a lack of appreciation for the complexities behind transabled compulsions. An interesting juxtaposition is the remark of Fred, a 'successful' self-amputee:

> ... by becoming an amputee [I] got rid of the torture of the obsession with it which was the main thing I suffered from – being an amputee is a piece of cake in comparison to what [I] went through.
>
> (Fred, email, 30/8/1998)

The investment by many transabled people in the disability community and exposure to ideas generated from disability studies has led to the expectation of acceptance on the grounds that many disability studies researchers consider disability to be a neutral signifier and something that can elicit pride. Imagine the surprise then at discovering the degree of internalisation of disability negativity:

> From time to time I get negative emails and comments calling me crazy and things of that nature because I wish to intentionally damage my hearing.... I noticed a large number of hits coming from a popular deaf message board this morning and to say that the thread about my blog was positive would be laughable. I don't understand,

though. I've read a few of the threads and many people seem proud of their deafness and seem to reject attempts to make them hearing. I wonder if they are the same people who say that I am crazy for wishing to be deaf? Seems like a double standard.

(Michele, October 9, 2007)

'Dirk's' comments sums up the irony well:

I find it hard to reconcile that these people (disability studies activists) are both saying that 'disability is neutral and ok', yet get so venomous against transabled people. The only thing I can attribute this to is internalised...ableism.

(Dirk, 9/7/08)

The disability offence: Rationality and ableism

'You are a rational man. You should be able to control it', remarked the wife of 'Jerry' who wished to use prosthesis to walk outside when the snow was falling on the way to a Christmas function. This comment sparked a lively conversation on the Fighting-IT e-list and 'Jerry' has permitted some of his thought to be shared with a broader audience. He says,

Indeed. I am rational, and I should be able to control it. I controlled it for the first 65 years of my life when I thought my daydreams of being an amputee seemed totally crazy to me...But what has been brewing inside of me since then is the question, 'Why should I want to control it?'...Why should you assume that a 'rational man' would not want this outcome [amputation] and would control it? Why?

(Jerry, 30/12/08, e-list)

Throughout this book both at the level of theory and also through the case studies on cochlear implants, transplant technology, conjoined twins and wrongful life torts there has been an intensive discussion about ableist compulsions to mitigate impairment and mimic ableness. In this small study of transabled subjectivity it becomes clear that many transabled people, at least people who are 'out' enough to engage in e-list discussions and surveys, have had to venture into territories both personal and societal to deconstruction ableist perspectives on the 'whole' body and attitudes towards disability. Many of the transabled people I have encountered have crossed over into a kind of 'trans-abled' world, into a realm beyond able-ness. Transabledness remains an affront to the culture of cure because of the implicit desire to value disability.

The 'problem' with conjoined, devotee and transabled desire seems not to be with desiring as such, but the object/subject of that desire – that is the disabled body. The disabled body as I have previously documented has been configured as the site of monstrosity and unthinkability... so inherently untenable that it has on occasions been pronounced ritually dead (Turner, 1987). Elsewhere (Campbell, 1999) I have written about a kind of endemic desire in the form of voyeurism that inaugurates confessional discourses accessing the 'truth' of living with impairment. The desire to know, I argued, becomes in effect a source of pleasure. Foucault's description captures this pleasure imperative '[we have]...the fascination of seeing it and telling it, of captivating and capturing others by it, of confiding it in secret, of luring it out in the open...' (Foucault, 1976, p. 71). Conjoined twins, devotee and transabled people have called into question the ontological position of their communities.

I posed the question earlier on in this chapter whether conjoined, devotee and transabled people have anything to contribute towards the development of a positive ascetic of impairment. It is my conclusion that the marginal populations have much to contribute – albeit with a caveat. As disabled people are experimenting/exploring a new visualisation, a new experience of the erotic, conjoined, devotee and transabled people have the opportunity, together with other people with disability, to disrupt and subvert notions of wholeness and beauty. This will only happen when both communities challenge traditional gendered notions of the body beautiful and embrace beautiful in all its different forms. Meanwhile, transabled people, conjoined twins and devotees tend to recall the disgust of disability. Instead of denying such a reaction because it might appear to offend modern sensibilities of relative inclusion it would be better to turn towards disgust and make it a 'good place' a site of rumination, witnessing and reflection that unveils subtle ableist impulses.

A disability orientation

In a world that make claims to integrity using the argument based of equality as sameness (we are normal, we are like you, we are everyday people), it would be seen a bit bold or offensive to suggest that people with disability are different from the run-of-mill ableist norm emulaters.

I suggest ableness is a social and bodily orientation that extends what is within reach. Ahmed (2006) points to an alternate prism, a 'migrant orientation' to capture a disorientation faced by all disabled people – the lived experience of facing at least two directions: towards a home that has been lost (ableist compulsions), and to a place that is not yet home. As Ahmed (2006, p. 20) puts it, 'inhabiting a body that is not extended by the social means the world acquires a new shape and makes new impressions'.

This chapter has been about attempts to build a new home, to make room by crafting a territory that is antithetical to ableist normativities. We could propose that the world extends the form of some bodies and mentalities more than others, and such bodies/mentalities in turn feel at home in the world. Staring down ableism (because it really cannot be escaped) involves, following Heidegger an alternate *significance* (the sum total of equipment, norms and social roles). Intelligibility shaped through significance then takes on a different culture or form of life. Making room in the world is not about squeezing in, inserting the crip into the polis. The disabled body is already spatialised even in its set-offness and hiddeness. Heidegger (1962) indicated that the average compulsion of Dasein (beingness) is to obey rules and standards; however, the *resolute* person who turns away from banality and respond to the concrete situation of taking action through refining responses over time the resolute individual can arise from ableism, come out the other side with an post-ableist consciousness. Conjoined twins, devotee and transabled people are definitely resolute peoples.

In this chapter, I have attempted to refute the idea that the joining of disability and desire is oxymoric by introducing and exploring attempts by disabled people themselves to journey into the erotica of impairment and play with a positive ascetic. In addition, I have introduced the communities of devotees, conjoined twins and transabled people into our discussion as oppositional trajectories of desire in order to push the envelope further around affirmations of disability desire. No doubt if we start to put desire back into disability – this invocation might gain a foothold. Butler informs us

> ... that language only persists through repeated occasions of that invocations. That language gains its temporal life only in and through the utterances that reinvokes and restructures the conditions of its own possibility.
>
> (Butler, 1997b, p. 140)

Still more work needs to be done, more research relating to the phenomena of desiring impairment is required. It was not long ago that to be a gay man, lesbian or transgendered person was viewed by society as subnormal or at best, deviant. Today the commodification of gay culture has meant that this former abomination is now considered sexy fashion (albeit transitory for some individuals). It is uncertain what the future will hold for the creation of an ethic of affirming disability. By inverting the dominant gaze of disability as negative ontology maybe, we will witness in the future (for better or worse) disability envy, sites where disabled bodies are lovable, hot, inspiring, 'chic' and sexy.

Afterword: From Disability Studies to Studies in Ableism

> ...we, the survivors, are not the true witnesses... We survivors are not only an exiguous but also an anomalous minority: we are those who by their prevarications or abilities or good luck did not touch bottom.
>
> (Levi, 1989, pp. 63–64)

Today ambivalent survivors are charged with passing on knowledge and memories of how life was so that 'we' can dream of another way to be. Thus stories of disability and abledness are like maps providing safety so the traveller will not inadvertently turn off the road, go astray or navigate haphazardly into areas unknown or secured for the sole use of other, inhabitants. Like the map, stories provide clarity about the journey taken and the road ahead. The banter helps us make sense of the world and the way in which we interpret the 'nature' of things and interpolate ways of difference. Sometimes these stories are explicitly named and actively exchanged. Others are more mundane, somewhat insidious; passing on in a multitude of remnants, connected, disconnected, contrary and multiple, eventually taking on the status of a naturalised state of affairs. Even though the terrain may be winding and rocky, there is at least an illusion of certainty in the map which can be re-read and consulted again and again to ensure ordered spaces, corrected tracking, helping us re-cognise the signposts as we travel.

Ableism is a map of a simulated territory that denotes the home-lands of humanness, the dispensable beasts and changelings existing on the perimeter. Ableist landscapes communicate the values of culture, its characterological objects, and secure the transmission of the 'memory' of a body of people. In these landscapes rest a form of anamnesis that orientates between the past, the present and the future. *Contours of Ableism* has been preoccupied with matters of ordering and disorder, the constitutional compartmentalisation between the 'normal' and the 'pathological' and the ways that stories about wholeness, health, enhancement and perfection are told. This work inverts the usual gaze used in the study of disability, namely empirical observations of those bodies considered as aberrant or pathological. The work is a story (stories) about the creation and production of a certain kind of difference known under the contemporary neologism 'able (bodiedness)' and its counterpoint 'disability'. In the tradition of critical disability studies, a study of ableism such as *Contours of Ableism* has worked on disputing the self-evidence of categories/entities of disability and impairment, opens up dialogue around broader questions of anomaly and the place of both disgust and desire. *Contours of Ableism* has made a cartographic journey into the battlegrounds that seek to ensure the line of defence, between notions and epistemologies of ableism and disability. This journey seeks to remove grey zones that foreground hybrids, reduce uncertainties and enact what Owen Wrigley calls *outlaw ontologies*.

Argument within this work views the production of the abled-body as part of a tussle over ordering, a desire to create order from an assumed disorder; a flimsy but often convincing attempt to shore up the so-called *optimal ontologies*. Conversely, the work is interested in ways 'disability' rubs up against and provokes other seemingly unrelated concepts such as wellness, ableness, perfection, competency, causation, productivity and use value. It examines the ways 'abled-ness' is known and focuses attention on the practices and formations of ableism. Hence, studies in ableism offers a new direction in research on aberrancy in its focus on a normate ethos. Uncritical stories and namings of abled-ness are stories of *abled fabrication*; stories that seem to objectively tell us how 'abled-ness' and its kindred twin 'disability' are to be framed and thus understood. Undeniably a significant amount of storytelling that masquerades as disability is not really about impairment or disablement. The 'real' story being told is about ableism – the ways our bodies *should* be or at least strive to become. The ableist story unfolds as a comportment of living from our early years as a child and into adulthood, creating a code that helps each of us to make sense of the contingencies and exigencies of living. The underbelly of ableism discloses various sites of discomfort that are able to be revealed in a different way from traditional disability studies – unveiling discomforts that seep into other kinds of human ambiguity.

This work represents a major shift in the study of disability because of its concentration on the production of abled-ness – and is the *first* book of its kind on the market. The reality is that studies in ableism offers more than a contribution to re-thinking disability. These studies provide a platform for reconsidering the way we think about *all* bodies and mentalities within the parameters of nature/culture. In that sense, studies in ableism has the capacity to reconfigure both race and gender studies. A note of caution remains. Emerging is a growing field concerned with somatechnics and 'wrong' bodies. Without over generalising, much of this new work originates from cultural and feminist studies of the body. In the process of writing this book, I have utilised a number of thinkers from those traditions. A move towards studies in ableism *must not* spell a separation with disability studies, rather the focus on ableism is meant to reconfigure a disability studies perspective and extend it. There is a real danger of those who come to studies in ableism without being exposed to the rich canon of critical disability studies will not feel inclined, accountable or committed to broader disability studies scholarship. The narratives and the lived experiences of people with disability can be more intimately embraced and understood through critical disability studies. There is an ethos in critical disability studies whereby people with disability are both subject and object of the process of theorisation. The denial or ignorance of such could lead to the erasure of the centralised positioning of the materialised disabled body.

Notes

2 Internalised Ableism: The Tyranny Within

1. I am adopting the convention of using 'disabled people' instead of 'people with disability' in recognition that ableist processes and practices do indeed produce disabled people. Additionally, as it will be become evident in this chapter, disability and impairment are indeed difficult to separate from a person's being-ness.
2. The practice of partitioning, classifying and dividing groups into races and making 'raced' people not only shapes our sense of self, but it can tell us 'who' and 'what' we are and are not.
3. Thomson cited a number of strategies such as charm, humour, deference to relieve the discomfort of able bodied people (Thomson, 1997, pp. 12–13). See also Thomson, 2009).

3 Tentative Disability – Mitigation and Its Discontents

1. *Carrie Buck* v. *James Hendren Bell, Superintendent of State Colony for Epileptics and Feeble Minded*, 274 U.S. 200.
2. *Richmond* v.*Croson*, 488 U.S. 469 (1989).
3. The 1432 sense of the word is "make mild or gentle, whilst soft, mild": is attested to in the 1362 understanding. *Online Etymology Dictionary, available online at* http://www.etymonline.com/index.php?term=mitigate, (visited on 05/05/2005).
4. We can categorise three distinct groups deemed to have 'elective' disability: (1) *non-mitigators* – people who choose to remain impaired; (2) *disabled pro-creators* – women who choose to bear children with disability and (3) the *transabled* – able-bodied individuals who desire to be disabled.
5. Known as the 'mitigation of disability cases' the parameters of defining 'disability' under the *ADA* have been realigned, in respect to 'corrective measures' to mitigate 'disabling conditions': *Sutton* v. *United Airlines Inc*, 527 U.S. 471 (1999); *Murphy* v. *United Parcel Service*, 527 U.S. 516 (1999); *Albertson's Inc v Kirkingburg*, 527 U.S. 555 (1999). I would argue in addition that the 'disability' concept is already occluded – as prong of the definition is tied to the notion of substantially limiting a major life activity'. s3 (2)(a) of the *ADA*.
6. *Purvis v New South Wales (Department of Education and Training)*, 2003 (202 ALR 133).
7. *Lawson v. CSX Transportation* 101 F.Supp. 2d 1089 (S.D. Ind. 2000).
8. *Lawson, id*, at p. 1104.
9. *Lawson, id*, at pp. 1103–1104.
10. In one recent *ADA* case, the Arizona District Court upheld a claim of 'disability' (and therefore coverage under anti-discrimination legislation)

irrespective of the use of compensating/mitigating measures such as prostheses. In *Finical* v. *Collection Unlimited*, 65 FSupp 2d 1032 (1999), the plaintiff who was hearing impaired decided against using a hearing aid on the basis that such a device picked up background noise and therefore was annoying. The defendants argued that hearing aids should be included as a mitigating measure. The court however held that an employee with a hearing impairment was disabled irrespective of their use of 'hearing' devices.

4 Love Objects and Transhuman Beasts? Riding the Technologies

1. I am following Bruno Latour's (1993) delineation 'artefact' to refer to those objects/subjects of the non-human, transhuman kind.
2. Any device specifically designed for disabled people in contrast with technologies designed for the broader population that have been embraced by the dis/community.
3. Space does not allow for a extensive discussion of 'enframing' as developed by Heidegger, suffice to say *enframing* (*gestell*) denotes a mode thinking, an armature or framework that seeks to systematise, compartmentalise and classify the world (animate and inanimate) in order to maximum order and control. c. f. *Concerning Technology*, pp. 301–305.
4. The 'notion of standing in reserve' – something has value only so far as it is good for something. Human ontology becomes transformed to that of 'human resources'.
5. Un nouveau concept s'est progressivement imposé qui définit le handicap comme étant une confrontation entre les aptitudes d'une personne et les situations qu'elle rencontre dans la vie : "macro-situations", comme le travail ou la scolarisation, ou "micro-situations" telles que couper sa viande ou utiliser le clavier d'un ordinateur. Les situations handicapantes ne sont pas que structurelles et matérielles, elles sont aussi (et surtout) culturelles. Bien des rejets sont le fait des "autres" et de leurs préjugé.
6. How one perceives the impact of difference in their body.
7. United Nations General Assembly, *Convention on the Rights of Persons with Disabilities*, 6 December 2006, <http://www.un.org/esa/socdev/enable/rights/convtexte.htm> (29 April 2008) at [e].
8. The case professor Kevin Warwick from the cybernetics department of Reading University (UK) who self-implanted a computer chip into the nervous system of himself and his wife Irena comes to mind (Hanlon, 2002). See also the National Library of Medicine (USA) awarded a contract to the University of Colorado Health Sciences Centre in 1991 to create the digital cross-sections of a 39-year-old convicted murderer (on death row) who had donated his body to science. This research became the *Visible Human Project®*, a creation of complete, anatomically detailed, three-dimensional representations of male and female human bodies. http://www.nlm.nih.gov/research/visible/visible_human.html.
9. There is an endurance of victorious and triumphant images that cast out feebleness/nationalist. These images often draw upon various forms of war metaphor to rid nations of disability.

10. I have problematised this point as I am in agreement with Latour (1993, p. 11) when he says that the modern critical stance is to keep the practices of translation (hybridisation) and purification separate. To attend to both processes we stop being modern and move into a different mode.
11. I should clarify this point. The preferability of hearing would have it that sign language interpretation is but an interim measure – for the goal is to have the Deaf speak and hear.

5   The Deaf Trade: Selling the Cochlear Implant

1. In line with established conventions, I employ 'Deaf' to refer to people who identify with the Deaf community, language and culture, in distinction from *audiological deafness* represented by a lower case 'd'.
2. This phrase was the description used by CI users on a Yahoo group electronic discussion list.

6   Print Media Representations of the 'Uncooperative' Disabled Patient: The Case of Clint Hallam

1. The team of was led by Jean-Michel Dubernard of Lyon and Earl Owen of Sydney and included Nadey Hakim (UK), Marco Lanzetta (Italy) Hari Kapila (Australia), Guillaume Herzberg, Marwan Dawahra, Xavier Martin (France).
2. Media reports do not indicate whether Clint identified as a 'disabled person'. Certainly, as an amputee his 'disabled' status would be recognised by some government and non-government organisations. Titchkosky (2001, p. 129) uses the example of the expression 'I'm not disabled, I am a person whose leg happens to be missing' and points out that irrespective of this stance, the 'missing leg' would be enumerated among the ranks of the mobility impaired.
3. The initial amputated hand was restitched and then re-amputated after loss of sensation.
4. It is often the case that the 'voice' of the subject is never direct but mediated by the 'voice' of so-called knowable others such as doctors, journalists and other social commentators.
5. Indeed the question of ownership of the hand arises when Hallam later wants it removed.
6. The notion of a hybrid actant, this case the transplanted limb, creates a space for the limb to come alive in terms of agency and as an active part in a network of relations. This approach is derived from actor network theory, especially the work of Bruno Latour (1992).
7. This is the title of a proposed book by Clint Hallam.

7   Disability *Matters*: Embodiment, Teaching and Standpoint

1. A word about terminology. Where I have deemed relevant I have used person first language, that is person with disability. However, as this is a theoretical

chapter written within a poststructuralist genre, I often refer to the disabled body in a similar way to the common usage of the raced and sexed body. Usually in these instances I am not referring to a person with disability *per se*, but a more abstracted ontological notion of difference.

2. Although the piece might seem dated, the debate in many countries has not really moved forward, rather sensitivities about 'dealing' with the issues had pushed it somewhat underground.

8 Pathological Femaleness: Disability Jurisprudence and Ontological Envelopment

1. Gk: meaning unevenness, asperity, for example anomaly.
2. There are other classes of disaffected workers as well whose bodied are marked by race, where notions of identify emerges from community – this means that the person is never unencumbered in an atomistic sense.
3. Richardson (1995) provides a good summary of the medical arraignment of PMS.
4. *Commonwealth v. Richter*, No. T90-215256 (Fairfax County Gen. Dist.Ct. 4 June 1991, Unreported.
5. *Regina v. Craddock* [1981] 1 C.L. 49.
6. *Regina v. Smith (Sandie)*, 1982 WL221797 (CA (Crim div)), [1982] (Crim. L.R.531).
7. *Regina v. English* (Unreported, Norwich Crown Court, 10 November 1981). The defendant was charged with murder after pinning the victim against a pole with her car. English was able to show that she suffered PMS for an extensive period of time and charges were reduced to manslaughter resulting in a sentence of 12 probation.
8. *People v. Santos*, No. TK046229 of 1981 (N.Y. County Crim. Ct. Pleas entered Nov 3, 1982).
9. *Re Lovato v. Irvin*, 31 B.R. 251 (Bankr. D. Colo. 1983).
10. *Irvin*, 31 B.R. at 259, 261.
11. AB1947 *Vehicles Parking Privileges People with Disabilities*, California Legislature – 2003–04 Regular Session.
12. AB1940. *An Act to amend Section 22511.59 of the Vehicle Code, relating to vehicles*, California Legislature – 2007–08 Regular Session, at 99.
13. Who is the 'we' – non-disabled people, the law?

9 Disability Harm and Wrongful Life Torts

1. These cases are sometimes referred to as 'wrongful conception' cases, although his distinction is sometimes blurred (Weybury & Witting, 1995, p. 53).
2. (1994), 21 C.C.L.T. (2d) 66 (B.C.S.C.); (1997), 148 D.L.R. (4th) (S.C.C).
3. (1994) Aust Tort Reports 81 – 309.
4. (1995) Aust Tort Reports 81 – 360 (CA NSW).
5. 165 Cal.Rept. 477 (1980), appeal denied 2 Civ. 58192 (4 September 1980)
6. (1982) 1 QB 1166; (1982) *All ER* 771.

7. (*Valentini c. Castaldini*, 15/10/1990).
8. Exp Perruche c/ Mutualle d'assuance du corps sanitaire francais et al. (Cour de Cassation, arret n. 457 P, Juris-Data n. 006884, 17.11.2000).
9. Aust Torts Reports 81 – 079.
10. Aust Torts Reports 81 – 309.
11. 41Ill.App.2d 240, 190 N.E. 2d 849 (1963), cert denied, 379 U.S. 945 (1964). In that case a child sued her own father because she was born illegitimately, and alleged harm on that basis.
12. 49 N.J. 22, 227 A.2d 689 (1967).
13. See also another Californian case: *Turpin v Sortini*, 31 Cal. 3d 220, 643 P.2d 954, 182 Cal. Rptr. 337 (1982).
14. 165 Cal.Rept. 477 (1980), appeal denied 2 Civ. 58192 (4 September 1980)
15. *Berman v Allan* 80 NJ 421; 404 A 2d 8 (1979) and *Azzolino v Dingfelder* 315 NC 103; 337 SE 2d 528 (1985).
16. *Procanik by Procanik v Cillo* 478 A.2d 755 (N.J. 1984); *Turpin v Sortini*, 31 Cal. 3d 220, 643 P.2d 954, 182 Cal. Rptr. 337 (1982); *Harbeson v Parke-Davis, Inc.*, 656 P.2d 483 (Wash 1983).
17. 478 A.2d 755 (N.J. 1984).
18. *Taylor v Kurapati*, No. 204908, CA 1999 Mich. App LEXIS 170 (25 June); and *Etkind v Suarez*, S98G1978, 1999 Ga. LEXIS 627 (6 July).
19. (1982) 1 QB 1166; (1982) *All ER* 771.
20. [1972] V.R. 353.
21. Loosely translated as "comments on the aside".
22. LJ Griffiths agreed with LJ Stephenson adding that WL actions were premised on the belief that the child is "...better dead than alive" (Griffiths, at 1193).
23. Aust Torts Reports 81 – 079.
24. (1994) Aust Tort Reports 81 – 309.
25. *Edwards v Blomeley* [2002] NSWSC 460; *Harriton v Stephens* [2002] NSWSC 461; *Waller v James* [2002] NSWSC 462.
26. 332 Md. 226, (1993).
27. *Edwards v Blomeley* [2002] NSWSC 460; *Harriton v Stephens* [2002] NSWSC 461; *Waller v James* [2002] NSWSC 462. Justice Studdert heard all three cases together but delivered three independent judgments. Edwards would be considered the lead case.
28. 386 N.E. 2d 807 (N.Y. 1978).
29. Emma Ganderton (2000) proposes assigning values to life (+) and life with defects(-) [sic] where the assumption was that the more 'severe the deformity' the greater burden and therefore the less valuable a life.

10 Searching for Subjectivity: The Enigma of Devoteeism, Conjoinment and Transableism

1. *Purvis v New South Wales (Department of Education and Training)* 2003 (202 *ALR* 133).
2. Dividing practices are situations where "the subject is either divided inside himself or divided from others" (Foucault, 1983: 208).
3. Translation: "the visual representation of disabled people in pornographic materials is considered *a priori* impossible".

4. *Re A (Children) (Conjoined Twins: Surgical Separation)* 4 All ER 961.
5. The gendering of social and psychological research is a pertinent issue here.
6. Dr Money of the John Hopkins University described the paraphilia associated with attraction to disabled people and their appliances. Defined as "A paraphilia of the eligibilic/stigmatic type in which sexuoerotic arousal and facilitation or attainment of orgasm are responsive to and contingent on the partner being lame, with a limp, or crippled (from Greek, *abasios* lameness + -*philia*)" (c.f. Money, 1996).
7. My lack of comment at this point should not be taken to mean that I consider these theories to be unimportant, comintantly; they are critical to the inscribing the D-P-T as deviant. Rather a strategic 'silence' has been adopted to avoid my attention from being subsumed by this debate and away from my focal concerns around ontological representations of disability (and desire).
8. In contrast to the suggestion that disabled women are being exploited by devotee. Aguilera (2000) and Kafer (2002) independently note that the vast number of businesses and social organisations are owned or managed by the women themselves.

Bibliography

AAP/Ninemsn. 2001. Hand Transplant Surgeon says he was Used. *Ninemsn News*. 5/2/2001, http://news.ninemsn.com.au/world/story_8151.asp [Accessed 12/4/2002].

Abelove, H., Barale, M.A. & Halperin, D.M. 1993. *The Lesbian and Gay Studies Reader*. New York: Routledge.

Access Economics. 2006. *Listen Hear! The Economic Impact and Cost of Hearing Loss in Australia*, A report by Access Economics Pty Ltd, February.

Agamben, G. 2005. *State of Exception*. Chicago: The University of Chicago.

Agamben, G. 1998. *Homo Sacer: Sovereign Power and Bare Life*. Stanford: Stanford University Press.

Agnew, W. & McCreery, D. 1990. *Neural Prostheses: Fundamental Studies*. Englewood Cliffs, N.J: Prentice Hall.

Aguilera, R. 2000. Disability and delight: Staring back at the devotee community. *Sexuality and Disability*. 18, 255–261.

Ahmed, S. 2006. *Queer Phenomenology*. Durham: Duke University.

Alcoff, L. 1991. The problem of speaking for others. *Cultural Critique*. 2, 5–34.

Altman, B. 2001. Disability definitions, models, classification schemes, and applications. In G. Albrecht, K. Seelman & M. Bury, eds. *Handbook of Disability Studies*. Thousand Oaks: Sage, pp. 97–122.

Amundson, R. & Taira, G. 2005. Our lives and ideologies: The effects of life experience on the perceived morality of the policy of physician – assisted suicide. *Journal of Policy Studies*. 16(1), 53–57.

Angel, M. 1994. IPedagogies of the obscene: The specular body and demonstration. In J. Matthews, ed. *Jane Gallop Seminar Papers, proceedings of the Jane Gallop Seminar and Public Lecture 'The Teachers Breasts'*. Canberra: The Humanities Research Centre, pp. 61–72.

Ann-Lewis, V. 1988. People with disabilities in the Media and Performing Arts. *Australian Disability Review*. 1(2), 1–2.

Anstey, K. 2002. Are attempts to have impaired children justifiable? *Journal of Medical Ethics*. 28(5), 286–288.

Aoki, K. 2000. Space invaders critical geography, the 'third world' in international law and critical race theory. *Villanova Law Review*. 913, 45.

Appel, J. 2008. When the boss turns pusher: a proposal for Employee protections in the age of Cosmetic neurology. *Journal of Medical Ethics*. 34(6), 616–618.

Appelbaum, E., Thomas Bailey, T., Berg, P. & Kalleberg, A. 2002. *Shared Work – Valued Care: New Norms for Organizing Market Work and Unpaid Care Work*. Washington DC: The Economic Policy Institute.

Aristotle. 1998. *Generation of Animals*. Oxford: Oxford University Press.

Assante, V. 2000. *Situations de handicap et cadre de vie* (Situations of Disability and Life Framework) [French only], Report to Conseil Economique et Social. Les éditions des Journaux officiels Avis et rapports du CES, no. 10. Online at: http://www.conseil-economique-etsocial.fr/ces_dat2/2-3based/frame_rech_avis.htm. [Accessed 2003].

Auslander, G. & Gold, N. 1999. Disability terminology in the media: A comparison of newspaper reports in Canada and Israel. *Social Science & Medicine*. 48, 1395–1405.

Baker, B. & Campbell, F. 2006. Transgressing noncrossable borders: disability, law, schooling and nations. In S. Danforth & S. Gabel, eds. *Vital Questions Facing Disability Studies in Education*. New York: Peter Lang Publishing, pp. 319–347.

Barclay, L. 2000. Autonomy and the social self, relational autonomy. In C. Mackenzie & N. Stoljar eds. *Relational Autonomy: Feminist Perspectives on Autonomy, Agency and the Social Self*. New York: Oxford University Press, pp. 52–71.

Barhorst, S. 1999–2000. What does disability mean: The Americans with Disabilities Act of 1990 in the aftermath of Sutton, Murphy, and Albertsons. *Drake Law Review*. 48, 138–171.

Barnes, C. 1992. *Disabling Imagery and the Media: An Exploration of Media Representations of Disabled People*. Belper: British Council of Organisations of Disabled People.

Baster, J. 1954. Recent literature on the economic development of backward areas. *Quarterly Journal of Economics*. 68(4), 585–560.

Bauby, J. 1997. *The Diving Bell and Butterfly*. London: Harper Perennial.

Bayne, T. & Levy, N. 2005. Amputees by choice: Body integrity identity disorder and the ethics of amputation. *Journal of Applied Philosophy*. 22(1), 75–86.

BBC News 2001. 'Surgeon Agrees to Sever Transplant Hand', *BBC News Online*, 21/10/2000; Online at: htttp://news.bbc.co.uk/hi/english/world/europe/newsid_982000/982817.stm, [Accessed 2/3/2003].

Bell, C. 2000. Eclipse: A Theatre Workshop on Disability. In S. Crutchfield & M. Epstein, eds. *Points of Contact: Disability, Art and Culture*. Ann Arbor: The University of Michigan Press.

Bell, D. 1995. Whose afraid of critical race theory? *University of Illinois Law Review*. 4, 893–910.

Belsey, C. 1994. *Desire: Love Stories in Western Culture*. Oxford: Blackwell.

Bendle, M. 2002. Teleportation, cyborgs and the posthuman ideology. *Social Semiotics*. 12, 45–62.

Berger, T. & Glanzman, D. 2005. *Toward Replacement Parts for the Brain: Implantable Biomimetic Electronics as Neural Prostheses*. Mass: The MIT Press.

Bertling, T. 1994. *A Child Sacrificed: To the Deaf Culture*. Wilsonville, OR: Kodiak Media Group.

Bishop, H. 1999. *Posting to the Colloquy: Whose Field is it Anyway? Disability Studies and the Academy, The Chronicle of Higher Education*, 24/4/99, Online at: http://chronicle.com/colloquy/99/disability/35.htm [Accessed 2/3/2003].

Blume, S. 1997. The rhetoric and counter rhetoric of a 'Bionic' Technology. *Science, Technology and Human Values*. 22, 31–56.

Blume, S. 1994. Making the deaf hear: The cochlear implant as promise and threat. *Medische Antrhopologie*. 6, 108–121.

Bogies, M., Baker, J. & Balkany, T. 1989. Loss of residual hearing after cochlear implantation. *Laryngoscope*. 99, 1002–1005.

Bolderson, H. 1991. *Social Security, Disability and Rehabilitation: Conflicts in the Development of Social Policy 1914–1946*. London: Jessica Kingsley.

Boothroyd, A. 1993. Profound deafness. In R. Tyler, ed. *Cochlear Implants: Audiological Foundations*. San Diego: Singular, pp. 1–33.

Boothroyd, A. 1991. Assessment of speech perception capacity in profoundly deaf children. *American Journal of Otology, Supplement*. 12, 67–72.

Borenstein, J. 2005. Estimating direct and indirect costs of Premenstrual Syndrome. *Journal of Occupational and Environmental Medicine*. 47(1), 26–33.

Bostrom, N. 2006. Welcome to the world of exponential change. In P. Miller & J. Wilsdon, eds. *Better Humans? The Politics of Human Enhancement and Life Extension*. Demos Collection 21, London: Demos, pp. 40–50.

Bostrom, N. 2005. A history of transhumanist thought. *Journal of Evolution and Technology*. 14(1), 1–25.

Bostrom, N. 2003. Human gemnetoic enhancements: A tranhumanist perspective. *Journal of Value Enquiry*. 3794, 493–506.

Bostrom, N. 2002. *Anthropic Bias: Observation Selection Effects in Science and Philosophy*. New York: Routledge.

Botkin, J. 1988. The legal concept of wrongful life. *The Journal of the American Medical Association*. 259, 1541–1545.

Braun, J. 2007. The imperatives of narrative: Health interest groups and morality in network news. *The American Journal of Bioethics*. 7(8), 6–14.

Breckenridge, C. & Vogler, C. 2001. The critical limits of embodiment: Disability's criticism. *Public Culture*. 13(3), 349–357.

Bridy, A. 2004. Confounding extremities: Surgery at the medico-ethical limits of self-modification. *Journal of Law, Medicine & Ethics*. 32, 148–158.

Brown, W. 1995. *State of Injury: Power and Freedom in Late Modernity*. Princeton: Princeton University Press.

Brown, W. 1993. Wounded attachments; oppositional political formations in late modern democracy. *Political Theory*. 21, 390–410.

Bruce, R.V. 1974. *Alexander Graham Bell, Teacher of the Deaf*. Northampton, Mass: The Clarke School for the Deaf.

Bruegemann, B. Feldmaneier-White, B. Dunn, P. Heifferon, B. & Cheu, J. 2001. Becoming visible: Lessons in disability, *CCC (College Composition and Communication)*. 52(3), 368–398.

Bruno, R. 1997. Devotees, pretenders and wannabees: Two cases of factitious disorder. *Journal of Sexuality and Disability*. 15, 243–260.

Burbules, N. & Bruce, B. 2001. Theory and research on teaching as dialogue. In V. Richardson, ed. *Handbook of Research on Teaching* (4th edition). Washington DC: American Educational Research Association, pp. 1102–1121.

Burstow, B. 2003. Toward a radical understanding of Trauma and Trauma Work. *Violence Against Women*. 9(11), 1293–1317.

Butler, B. 1998. Hand gained, home likely lost. *The New Zealand Herald*. 23.12.98, 10.

Butler, J. 1997a. *Excitable Speech: A Politics of the Performative*. New York: Routledge.

Butler, J. 1997b. *The Psychic Life of Power: Theories in Subjection*. California: Stanford University Press.

Butler, J. 1995. Stubborn attachment, bodily subjection: Hegel on the unhappy consciousness. In T. Rajan & D. Clark, eds. *Intersections: Nineteenth Century Philosophy and Contemporary Theory*. Albany: State University of New York Press, pp. 173–196.

Butler, J. 1990. *Gender Trouble: Feminism and the Subversion of Identity*. New York: Routledge.

Butler, J. 1987. *Subjects of Desire: Hegelian Reflections in Twentieth-Century France.* New York: Columbia University Press.

Butler, L. 1992. Torts – *Cowe by Cowe v. Forum Group, Inc*: wrongful life dilemma of comparing impaired with non-Existence. *Memphis State University Law Review.* 22, 881–887.

Butler, R. & Parr, H. 1999. *Mind and Body Spaces: Geographies of Illness, Impairment and Disability.* London, New York: Routledge.

Byrnes, T. 2000. *Frontispiece,* Online at: http://www.theresbyrne.com [Accessed March 2006].

Cain, M. 1994. The symbol traders. In M. Cain & M. Harrington, eds. *Lawyers in a Post-Modern World.* Buckingham: Oxford University Press, pp. 15–48.

Calabro, J. 1999. Posting to the colloquy: Whose field is it anyway? Disability studies and the academy. *The Chronicle of Higher Education.* 29/3/99, Online at: http://chronicle.com/colloquy/99/disability/29.htm [Accessed 2/11/2004].

Callon, M., Law, J. & Rip, A. 1986. *Mapping the Dynamics of Science and Technology: Sociology of Science in the Real World.* Basingstoke, Hampshire: Macmillan.

Campbell, F. Kumari. 2008. Exploring internalised ableism using critical race theory. *Disability & Society.* 23(2), 151–162.

Campbell, F. Kumari. 2007. States of exceptionality: Provisional Disability, its mitigation and citizenship. *Socio Legal Review.* 3, 28–50.

Campbell, F. Kumari. 2006. Litigation neurosis: Pathological responses or rational subversion? *Disability Studies Quarterly: Special Issue Law and Disability.* 25(4), [Online version].

Campbell, F. Kumari. 2005a. Legislating disability: Negative ontologies and the government of Legal identities. In S. Tremain, ed. *Foucault and the Government of Disability.* Ann Arbor: The University of Michigan Press, pp. 108–130.

Campbell, F. Kumari. 2005b. Selling the cochlear implant. *Disability Studies Quarterly* (online version) 25(3).

Campbell, F. Kumari. 2004. The case of Clint Hallam's wayward hand: Print media representations of the 'Unco-operative' Patient'. *Continuum: Journal of Media & Cultural Studies.* 11(3), 443–458.

Campbell, F. Kumari. 2001. Inciting legal fictions: Disability's date with ontology and the ableist body of the law. *Griffith Law Review.* 10, 42–62.

Campbell, F. Kumari. 1999. 'Refleshingly Disabled': Interrogations into the corporeality of 'disablised' bodies. *Australian Feminist Law Journal.* 12 March, 57–80.

Canguilhem, G. 1978. *On the Normal and the Pathological.* London: D. Reidel Publishing.

Carver, R. 1990. Cochlear implants in prelingual deaf children: A deaf perspective. Address presented to the Cochlear Implant Forum, Canadian Hearing Society, Toronto, March 31, 1990. Deaf World Web, Online at: http://dww.deafworldweb.org/pub/c/rjc/cicarver.html [Accessed 2/3/2003].

Cassuto, L. 1999. Whose field is it anyway? Disability studies and the academy. *The Chronicle of Higher Education* 44(28), A60.

Chatterjee, A. 2007. Cosmetic neurology and cosmetic surgery: Parallels, predictions and challenges. *Cambridge Quarterly of Health Care Ethics.* 16, 129–137.

Chatterjee, A. 2004. Cosmetic neurology: The controversy over enhancing movement, mentation and mood. *Neurology.* 63(September), 968–974.

Cherney, J. 1999. Deaf culture and the cochlear implant debate: Cyborg politics and the identity of people with disabilities. *Argumentation and Advocacy.* 36 (Summer), 22–34.

Child, M. & King, R. 1992. 'OverGround's Manifesto'. *OverGround.* 2, 4.

Chouinard, V. 1997. Making space for disabling difference: Challenges ableist geographies. *Environment and Planning D: Society and Space.* 15, 379–387.

Chrisler, J. Dutch, S. & Grant, M. 2006. The PMS illusion: social cognition maintains social construction. *Sex Roles.* 54, 371–376.

Christiansen, J., Leigh, I. & Spencer, P.E. 2002. *Cochlear Implants in Children: Ethics and Choices.* Washington, DC: Gallaudet University Press.

Chwang, E. 1997. *The Peculiarities of 'Wrongful Life' Cases.* http://www.princeton.edu/~ elchwang/wrongful_life.htm.

Clark, G. 2000. *Sounds from Silence: Graeme Clark and the Bionic Ear Story.* Sydney: Allen & Unwin.

Clark, G. 1987. *The University of Melbourne-Nucleus Multi-Electrode Cochlear Implant.* New York: Karger.

Clark, G. & Tong, Y. 2000. *History of the University of Melbourne/Cochlear Limited Cochlear Implant.* The Bionic Ear Institute. Online at: http://www.medoto.unimelb.edu.au/info/history3.htm [Accessed 2003].

Clarke, A. & Fujimura, J. 1992. *The Right Tools for the Job: At Work in Twentieth-Century Life Sciences.* Princeton, N.J.: Princeton University Press.

Clear, M. 1999. The 'normal' and the monstrous in disability research. *Disability & Society.* 14(4), 435–448.

Clifton, J. 1968. *Introduction to Cultural Anthropology.* New York: Houghton Mifflin.

Cochlear Implant Association Inc. 1997. *What is a Cochlear Implant?* Cochlear Implant Association Inc, Washington DC. Online at: http://www.cici.org/english/whatis.htm [Accessed 2/3/2003].

Cochlear Implant Clinic. 2000. *What is a Cochlear Implant?* Melbourne: The Bionic Ear Institute.

Cochlear Limited. 2002. *What is a Cochlear Implant?* Online at: http://www.cochlear.com.au/NewToCochlear/161.asp [Accessed 2003].

Cochlear Limited. 2000. *Annual Report 1999/2000: Executive Summary.* Cochlear Limited.

Code, L. 1991. *What Can She Know?: Feminist Theory and the Construction of Knowledge.* Ithaca: Cornell University Press.

Cohen, C. Wilk, R. & Stoeltje, B. 1996. *Beauty Queens on the Global Stage: Gender, Contests, and Power.* New York: Routledge.

Cohen, L. McAuley, J. & Duberley, J. 2001. Continuity in Discontinuity: Changing Discourses of Science in a Market Economy. *Science, Technology & Human Values.* 26, 145–166.

Coldron, J. & R. Smith. 1999. Active location in teachers' construction of their professional identities. *Journal of Curriculum Studies.* 31(6), 711–726.

Comaroff, J. 2001. Symposium introduction, colonialism, culture and the law: A forward. *Law & Social Inquiry.* 305.

Compston, A. 1994. Brain repair, an overview. *Journal of Neurology.* 242, s1–s4.

Concar, D. 1998. Hands Today, Faces Tomorrow. *New Scientist.* 13th October 98, 160, 13.

Conjoined twins, Horizon. 2000. [Film]. Van der Pool. United Kingdom: BBC Science. Transcript: http://www.bbc.co.uk/science/horizon/2000/conjoined_twins_transcript.shtml [Accessed 11/3/2009].

Collins, E.F. 1983–1984. An overview and analysis: Prenatal torts, preconception torts, wrongful life, wrongful death, and wrongful birth: Time for a new framework. *Journal of Family Law.* 22, 677–711.

Connolly, E. 2000. Transplant man fled to avoid arrest. *Sydney Morning Herald,* Online at: http://www.smh.com.au.news/0005/09/national/national09.html [Accesssed, 2/3/2003].

Cooper, S. 2002. The small matter of humanity. *Arena Magazine.* 59, 34–38.

Corbett, J. & Ralph, S. 1994. Empowering adults: The changing image of charity advertising. *Australian Disability Review.* 1, 5–13.

Corker, M. 2001. Sensing disability. *Hypatia.* 16, 34–52.

Corker, M. & Shakespeare, T. eds. 2002. *Disability/Postmodernity: Embodying Disability Theory.* London: Continuum.

Côte, I. 2002. Work loss associated with increased menstrual loss in the United States. *Obstetrics & Gynecology.* 100, 683–687.

Cox, O. 1948. *Caste, Class, and Race.* New York: Doubleday.

Cresswell, T. 2005. Moral geographies. In D. Atkinson, P. Jackson, D. Sibley & N. Washbourne, eds. *Cultural Geography: A Critical Dictionary of Key Concepts.* London: Taurus, pp. 128–134.

Crichton, S. 2001. Three disabled children to Sue for "Wrongful Life". *The Age.* Melbourne, Australia.

Crouch, R. 1997. Letting the deaf be deaf: Reconsidering the use of cochlear implants in prelingually deaf children. *Hastings Center Report.* 27, 14–21.

Crutchfield, S. & Epstein, M. 2000. *Points of Contact: Disability, Art and Culture.* Ann Arbor: Michigan University Press.

Dahlstrom, D. 1988. Lebenstechbik und essen: Toward a technological ethics after Heidegger. In P. Durbin, ed. *Technology and Contemporary Life.* Dordrecht: D. Reidel Publishing Company, pp. 145–159.

Dalton, K. 1986. Premenstrual syndrome. *Hamline Law Review.* 9, 143–154.

Degener, T. & Quinn, G. 2000. *A survey of international, comparative and regional disability law reform,* paper presented at "From principles to practice", An international disability law and policy symposium, October 22–26, Disability Rights and Education and Defence Fund, Online at: http://www.dredf.org/symposium/degener1,html [Accessed 5/4/2006].

Delgado, R. 2000. Storytelling for oppositionists and others: A plea for narrative. In R. Delgado & J. Stefancic, eds. *Critical Race Theory The Cutting Edge* (2nd edition). Philadelphia: Temple University Press, pp. 60–70.

Delgardo, R. & Stefancic, J. 2001. *Critical Race Theory; An Introduction.* New York: New York Press.

Delgado, R. & Stefancic, J. ed. 2000. *Critical Race Theory. The Cutting Edge* (2nd edition). Philadelphia: Temple University Press.

Department of Education, Science and Training (DEST). 2004. *Student Equity in Higher Education, Equity Statistics, Queensland,* Online at: http://www.dest.gov.au/sectors/higher_education/publications_resources/staistics/stduents [Accessed 25/08/2005].

Detienne, M. 1979. *Dionysos Slain.* Baltimore: John Hopkins University Press.

Djourno, A. & Eyries, C. 1957. Prostheses auditive par exicitation electrique a distance du nerf sensorial a l'aide d'un bobinage inclus a demeure. *Presse Medicule*. 65, 63.

Dolnick, E. 1993. Deafness as culture. *The Atlantic*. 272(3), 37–53.

Dreger, A. 2004. *One of us: Conjoined twins and the Future of the Normal*. Cambridge, MA: Harvard University Press.

Dreger, A. 1998. The Limits of Individuality: Ritual and sacrifice in the Lives and medical treatment of Conjoined twins. *Studies in History and Philosophy of Biological and Biomedical Sciences*. 29(1): 1–29.

Drengson, A. 1990. Four philosophies of technology. In L. Hickman, ed. *Technology As a Human Affair*. New York: McGraw-Hill, pp. 25–40.

Dreyfus, Hubert. 1995. Heidegger on gaining a free relation to technology. In A. Feenberg & A. Hannay, eds. *Technology and the Politics of Knowledge*. Indiana: Indiana University Press, pp. 97–107.

Dureau, G. & Lucie-Smith, E. 1995. *New Orleans: 50 Photographs*. San Francisco: Heretic Books.

Eddington, D. & Pierschalla, M. 1994. Cochlear implants restoring hearing to the deaf. *'On the Brain': The Harvard Mahoney Neuroscience Institute Newsletter*. 3, 3.

Eichhorn, L. 1998–1999. Major litigation activities regarding major life activities: the failure of the 'Disability' definition in the Americans with Disabilities Act of 1990. *North Carolina Law Review*. 77, 1405–1421.

Elias, N. 1991. *The Society of Individuals*. Oxford: Blackwell.

Elliott, C. 2000. A New Way to be Mad. *The Atlantic Monthly*. December, Online at http://www.theatlantic.com/doc/200012/madness [Accessed 15/2/2008].

Emecke, C. 2000. Between choice and coercion: Identities, injuries, and different forms of recognition. *Constellations*. 7(4), 483–495.

Epstein, J. 1989. *The Story of the Bionic Ear*. South Yarra, Vic.: Hyland House.

Erevelles, N. 2005. Understanding curriculum as normalizing text: Disability studies meet curriculum theory. *Journal of Curriculum Studies*. 37(4), 421–439.

Ewick, P. & Sibley, S. 1995. Sociology of narrative. *Law & Society Review*. 29, 200.

Extraordinary People: The Twins Who Share a Body. 2007. [Film] Pihlaja, R. United Kingdom: True North Productions.

Fanon, F. 1963. *The Wretched of the Earth*. London: Penguin.

Faunce, T. & Jefferys, S. 2007. Abandoning the common law: Medical negligence, genetic tests and wrongful life in the Australian High Court. *Journal of Law and Medicine*. 14(4), 469–477.

Fenton, A. & Alpert, S. 2008. Extending our view on using BCIs for locked-in syndrome. *Neuroethics*. 1, 119–132.

Ferrari, J. 1998. Hands – on Experience. *The Weekend Australian*. National: 17–18 October, pp. 28–29.

Figert, A. 2005. Premenstrual syndrome as scientific and cultural artifact. *Integrative Physiological & Behavioral Science*. 40(2), 102–113.

Fitzgerald, J. 1995. Selective abortion and wrongful birth in Queensland: *Vievers v Connolly*. *Queensland Law Society Journal*. 25, 189–197.

Flax, J. 1992. The End of Innocence. In J. Butler & J. Scott, eds. *Feminists Theorize the Political*. New York: Routledge, pp. 445–463.

Foucault, M. 2003. *Abnormal: Lectures at the College de France 1974–1975*. Picador: New York.

Foucault, M. 1998 (Orig 1966). The Thought of the outside. In J. Faubion, ed. *Michel Foucault Aesthetics, Method, and Epistemology*. London: Allen Lane/The Penguin Press, pp.147–169.

Foucault, M. 1997a. Technologies of the self. In P. Rabinow, ed. *Ethics: Subjectivity and Truth. Essential Works of Michel Foucault, 1954–1984, vol. 1*. London: Allen Lane/The Penguin Press, pp. 223–251.

Foucault, M. 1997b (orig 1982). Technologies of the self. In P. Rabinow, ed. *Michel Foucault Ethics: Subjectivity and Truth, Vol 1*. London: Allen Lane/The Penguin Press, pp. 223–251.

Foucault, M. 1991. Governmentality. In G. Burchell, C. Gordon & P. Miller, eds. *The Foucault Effect*. Hempstead: Harvester Wheatsheaf, pp. 87–104.

Foucault, M. 1988 (Orig 1981). The political technology of individuals [Omnes et Singulatim]. In L. Martin, H. Gutman & P. Hutton, eds. *Technologies of the Self: A Seminar with Michel Foucault*. London: Tavistock, pp. 145–162.

Foucault, M. 1985. *The History of Sexuality: The Use of Pleasure, Vol 2*. Middlesex: Penguin.

Foucault, M. 1983. The subject and power. In H. Dreyfus & P. Rabinow, eds. *Michel Foucault: Beyond Structuralism and Hermeneutics*. Chicago: The University of Chicago Press, pp. 208–226.

Foucault, M. 1980. Two lectures. In C. Gordon, ed. *Foucault; Power Knowledge: Selected Interviews an Other Writings 1972–1977*. New York: Pantheon Press, pp. 78–108.

Foucault, M. 1978. About the concept of dangerous individuals in 19th century legal psychiatry. In D. Weisstub, ed. *Law & Psychiatry*. New York: Pergamon Press.

Foucault, M. 1976. *The History of Sexuality: An Introduction, Vol 1*. Middlesex: Penguin.

Foucault, M. 1975. *The Birth of the Clinic: An Archaeology of Medical Perception*. New York: Vintage/Random House.

Foucault, M. 1971. *Madness and Civilization: A History of Insanity in the Age of Reason*. Cambridge: Rouledge.

Foucault, M. 1961. *Madness & Civilization: A History of Insanity in the Age of Reason*. London: Routledge.

Frank, A. 1990. Bringing bodies back in a decade review. *Theory, Culture and Society*. 7, 131–162.

Frank, R. 1931. The hormonal causes of premenstrual tension. *Archives of Neurology and Psychiatry*. 26, 1053–1057.

Frankenberg, R. 1993. *White Women, Race Matters: The Social Construction of Whiteness*. Minneapolis: University of Minnesota Press.

Freeman, M. & Jaoude, A. 2007. Justifying surgery's last taboo: The ethics of face transplants. *British Medical Journal*. 33, 76–81.

Freidson, E. 1970. *Profession of Medicine*. New York: Dodd Mead.

Freire, P. 1970. *Pedagogy for the Oppressed*. New York: Seabury.

French, T. 1994. The political economy of injury and compassion: Amputees on the Thai-Cambodian Border. In T. Cordas, ed. *Embodiment and Experience: The Existential Ground of Self and Culture*. Cambridge: Cambridge University Press.

Friedman, J. 1981. *The Monstrous Races in Medieval Art and Thought*. Cambridge: Harvard University Press.

Frug, G. 1989. A critical theory of law. *Legal Education Review*. 1(1), 43.

Fujimura, J. 1996. *Crafting Science: A Sociohistory of the Quest for the Genetics of Cancer.* Cambridge, MA: Harvard University Press.

Fujimura, J. 1992. Crafting science: Standardised packages, boundary objects, and 'translations'. In A. Pickering, ed. *Science as Practice and Culture*. Chicago: University of Chicago Press, pp. 168–211.

Fukuyama, F. 2002. *Our Posthuman Future*. London: Profile Books.

Fursman, L. 2001. *Conscious Decisions, Unconscious Paths: Pregnancy and Importance of Work for Women in Management*. Berkeley: Center for Working Families University of California.

Gabel, S. 2002. Some conceptual problems with critical pedagogy. *Curriculum Inquiry*. 32(2), pp. 177–201.

Garland-Thomson, R. 2001. *Re-shaping, Re-thinking, Redefining: Feminist Disability Studies*. Barbara Waxman Fiduccia Papers on Women and Girls with disabilities, Washington DC: Center for Women Policy Studies.

Giami, A. 2003. Pornographie et handicap. *Cités*. 3(15), 43–59 [French only].

Gibson, B. 2006. Disability, Connectivity and Transgressing the Autonomous Body. *Journal of Medical Humanities*. 27(3), 187–196.

Gibson, B., Upshur, R., Young, N. & McKeever, P. 2007. Disability, technology and place: Social and ethical implications of long-term dependency on medical devices. *Ethics, Place & Environment*. 10(1), 7–28.

Gleeson, B. 1999. *Geographies of Disability*. London: Routledge.

Goggin, G. & Newell, C. 2000. Crippling paralympics? media, disability and olympism. *Media International Australia*. 97(November), 71–83.

Gordon, B. & Rosenblum, K. 2001. Bringing disability into the sociological frame: A comparison of disability with race, sex, and sexual orientation statuses. *Disability and Society*. 16(1), 5–21.

Gordon, N. & Sagman, U. 2003. *Nanomedicine Taxonomy*. Briefing paper, Canadian NanoBusiness Alliance.

Greeley, A. 1997. *No Bigger than Necessary: An Alternative to Socialism, Capitalism and Anarchism*. New York: Meridian, New American Library.

Greene, B. Herek, G.M., & Society for the Psychological Study of Lesbian and Gay Issues. 1994. *Lesbian and Gay Psychology: Theory, Research, and Clinical Applications*. Thousand Oaks, Sage Publications.

Griffith, C. 2002a. Hearing the evil. *The Courier Mail* (Brisbane). 6th April, p. 6.

Griffith, C. 2002b. Lesbians admit plan to create a deaf child. *The Courier Mail* (Brisbane).

Grose, N. 1998–1999. Premenstrual dysphoric disorder as a mitigating factor in sentences: Following the lead of English Criminal Courts. *Valparaiso University Law Review*. 33, 201–230.

Grosz, E. 1996. Intolerable ambiguity: Freaks as/at the Limit. In R.G. Thomson, ed. *Freakery: The Cultural Spectacle of the Extraordinary Body*. New York: New York University Press, pp. 55–66.

Grosz, E. 1995. *Space, Time and Perversion: The Politics of Bodies*. St. Leonards: Allen & Unwin.

Grosz, E. 1994. *Volatile Bodies: Toward a Corporeal Feminism*. St Leonard: Allen & Unwin.

Gurevich, M. 1995. Rethinking the label: Who benefits from the PMS construct? *Women & Health*. 23(2), pp. 67–98.

Hahn, H. 1986. Public support for rehabilitation programmes: The analysis of U.S. disability policy. *Disability & Society*. 1(2), 121–137.

Halbbreich, U. 2006. History and trajectory of PMS: Towards a balanced adaptation and a biosocial hoeostasis. *Journal of Reproductive and Infant Psychology*. 24(4), 336–346.

Hamonet, C. 2006. À propos du handicap..., *Cofemer: Modele Handicap – Évaluation – Réadaptation–Réparation médico-légale*, 1–2, Online at www.cofemer.fr/UserFiles/File/Ha4Loi.pdf. [About Disability]. (French only) [Accessed 4/4/2007].

Handelman, S. 2007. The memory hacker. *Popular Science*. April, 66–71, 96, 100.

Hanlon, M. 2002. 'Mr & Mrs Cyborg!', *The Sunday Mail (QLD)*, 22 May, Brisbane, Australia.

Hansen, D. 2001. Teaching as moral activity. In V. Richardson, ed. *Handbook of Research on Teaching*, (4th edition), Washington: American Educational Research Association, pp. 826–857.

Haraway, D.1997. Modest_witness@Second_Millennium. FemaleMan_Meets_ OncoMouse. New York: Routledge.

Haraway, D. 1991a. *Simians, Cyborgs and Women; The Revolution of Nature*. New York: Routledge.

Haraway, D. 1991b. Situated knowledges: The science question in feminism and the privilege of partial perspective. In D. Haraway, ed. *Simians, Cyborgs and Women; The Revolution of Nature*. London: Free Association Books, pp. 183–195.

Haraway, D. 1989. *Primate Visions: Gender, Race, and Nature in the World of Modern Science*. New York: Routledge.

Harris, P. 2001. From relief to mutual obligation: Welfare rationalities and unemployment in 20th-Centruy Australia. *Journal of Sociology*. 37(6), 5–26.

Harvey, A. 1995. The issue of skin color in psychotherapy with African Americans: Families in society. *The Journal of Contemporary Human Services*. 76(1), 3–20.

Hasday, J. 2004. Mitigation and the Americans with disabilities act. *Michigan Law Review*. 103(2), 217–278.

Hasler, F. 1993. The place for information provision in the disability movement. *Information Enables Improving Access to Information Services for Disabled People, National Disability Information Projects*. Nottingham: Policy Studies institute London.

Hayles, K. 1999. *How we Became Posthuman: Virtual Bodies in Cybernetics, Literature, and Informatics*. Chicago: The University of Chicago Press.

Hays, C. 2002. A tale of three mothers. *Women's Quarterly*. (Spring), 2.

Hesslow, G. 1993. Do we need a concept of disease? *Theoretical Medicine*. 14, 1–14.

Heidegger, M. 1962. *Being and Time*, Translators J. Macquarie & E. Robinson. HarperSanFrancisco.

Heidegger, M. 1977 (Orig. 1953). The question concerning technology. In D. Krell, ed. *Martin Heidegger Basic Writings*. New York: Harper & Row, pp. 284–317.

Heidegger, M. 1966. *Discourse on Thinking*. New York: Harper & Row.

Henshaw, C. 2007. PMS: Diagnosis, aetiology, assessment and management: Revisiting premenstrual syndrome. *Advances in Psychiatric Treatment*. 13, 139–146.

Hersch, P. 1983. Comments: Tort liability for 'Wrongful Life'. *U.N.S.W. Law Journal*. 6, 135–142.

Hindess, B. 2000. The Liberal Government of Unfreedom, *The Ethos of Welfare Symposium*. University of Helsinki, Unpublished MS.

Hindmarsh, R., Lawrence, G. & Norton, J. 1998. Bio-Utopia: the Way Forward? In R. Hindmarsh, G. Lawrence & J. Norton, eds. *Altered Genes Reconstructing Nature: The Debate*. St Leonards: Allen & Unwin, pp. 3–23.

Hirsch, D. 2002. 'Submission in Wrongful Life Test Case – NSW Supreme Court': Maurice Blackburn Cashman Lawyers, Unpublished Manuscript.

Ho, A. 2008. The individualist's model of autonomy and the challenge of disability. *Journal of Bioethic Inquiry*. 5, 193–207.

Hocking, C. 1999. Function or feelings: Factors in abandonment of assistive devices. *Technology and Disability* 11(1–2), 3–11.

Hofmann, B. 2001. The technological invention of disease. *Journal of Medical Ethics: Medical Humanities*. 27, 10–19.

Holloway, G. 1994. Susto and the career path of the victim of an industrial accident: A sociological case study. *Social Science & Medicine*. 38(7), 989–997.

Holtzman, E. 1984. Premenstrual syndrome: The indefensible defense. *Harvard Women's Law Journal*. 7, 1–3.

Hooks, B.1990. *Yearning: Race, Gender and Cultural Politics*. Boston: South End Press.

Hopkins, P. 2008. A moral vision for transhumanism. *Journal of Evolution and Technology*. 19(1), September, 3–7, Online at: http://jetpress.org/v19/hopkins.htm [Accessed 7/8/2008].

Horn, R., Nozza, R. & Dolitsky, J. 1991. Audiological and medical considerations for children with cochlear implants. *American Annals of the Deaf*. 136, 82–86.

Hosp, C. 1992. Has the PMS defense gained a legitimate toehold in Virginia Criminal Law? *Commonwealth v. Richter, George Mason University Review of Law*. 1492, 427–446.

House, William. 1995. *Cochlear Implants: My Perspective*. AllHear Inc. Online at: http://www.serve.com/AllHear/monographs/m-95-htm.html [Accessed 2/3/2003].

Hughes, B. 2007. Being disabled: Toward a critical social ontology for disability studies. *Disability & Society*. 22(7), 673–684.

Hughes, B. 2000. Medicine and the aesthetic invalidation of disabled people. *Disability & Society*. 15(4), 555–568.

Hughes, J. 2004. *Citizen Cyborg*. Cambridge, MA: Westwiew Press.

Hughes, J. 2001. The future of death: Cryonics and the telos of liberal individualism. *Journal of Evolution and Technology*. 6. [Electronic]. http://jetpress.org/volume6/death.htm

Hughes, J. 1996. Embracing change with all four arms: Post-humanist defense of genetic engineering. *Eubios Journal of Asian and International Bioethics*. 64, 94–101.

Hughes, J. 1995. Brain death and technological change: Personal identity, neural prostheses and uploading. *Second International Symposium on Brain Death*. Havana, Cuba.

Ingebretson, E. 2001. *At Stake: Monsters and the Rhetoric of Fear in Public Culture*. Chicago: University of Chicago Press.

Infolink 2002. Bionic ear inventor vouches for Australian product. *Dialinfolinkmanufacturing (Reed Business Information)*. Online at: http://www.dialinfolink.com.au/articles/63/0c00f763.asp [Accessed 2/3/2003].

Iwasaki, Y & Mactavish, J. 2005. Ubiquitous yet unique: Perspectives of people with disabilities on stress. *Rehabilitation Counselling Bulletin.* 48(4), 194–208.

'J'. 2002. An Introduction To OverGround. *Overground.* http://www. overground.be/policy.php?code=336&lan=en

Jayasuriya, W. 1988. *The Psychology and Philosophy of Buddhism: An Introduction to the Abhidhamma.* Kuala Lumpur: Buddhist Missionary Society.

Johnson, T. 1987. Premenstrual syndrome as a western culture-specific disorder. *Culture, Medicine & Psychiatry.* 11(3), 337–356.

Johnson, L. & Moxon, E. 1998. In whose service? Technology, care and disabled people: the case for a disability politics perspective. *Disability and Society.* 13, 241–258.

Jones, J. 1972. *Prejudice and Racism.* Reading: Addison-Wesley Pubs.

Jones, M. 2008. *Skintight: An Anatomy of Cosmetic Surgery.* Oxford: Berg.

Jordan, J. 2004. The rhetorical limits of the 'Plastic Body'. *Quarterly Journal of Speech.* 90(3), 327–358.

Josephus, F. 1974. Jewish antiquities, xvii. v. §5. In *Selections from His Works,* with introduction and notes by Abraham Wasserstein. New York: Viking Press.

Kafer, A. 2000. Amputated desire, resistant desire: Female amputees in the devotee community. *Society for Disability Studies Conference Paper.* Chicago.

Kalekin-Fishman, D. 2001. The hidden injuries of a 'slight limp'. In M. Priestley, ed. *Disability and the Life Course: Global Perspectives.* Cambridge: Cambridge University Press, pp. 136–148.

Karpin, I. 1994. Reimagining maternal selfhood: Transgressing body boundaries and the law. *The Australian Feminist Law Journal.* 2, 36–62.

Kant, I. 1996. What is enlightenment? (Orig. 1784). In J. Appleby, E. Covington, D. Hoyt, M. Lantham & A. Sneider, eds. *Knowledge and Postmodernism in Historical Perspective.* New York: Routledge, pp.106–109.

Kendall, G. & Michael, M. 2000. Order and disorder: Time technology and self. Unpublished MS.

Key, E. 1996. Voluntary disabilities and the ADA: a reasonable interpretation of 'reasonable accommodation'. *Hastings Law Journal.* 48, pp. 75–104.

Keywood, K. 2000. More than a woman? embodiment and sexual difference in medical law. *Feminist Legal Studies.* 8, 319–342.

Kovel, J. 1970. *White Racism, a Psychohistory.* New York: Columbia University.

Krieger, N. 1999. Embodying inequality: A review of concepts, measures, and methods for studying health consequences of discrimination. *International Journal of Health Services.* 29(2), 295–352.

Kurzweil, R. 2005. *The Singularity is Near: When Humans transcend Biology.* New York: Viking.

Kurzweil, R. 1999a. *The Age of Spiritual Machines: When Computers Exceed Human Intelligence.* New York: Viking.

Kurzweil, R. 1999b. The coming merging of mind and machine. *Scientific American.* 10, 56–60.

Kuppers, P. 2003. *Disability and Contemporary Performance Bodies on the Edge.* New York: Routledge.

Kuusisto, S. 1998. *Planet of the Blind.* London: Faber & Faber.

Kyle, D. 1993. *Human Robots & Holy Mechanics: Reclaiming Our Souls in a Machine World.* Portland: Swan/Raven.

Lane, H. 1992. *The Mask of Benevolence: Disabling the Deaf Community*. New York: Alfred Knopf.

Lane, H. & Grodin, M. 1997. Ethical issues in cochlear implant surgery: An exploration into disease, disability, and the best interests of the child. *Kennedy Institute of Ethics Journal*. 7, 231–251.

Lane, H., Hoffmeister, R. & Bahan, B. 1996. *A Journey into the Deaf-World*. San Diego: DawnSign Press.

Latour, B. 1999. *Body, Cyborgs and the Politics of Incarnation*. Darwin Lecture, Darwin College Cambridge. 19th February, 1999. Online at: http://www.ensmp.fr/~ latour/artpop/P-80CYBORGS.html [Accessed 2/3/2003].

Latour, B. 1996. *Aramis or the Love of Technology*. Cambridge: Harvard University Press.

Latour, B.1993. *We Have Never Been Modern*. New York: Harvester Wheatsheaf.

Latour, B. 1992. Where are the missing masses? The sociology of a few mundane artefacts. In W. Bijker & J. Law, ed. *Shaping Technology/Building Society: Studies in Sociotechnical Change*. Cambridge MA: MIT Press, pp. 225–258.

Latour, B. 1988. *The Pasteurisation of France*. Cambridge: Harvard University Press.

Law, J. 1999. *Political Philosophy and Disabled Specificities (draft)*. Lancaster: Department of Sociology and Centre for Science Studies, Lancaster University. Online at: http://www.comp.lancs.ac.uk/sociology/soc026jl.html [Accessed 2003].

Laws, S. 1983. The sexual politics of pre-menstrual tension. *Women Studies International Forum*. 6(1), 19–31.

Leary, K. 1999. Passing, posing, and 'Keeping it Real'. *Constellations*. 6, 85–96.

Leder, D. 1999. Whose body? What body? The metaphysics of organ transplantation. In M. Cherry, ed. *Persons and their Bodies: Rights, Responsibilities, Relationships*. Dordrecht: Kluwer, pp. 233–264.

Lee, S. 2002. Health & sickness: the meaning of menstruation and premenstrual syndrome in women's lives. *Sex Roles*. 46(1/2), pp. 25–46.

Lee, A. & Poynton, C. 2000. *Culture and Text: Discourses and Methodology in Social Research and Cultural Studies*. St Leonards: Allen & Unwin.

Levi, P. 1989. *The Drowned and the Saved*. London: Abacus.

Levy, N. 2002. Deafness, culture, and choice. *Journal of Medical Ethics*. 28, 284–285.

Linton, S. 1998a. Disability studies/not disability studies. *Disability and Society*. 13(4), 525–540.

Linton, S. 1998b. *Claiming Disability: Knowledge and Identity*. New York: New York University Press.

Lloyd, K. 2001. Cochlear implants – the AAD View. *Vicdeaf News*, Victoria (Australia), October. Online at: http://www.aad.org.au [Accessed 2003].

Lochrie, K. 1999. *Covert Operations: The Mediaeval Uses of Secrecy*. University of Philadelphia, Pennsylvania Press.

Locke, J.1979. (orig. 1689). *An Essay Concerning Human Understanding*. Oxford: Clarendon Press.

Longmore, P. 2003. *Why I Burned My Book and Other Essays on Disability*. Philadelphia: Temple University Press.

Luczak, R. 2007. *Eyes of Desire 2 A Deaf GLBT Reader*. Minneapolis: Handtype Press.

Lunbeck, E. 1994. *The Psychiatric Persuasion: Knowledge, Gender and Power in Modern America.* Princeton: Princeton University Press.

Mackay, James. A. 1997. *Alexander Graham Bell: A life.* New York: J. Wiley.

MacKenzie, R. 2008. Somatechnics of medico-legal taxonomies: Elective amputation and transableism. *Medical Law Review.* 16, 390–412.

MacKenzie, R. & Cox, S. 2007. Transableism, disability and paternalism in public health ethics: Taxonomies, identity disorders and persistent unexplained physical symptoms. *International Journal of Law in Context.* 294, 363–375.

Mackenzie, R. 1999. From sanctity to screening: Genetic disabilities, risk and rhetorical strategies in wrongful birth and wrongful conception cases. *Feminist Legal Studies.* 7, 175–191.

MacKinnon, C. 1989. *Towards a Feminist Theory of the State.* Cambridge: Harvard University Press.

Macpherson, C.B. 1964. *The Political Theory of Possessive Individualism.* Oxford: Oxford University Press.

Maih, A. 2003. Be afraid: Cyborg athletes, transhuman ideals and posthumanity. *Journal of Evolution & Technology.* 13, Online at: http://jetpress.org/volume13/miah.htm [Accessed 4/4/2007].

Mairs, N. 1996. *Waist-High in the World: A Life among the Nondisabled.* Boston: Beacon Press.

Marks, D. 1999. *Disability: Controversial Debates and Psychosocial Perspectives.* London: Routledge.

Marks D. 1996. Abled-bodied Dilemmas in teaching disability studies. *Feminism & Psychology.* 6, 69–73.

Marshall, T.H. 1963. *Sociology at the Crossroads, and Other Essays.* London: Heinemann.

Marzano-Parisoli, M.M. 2001. Disability, wrongful-life lawsuits, and human difference: An exercise in ethical perplexity. *Social Theory and Practice.* 27, 637–659.

Mason, C. 2000. Cracked babies and the partial birth of a nation: Millennialism and fetal citizenship. *Cultural Studies.* 14, 35–60.

Massey, D. 1997. Space/power, identity/difference: Tensions in the city. In A. Merrifield & E Swyngedouw, eds. *The Urbanization of Injustice.* London: Lawrence and Wishart.

Maughan, A. 2008. Pregnant women won't get disabled parking, *WomenCo* Online at: http://www.womenco.com/topics/350-pregnant-women-wont-get-disabled-parking/posts [Accessed 8/9/2008].

May, T. 1998. *Social Research: Issues, Methods and Process.* Buckingham, UK: Open University Press.

Mayerson, A. & Mayer, K. 2000. *Defining Disability in the Aftermath of Sutton: Where Do We Go from Here?* , Online at: http://www.dredf.org/mayerson.html [Accessed 20/11/2000].

McBarnet, D. 1983. *Conviction.* London: Macmillan.

McClintock, A. 1995. *Imperial Leather: Race, Gender and Sexuality in the Colonial Context.* New York: Routledge.

McGinn, R. 1991. *Science, Technology and Society.* Englewood Cliffs, NJ: Prentice Hall.

McGinn, R. 1990. What is technology? In L. Hickman, ed. *Technology As a Human Affair.* New York: McGraw Hill, pp. 10–25.

McGivern, B. 2002. Tortious liability for (selected) genetic harm: Exploring the arguments. *Torts Law Journal.* 10, 41–63.

McGrath, A. 1994. *Christian Theology: An Introduction.* Oxford: Blackwell Publishers.

McKie, R. & Paton Walsh, N. 2001. Trickster has Transplant Hand Cut Off, *The Observer,* UK: Online at: http://www.observer.co.uk/Print/0,3858, 4130516,00.html [Accessed 2/3/2003].

McLellan, F. 2002. Controversy over deliberate conception of deaf child. *The Lancet.* 359, 1315.

McRuer, R. 2006. *Crip Theory: Cultural Signs of Queerness & Disability.* New York: New York University Press.

McRuer, R. 2002. Compulsory able-bodiedness and queer/disabled existence. In S. Snyder, B. Brueggemann & R. Garland-Thomson, eds. *Disability Studies: Enabling the Humanities.* New York: Modern Language Association, pp. 88–90.

McRuer, R. & Wilkerson, A. 2002. *Desiring Disability: Queer Theory Meets Disability Studies.* Durham, NC: Duke University Press.

McSherry, B. 1994. Premenstrual syndrome and criminal responsibility. *Psychiatry, Psychology and Law.* 193, 139–151.

McSherry, B. 1993. The return of the raging hormones theory, premenstrual syndrome, postpartum disorders and criminal responsibility. *Sydney Law Review.* 15, 292–316.

McWilliam, E. 1996. Admitting impediments: or things to do with bodies in the classroom. *Cambridge Journal of Education.* 26(3), 367–378.

McWilliam, E. 1995. (S)education: a risky inquiry into pleasurable teaching. *Education and Society.* 14(1), 15–24.

McWilliam, E & Taylor, P. 1998. *Teacher Im/material: Academic Teaching and the New Pedagogies of Instructional Design,* Online Paper, American Education Research Association. Online at: http://aera.net/ [Accessed 2/3/2006].

Meekosha, H & Dowse, L. 1997. Distorting images, invisible images: Gender, disability and the media. *Media International Australia.* 84(May), 91–101.

Mialet, H. 2003. Reading Hawking's presence: An interview with a self-effacing man. *Critical Inquiry.* 29(Summer), 571–598.

Mialet, H. 1999. Do angels have bodies? Two stories about subjectivity in science: The cases of William X & Mister H. *Social studies of Science.* 29(4), 551–581.

Michalko, R. 1999. *The Two-in-one: Walking with Smokie, Walking with Blindness.* Philadelphia: Temple University Press.

Middap, C. 2000. Hand of fate. *The Courier-Mail (QLD).* Brisbane, 28/10/00, p. 31.

Mill, J., 1975 (Orig. 1859). *On Liberty. Three Essays.* Oxford: Oxford University Press.

Miller, G. 2003. Norm enforcement in the public sphere: The case of handicapped parking. *George Washington Law Review.* 71(6), 895–933.

Minow, M. 1990. *Making All the Difference: Inclusion, Exclusion, and American Law.* Ithaca: Cornell University Press.

Minsky, M. 1988. *The Society of Mind.* New York: Simon & Schuster.

Mirzoeff, N. 1995. Framed: The deaf in the harem. In J. Terry & J. Urla, eds. *Deviant Bodies: Critical Perspectives in Science and Popular Culture.* Bloomington, IN: Indiana University Press, pp. 49–77.

Mishler, E. 1984. *The Discourse of Medicine: Dialectics of Medical Interviews.* Norwood: Ablex Publishing.

Mitchell, D. 2002. Narrative prosthesis and the materiality of metaphor. In S. Snyder, B. Brueggemann & R. Garland-Thomson, eds. *Disability Studies: Enabling the Humanities*. New York: Modern Language Association, pp. 15–30.

Mitchell, D & Snyder, S. 2003. The eugenic Atlantic: Race, disability, and the making of an international eugenic science, 1800–1945. *Disability & Society*. 18(7), 843–864.

Moffett, G. 1994. UN population conference meets religious resistance. *Christian Science Monitor*. Sep. 6(1), 4.

Moje, E. 2000. Changing our minds, changing our bodies: power as embodied in research relations. *Qualitative Studies in Education*. 13(2), 25–42.

Monaghan, P. 1998. Pioneering field of disability studies challenges established approaches and attitudes. *The Chronicle of Higher Education*. 44(20), A15–16.

Money, J. 1996. *Love Maps: Clinical Concepts of Sexual/Erotic Health and Pathology, Paraphilia, and Gender Transposition in Childhood, Adolescence and Maturity*. Buffalo: Pronetheus Books.

Montaigne, de M. 1588. 'Of cripples' *Essays* Book III. Viewed 2007. http://www.gutenberg.org/files/3600/3600-h/3600-h.htm [Accessed 12/12/2007].

More, M. 2005. *The Proactionary Principle, Version 1.2, July 29, 2005*. Online at: http://www.maxmore.com/proactionary.html [Accessed 2/3/2003].

More, M. 1999. The extropian Principles, 3.0 A transhumanist declaration. Extropy Institute. Online at: http://eee.extropy.com/ideas/principles.html [Accessed 2003].

Morris, J. 1992. Personal and political: A feminist perspective on researching physical disability. *Disability, Handicap and Society*. 7, 157–166.

Moser, I. 2000. Against normalisation: Subverting norms of ability and disability. *Science as Culture*. 9, 201–240.

Murray, C. 2001. The experience of body boundaries by Siamese Twins. *New Ideas in Psychology*. 19, 117–130.

Narayan, U. 1988. Working together across difference: Some considerations on emotions and political practice. *Hypatia*. 3(2), 31–48.

Narayan, U. 1997. *Dislocating Cultures: Identities, Traditions and Third World Feminism*. New York: Routledge.

Nelson, E. & Robertson, G. 2001. Liability for wrongful birth and wrongful life. *Isuma*. 2, 102–105.

Newell, C. 2000. Access to opportunity or oppression? An Australian policy analysis of the ethics of the cochlear implant. *Interaction*. 13(3), 16–23.

Nursing Health Policy (2008). *July 2nd-Analysis of Pending Health Care Legislation*. Online at: http://nursinghealthpolicy.wikispaces.com/July+2nd+Analysis+of+Pending+Health [Accessed 4/3/2007].

O'Brien, P. & Murray, R. eds. 1996. *Human Services: Towards Partnership & Support*. Palmerston North (NZ): The Dunmore Press.

Oliver, K. 2004. Witnessing and testimony. *Parallax*. 10(1), 78–87.

Oliver, M. 1996. *Understanding Disability: From Theory to Practice*. Basingstoke: Macmillan.

Oliver, M. 1993. *What's So Wonderful about Walking? Inaugural Professorial Lecture*. London: University of Greenwich.

Oliver, M. 1990. *The Politics of Disablement*. Basingstoke: Macmillan.

Ossorio, P. 2000. Prenatal genetic testing and the courts. In E. Parens & A. Asch, eds. *Prenatal Testing and Disability Rights*. Washington DC: Georgetown University Press, pp. 308–333.

Overboe, J. 2007. Vitalism: Subjectivity exceeding racism, sexism and (psychiatric) ableism. *Wag.a.du: A Journal of Trasnational Women's & Gender Studies*. 4, 23–34.

Overboe, J. 1999. Difference in itself: Validating disabled people's lived experience. *Body and Society*. 5, 17–29.

Oxford English Dictionary Online (2nd edition). 1989. Online at: http://dictionary.oed.com/entrance.dtl [Accessed 6/7/2004].

Parker, L. & Stovall, D. 2004. Actions following words: Critical Race theory connects to critical pedagogy. *Educational Philosophy and Theory*. 36(2), 167–182.

Parsons, I. 1999. *Cripples, Coons, Fags and Fems; A Look at How Four Human Rights Movements Have Fought Prejudice*. Geelong: Villamata Legal Service.

Paton, C. 1990. *Inventing AIDS*. New York: Routledge.

Paul. 2002. Disability as a Symbol of the Ultimate Other. *OverGround*. http://www.overground.be/article.php?code=75&lan=en

Perz, J. & Ussher, J. 2006. Women's experiences of premenstrual syndrome as a case of silence self. *Journal of reproductive and Infant Psychology*. 24(4), 289–303.

Pfeiffer, D. 1998. The ICIDH and the need for its revision. *Disability and Society*. 13(4), 503–523.

Phillips, C. 2001. Re-imagining the (dis)abled body. *Journal of Medical Humanities*. 22(3), 195–208.

Pillow, W. 2004. *Unfit Subjects: Educational Policy and the Teen Mother*. New York: Routledge.

Pinch, T. & Bijker, W. 1987. The social construction of facts and artefacts: Or how the sociology of science and the sociology of technology might benefit each other. In W. Bijker, T. Hughes & T. Pinch, eds. *The Social Construction of Technological Systems*. Cambridge, MA: The MIT Press, pp. 17–50.

Pointon, A & Davies, C. 1997. *Framed: Interrogating Disability in the Media*. London: British Film Institute.

Pue, W. 1990. Wrestling with law: (geographical) specificity vs. (legal) abstraction. *Urban Geography*. 11, 566.

Purdy, L. 1996. *'Loving Future People' Reproducing Persons*. Ithaca: Cornell University Press.

Pyke, K. & Dang, T. 2003. 'FOB' and 'Whitewashed': Identity and internalized racism among second generation Asian Americans. *Qualitative Sociology*. 26(2), 147–172.

Quid Pro Quo. 2008. [Film]. Brooks, R. USA; HDNet Films/Sanford/Pillsbury Productions.

Ray, J., Wright, T., Fielden, C., Cooper, H., Donaldson, I., & Proops, D.W. 2006. Non-users and limited users of cochlear implants. *Cochlear Implants International*. 7(1), 49–58.

Raz, J. 1997. The rule of law and its virtue. *The Law Quartley Review*. 93, 210 – 229.

Razack, S. 1998. Race, space and prostitution: The making of the Bourgeois subject. *Canadian Journal of Women & Law*. 10, 338–376.

Reagan, T. 2002. Toward an 'archaeology of deafness': Etic and emic constructions of identity in conflict. *Journal of Language, Identity, and Education*. 1, 46–66.

Reagan, T. 1995. A sociocultural understanding of deafness: American sign language and the culture of deaf people. *International Journal of Intercultural Relations*. 19, 239–251.

Ree, J. 1999. *I See a Voice: Deafness, Language and the Senses: A Philosophical History*. New York: Metropolitan Books.

Resoftlinks News 1998. The first hand transplant in Lyon, *Resoftlinks News*, Online at: http://news.resoftlinks.com/980925/hand.shtml [Accessed 2/3/2003].

Réaume, D. 2002. Of pigeonholes and principles: A reconsideration of discrimination law. *Osgoode Hall Law Journal*, 40(2), 113–143.

Richardson, J. 1995. The premenstrual syndrome: A brief history. *Social Sciences & Medicine*. 41(6), 761–767.

Rittenhouse, A. 1991. The emergence of premenstrual syndrome as a social problem. *Social Problems*. 38(3), 412–425.

Rodin, J. 1993. Cultural and psychosocial determinants of weight concerns. *Annals of Internal Medicine*. 119(7/2), 643–645.

Rodin, M. 1992. The social construction of premenstrual syndrome. *Social Sciences & Medicine*. 359(10), 49–56.

Roman, L. 2009. Go Figure! Public pedagogies, invisible impairments and the performative paradoxes of visibility as veracity. *International Journal of Inclusive Education*, forthcoming.

Rose, G. & Gregson, N. 2000. Taking butler elsewhere: performativitites, spatialities and subjectivities. *Environment and Planning D: Society and Space*. 18, 433–452.

Rosenwasser, P. 2000. Tool for transformation: Co-operative inquiry as a process for healing from internalized oppression. *Adult Education Research Conference (AERC)*. University of British Columbia. Online at: http://www.edst.edu.ubc.ca/aerc/2000/rosenwasserpl-final.PDF [Accessed 2/3/2003].

Ross, K. 2001. All ears: Radio, reception and discourses of disability. *Media, Culture and Society*. 23(4), 419–437.

Ross, K. 1997. But Where's me in it? Disability, broadcasting and the audience. *Media, Culture and Society*. 19(4), 669–677.

Rovner, L. 2001. Perpetuating stigma: Client identity in disability rights litigation. *Utah Law Review*. 2, 247.

Rubin, G. 1975. The traffic in women: Notes on the political economy of sex. In R. Reither, ed. *Towards and Anthropology of Women*. 157–210.

Ryan, L. 1918. Plastic surgery. *Illinois Medical Journal*. 34, 69.

Sanders, J. 2008a. California bill would give free parking to moms-to-be. *The Sacramento Bee*, Thursday, March 20, Online at: http://www.sacbee.com/capolitics/7999215.html [Accessed 4/4/2008].

Sanders, J. 2008b. No disabled parking placards permits to late-term pregnant women. *The Sacramento Bee*, Wednesday, March 26, Online at: http://www1.pressdemocrat.com/apps/pbcs.dll/article? [Accessed 4/4/2008].

Sass, L. 1994. Civilized madness: Schizophrenia, self-consciousness and the modern mind. *History of the Human Sciences*. 7(2): 83–120.

Savulescu, J. 2006. Justice, fairness and enhancement. *Annual of the N.Y. Academy of Science*. 1093, 321–338.

Sayer, N., Spoont, M. & Nelson, D. 2004. Veterans seeking disability benefits for post-traumatic stress disorder: who applies and the self-reported meaning of disability compensation. *Social Science & Medicine*. 58, 2133–2143.

Scheerenberger, R. 1983. *A History of Mental Retardation*. Baltimore: Paul H. Brookes Publishing.

Schumacher, E. 1973. *Small Is Beautiful: A Study of Economic As If People Mattered*. London: Abacus.

Schwalbe, M. & Mason-Schrock, D. 1996. Identity work as group process. *Advances in Group Processes*. 13, 113–147.

Scott, J. 1992. Experience. In J. Butler & J. Scott, eds. *Feminists Theorize the Political*. New York: Routledge, pp. 22–40.

Seltzer, M. 1992. *Bodies and Machines*. New York: Routledge.

Serlin, D. 2004. *Replaceable You: Engineering the Body in Postwar America*. Chicago: The University of Chicago Press.

Seymour, W. 1998. *Remaking the Body: Rehabilitation and Change*. Sydney: Allen and Unwin.

Shain, A. 2002. *Intimate Encounter Participant Quotes*. Intimate Encounters (Photographic Exhibition), B. Mason-Lovering, Producer. Online at: http://www.intimateencounters.com.au/participants/quotes.html [Accessed 2003].

Shakespeare, T. 1999. Losing the plot? Medical and activist discourses of contemporary genetics and disability. *Sociology of Health & Illness*. 21(5), 669–688.

Shannon, R. 1999. *Keynote speech at the Cochlear Implant Conference Institute, Manhattan Beach*. Cochlear Implant Association. Online at: http://www.cici.org/docs/Shannon.pdf [Accessed 2003].

Shapiro, S. 1994. Re-membering the body in Critical Pedagogy. *Education and Society*. 12, 61–79.

Showalter, E. 1987. *The female malady*: Women, madness and English culture 1830–1980. London: Virago Press.

Silverman, H. 2000. *Philosophy and Desire*. New York: Routledge.

Silvers, A. 1998a. Formal justice. In A. Silvers & D. Wasserman et al., eds. *Disability, Difference, Discrimination: Perspectives on Justice in Bioethics and Public Policy*. Lanham: Rowman & Littlefield Publishers, pp. 13–145.

Silvers, A. 1998b. Reprising women's disability: Feminist identity strategy and disability rights. *Berkeley Women's Law Journal*. 13, 81–116.

Singer, P. 2000. *A Darwinian Left: Politics Evolution and Co-operation*. New Haven: Yale University Press.

Singer, P. & Kuhse, H. 2002. *Unsanctifying Human Life: Essays on Ethics*. Oxford, UK: Blackwell.

Smith, D. 1997. Geography and ethics: A moral turn? *Progress in Human Geography*. 21(4), 583–590.

Smith, G.P. 1981. *Genetics, Ethics and the Law*. Gaithersburg, MD: Associated Faculty Press; Frederick, MD: [Distributed by] University Publications of America.

Smith, M. 2001. Clint Hands Gift Back to Doctors. *Herald Sun (Melbourne)*. 5/2/2001. Online at http://www.heraldsun.com.au/common/story_page/0,4511,1677532%255E663,00.html [Accessed 2003].

Smith, J. & Stovall, D. 2008. Coming home to new homes and schools; critical race theory and the new politics of containment. *Journal of Education Policy*. 23(2), 135–152.

Snyder, S. & Mitchell, D. 2001. Re-engaging the body: Disability studies and the resistance to embodiment. *Public Culture.* 13(3), 367–389.

Soifer, A. 2003. *Disabling the ADA: essences, better angels, and unprincipled neutrality claims,* Research Chapter, No 8., Boston College Law School (2003) Online at: http://ssm.com/abstract-id=389400 [Accessed 2003].

Solis, S. 2006. I'm coming out as disabled but I'm staying in to rest: reflecting on elected and imposed segregation. *Equity & Excellence in Education.* 39, 146–153.

Solomon, A. 1994. Defiantly Deaf. *The New York Times,* August 28, 1994, alternative URL. Online at: http://dww.deafworldweb.org/pub/d/nytimes.html [Accessed 3/4/2003].

Solomon, R. 1988. *Continental Philosophy Since 1750: The Rise and Fall of the Self.* Oxford: Oxford University Press.

Solvang, P. 2002. The amputee body desired: Beauty destabilised? disability re-valued?, *XV World Congress of Sociology.* Brisbane, Australia.

Somerville, M.A. 1983. Joiner of issue at the frontiers of biomedicine: A review essay on 'Genetics, Ethics and the Law', by George P. Smith, II. *U.N.S.W. Law Journal.* 6, 103–118.

Spriggs, M. 2002. Lesbian couple create a child who is deaf like them. *Journal of Medical Ethics.* 28, p283.

Spivak, G. 1990. Questions of multi-culturalism. In S. Harasyn, ed. *Gayatri Chakravorty Spivak. The Post Colonial critic Interviews, Strategies, Dialogues.* New York: Routledge.

Star Johnson, T. 2005. The 'Problem' of bodies and desires in teaching. *Teaching Education.* 16(2), 131–149.

Star, S. & Griesmer, J. 1989. Institutional ecology, 'translations' and boundary objects: Amateurs and professionals in Berkeley's Museum of Vertebrate Zoology, 1907–39. *Social Studies of Science.* 19, 387–420.

Sterne, J. 2001. A machine to hear for them: On the very possibility of sound's reproduction. *Cultural Studies.* 15, 259–294.

Stiker, H. 1999. *A History of Disability.* Ann Arbor: The University of Michigan Press.

Stock, G. 2002. *Redesigning Humans: Choosing Our Children's Genes.* BBC Science Horizon. Online at: http://www.bbb.co.uk/science/horizon/1999/stock.shtml [Accessed 2003].

Stoetzler, M. & Yuval-Davis, N. 2002. Standpoint Theory, Situated knowledge and the situated imagination. *Feminist Theory.* 3(3), 315–333.

Stone, R. 1996. *The War of Desire and Technology at the Close of the Mechanical Age.* Cambridge: MIT Press.

Storrs, B. 1996. *Devotees of Disability: Caveat Dater.* New Mobility Magazine, http://www2.ios.com/~ mauro/adevote.htm [Accessed 11/12/2002].

Suchman, L. 2000. *Human/Machine Reconsidered* (draft) Department of Sociology, Lanchaster University. Online at: http:// www.comp.lancaster.ac.uk/ sociology/soc0401s.html [Accessed 2003].

Sullivan, N. (2008). Dis-orientating Paraphilias? Disability, Desire, and the Question of (Bio)Ethics, *Bioethical Inquiry.* 5, 183–192.

Sveindóttir, H., Lundman, B. & Norberg, A. 2002. Whose voice? Whose experiences? Women's qualitative accounts of general and private discussions of premenstrual syndrome, Scandinavian. *Journal of Caring.* 16, 414–423.

Swain, J. & French, S. 2000. Towards an affirmation model of disability. *Disability & Society*. 15, 569–582.

Swann, C. 1997. Reading the bleeding body: Discourses on premenstrual syndrome. In J. Ussher, ed. *Body Talk: The Material and Discursive Regulation of Sexuality, Madness and Reproduction*. London: Routledge, pp. 176–198.

Szivos, S. 1992. The limits to integration? In H. Brown, , H. Smith, eds. *Normalisation: A Reader for the Nineties*. London: Routledge, pp.112–134.

Taylor, D. 2006. From 'it's all in your head' to 'taking back the month': Premenstrual syndrome (PMS) Research and the Contributions of the Society for menstrual Cycle research. *Sex Roles*. 54, 377–391.

Taylor, R. 1979. *Medicine out of Control: The Anatomy of a Malignant Technology*. Melbourne: Sun Books.

The New Zealand Herald. 1999. Hand at Risk as Hallam Bails out. *The New Zealand Herald*. 24/2/1999. Online at: http://www.nzherald.co.nz/storydisplay.cfm?thesection=news&thesubsection=storyID=293 [Accessed 2003].

Telegraph News [UK]. 2008. Hensel Twins Celebrate 18 years Together, 10/3/2008, *Telegraph News*, Online version: http://www.telegraph.co.uk/news/worldnews/1581218/Hensel-twins-celebrate-18-years-together.html [Accessed 05/02/2009].

Thera, N. 1998. *Adhidhamma Studies: Buddhist Explorations of Consciousness and Time*. Kandy Sri Lanka/Boston: Buddhist Publications Society/Wisdom Publications.

Thomas, C. 1999. *Female Forms: Experiencing and Understanding Disability*. Buckingham: Open University Press.

Thompson, F. 1917. The Hound of Heaven, Poem 239. In D. Nicholson, & A. Lee, eds. *The Oxford Book of English Mystical Verse*. Oxford: The Clarendon Press, 1917; Bartleby.com, 2000. Online at: www.bartleby.com/236/ [Accessed 9/11/2004].

Thomson, P. 2004. Severed heads and compliant bodies? A speculation about principal identities. *Discourse: Studies in the Cultural Politics of Education*. 25(1), 43–59.

Thomson, R.2009. *Staring: How We Look*, New York: Oxford University Press.

Thomson, R. 1997. *Extraordinary Bodies: Figuring Physical Disability in American Culture and Literature*. New York: Columbia University Press.

Thornton, M. 1996. *Dissonance and Distrust: Women in the Legal Profession*. Melbourne: Oxford University Press.

Titchkosky, T. 2001. Disability: A rose by any other name? People-first language in Canadian Society. *The Canadian Review of Sociology and Anthropology*. 38(2), 125–140.

Todd, A. 1989. *Intimate Adversaries: Cultural Conflicts Between Doctors and Women Patients*. Philadelphia: University of Pennsylvania Press.

Tong, R. 1999. Dealing with difference justly: Perspectives on disability. *Social Theory and Practice*. 25, 519–530.

Tremain, S. ed. 2005. *Foucault and the Government of Disability*. Ann Arbor: The University of Michigan Press, pp. 27–44.

Tucker, B. 1998. Deaf culture, cochlear implants, and elective disability. *Hastings Centre Report*. 28, 6–14.

Turner, B. 1992. *Regulating Bodies: Essays in Medical Sociology*. London: Routledge.

Turner, B. 1987. *Medical Power and Social Knowledge*. London: Sage.

Ungar, S. 1986. The professor of desire, the pedagogical contract: Teaching as a literary genre. *Yale French Studies*. 63, 81–97.

Ussher, J. 2006. *Managing the monstrous feminine: Regulating the reproductive body*. London: Routledge.

Ussher, J. 2003. The ongoing silence of women in families; an analysis and rethinking of premenstrual syndrome and therapy. *Journal of Family Therapy*. 25, 388–405.

Verga, M. 2000. *A Meeting with George Dureau*. Bentvoices.org, http://www.bentvoices.org/cultureclash/verga_georgedureau.htm [Accessed 12/2001].

Vogels, J. 2008. Your Wheelchair is Incredibly Hot. *See Magazine*. 1 (776), Online at: http://www.seemagazine.com/article/back/my-messy-bedroom/your-wheelchair-incredibly-hot/ [Accessed 4/3/2008].

Wasserman, D. 2000. Stigma without impairment: Broadening the scope of disability discrimination law. In L. Francis & A. Silvers, eds. *Americans with Disabilities: Implications of the Law for Institutions and Individuals*. New York: Routledge.

Watts, I. & Erevelles, N. 2004. These deadly times: Reconceptualizing school violence by using critical race theory and disability studies. *American Educational Research Journal*. 41(2), 271–299.

Watts – Jones, D. 2002. Healing internalized racism: The role of a within group sanctuary among people of African descent. *Family Process*. 41(4), 592–593.

Waxman Fiduccia, B. 1999. Sexual imagery of physically disabled women: Erotic? Perverse? Sexist?. *Sexuality and Disability*. 17, 277–282.

Wenzel, C. 2008. Pregnant women won't get disabled parking. *Silicon Valley Moms Blog*. March, 26, Online at: http://www.symoms.com/2008/03/pregnant-women.html [Accessed 8/9/2008].

Wertsch, J. 1998. *Mind as Action*. New York: Oxford University Press.

Weybury, D. & Witting, C. 1995. Wrongful conception actions. *Torts Law Journal*. 1, 53–74.

Whittell, G. 2000. Hand of fate. *The Weekend Australian*. November 11–12, Review section, pp. 4–5.

Williams, D. & Collins, C. 1995. U.S. Socio-economic and racial differences in health. *Annual Review of Sociology*. 21, 349–386.

Winzer, M. 1997. Disability and society before the eighteenth century: Dread and despair. In L. Davis, ed. *The Disability Studies Reader*. New York: Routledge, pp. 75–109.

Wolbring G. 2007. *The Triangle of New Emerging Technologies, Disabled People and the World Council of Churches; Ableism: A Prerequisite for Transhumanism*. WWC: Ebook.

Wolbring, G. 2006a. The unenhanced underclass. In P. Miller & J. Wilsdon, eds. *Better humans? The politics of human enhancement and life extension*. Demos Collection 21. London: Demos. pp.122–128.

Wolbring, G. 2006b. Emerging technologies (nano, bio, info, cogno) and the changing concepts of health and disability/impairment. *Health & Development*. 2(1&2), 19–37.

Wolbring, G. 2006c. Nanotechnology for Health & Development. *Development*. 49(4), 6–15.

Wolfensberger, W. 1972. *The Principle of Normalization in Human Services*. Toronto: National Institute on Mental Retardation.

Wolfensberger, W. & Thomas, S. 1983. *PASSING: Program Analysis of Service Systems' Implementation of Normalization Goals: A Method of Evaluating the Quality of Human Services According to the Principle of Normalization, Normalization Criteria and Ratings Manual*. Ontario: National Institute on Mental Retardation.

Wrigley, O. 1996. *The Politics of Deafness*. Washington, DC: Gallaudet University Press.

Young, C. 2002. Sound judgment: Does curing deafness really mean genocide? *Reason*. 33, 20–21.

Zahorik, P. & Jenison, R. 1998. Presence as being in the world. *Presence: Teleoperators and Virtual Environments*. 7, 78–89.

Zita, J. 1988. The premenstrual syndrome 'dis-easing' the female cycle. *Hypatia*. 3(1), 77–99.

Zugelder, M. & Champagne, P. 2003. Responding to the supreme court; employment practices and the ADA. *Business Horizons*. January–February, pp. 30–36.

Case Index

Index